LA BELLE SAISON

Also by Patricia Atkinson

The Ripening Sun

LA BELLE SAISON

Patricia Atkinson

arrow books

Published by Arrow in 2006

1 3 5 7 9 10 8 6 4 2

Copyright © Patricia Atkinson 2005

Patricia Atkinson has asserted her right under the Copyright, Designs
and Patents Act, 1988 to be identified as the author of this work

First published in the United Kingdom in 2004 by Century
The Random House Group Limited
20 Vauxhall Bridge Road, London, SW1V 2SA

Random House Australia (Pty) Limited
20 Alfred Street, Milsons Point, Sydney
New South Wales 2061, Australia

Random House New Zealand Limited
18 Poland Road, Glenfield
Auckland 10, New Zealand

Random House South Africa (Pty) Limited
Isle of Houghton, Corner of Boundary Road & Carse O'Gowrie,
Houghton 2198, South Africa

The Random House Group Limited Reg. No. 954009

www.randomhouse.co.uk

A CIP catalogue record for this book
is available from the British Library

Papers used by Random House
are natural, recyclable products made from wood grown in
sustainable forests. The manufacturing processes conform to
the environmental regulations of the country of origin

ISBN 0 09 945507 2
(export 0 09 949794 8)

Typeset by Palimpsest Book Production Limited, Polmont, Stirlingshire
Printed and bound in Great Britain by
Bookmarque Ltd, Croydon, Surrey

Acknowledgements

I would like to thank everyone who appears in this book — for their generosity of spirit, their kindness and their friendship. I would also like to thank Oliver Johnson, my friend and editor, whose patience, skill and arm-twisting are inexhaustible. And Eugenie Furniss, my agent, supportive and encouraging at every point. Not forgetting Red Shively who supplied the photographs that helped me with the personal bits — thank you, Red. My thanks also to Freddie Hawkins for his French corrections. Georges will be forever grateful, I know. And my thanks, as ever, to Nigel Farrow for his discerning support.

Illustration Sources

Duck, Goose, Truffle, Pig, Pigcuts, Cuve, Bottls, Oyster, Mushrooms, Wild Boar and Pressoir from Augé, Claude, *Petit Larousse Illustré* (Paris: Librarie Larousse, 1914)

Market, Town, Stonehouse and Townwall from Murray, A. H. Hallam, *Sketches on the Old Road Through France to Florence* (London: John Murray, 1904)

Hunter and Hillside from Long, William J., *Fowls of the Air* (Boston, Mass. and London: Ginn & Company, 1902)

Hare from Westell, W. Percival, *My Life as a Naturalist* (London: Cecil Palmer & Hayward, 1918)

Fish and Doves from Beach Thomas, W. and Collett, A.K, *The English Year: Spring* (London: T.C. & E.C. Jack, c. 1910)

For John and Chantal

For every thing there is a season, and a time for every
  matter under heaven:
A time to be born and time to die
A time to plant and a time to pluck up what is planted
A time to kill and a time to heal
A time to break down and a time to build up
A time to weep and a time to laugh
A time to mourn and a time to dance
A time to cast away stones and a time to gather stones
  together
A time to embrace and a time to refrain from embracing
A time to seek and a time to lose
A time to keep and a time to cast away
A time to rend and a time to sew
A time to keep silence and a time to speak
A time to love and a time to hate
A time for war and a time for peace
What gain has the worker from his toil?

Ecclesiastes, III: i–ix

Prologue

IT'S LATE AUGUST IN THE DORDOGNE AS I LOOK OUT OVER towards the valley of Bergerac from the highest point of my land. Green and fertile, it is bathed in summer light. The rays of the sun illuminate its fields and vineyards, quietly, as they have for centuries. Ancient limestone houses dotted in the landscape and whitewashed by the sun's rays contrast with the dark silhouette of woods on the skyline.

In the near distance gently sloping rows of vines spread out beneath an orchard of fruit trees. A calm over the valley with the stillness of late summer presages the cusp of the turning year. *La belle saison* is almost upon us. The vines shimmer in the summer haze, sweeping down in front of me, their sinuous curves lush and green. The rhythm of their ripening has come full circle again, the seasons and the land changing and nourishing them.

I often come here, as much for the view that stretches for miles over the gently rolling Périgordian landscape as for the calm stillness the view gives me. It is timeless. The pilgrims of Santiago de Compostela would have enjoyed the same view after their long climb from the valley bottom five hundred years ago. The same fields, the same farms, the same churches stood then as they do now. I imagine pilgrims resting after their exertions by the mission cross that stands a little behind me, next to Madame Cholet's house.

The cross reminds me of her. She died some years ago, peacefully, of old age. But mostly, it reminds me of Edge, my favourite vineyard worker and dear friend, also gone. His words have never been far from me in the years since he died. 'Boss,' he said. 'There's nothing that can't be achieved, you've just gotta stay positive. And go forward.' He had vitality and kindness, a passion for life. I think of him often, particularly at this time of year. I own the land on which the cross sits, along with Madame Cholet's house and the vines in front of me. Her son, Gilles, sold them to me before he moved to Sigoulès, ten kilometres away. He lived off the land, worked the vines as I do now. He often hunts here, or just wanders through the wood that sits to the right of the vines with his black Labrador, Prune. Its beauty and familiarity draw him back. He has known it all his life, hardly leaving this small part of rural France.

The landscape is as much a part of him as, after fifteen years in this village, it is becoming part of me. Gilles is short, dark and stocky. His voice is loud and deep and stentorian. He says what he thinks and feels. He epitomises the deep-rooted traditions of rural culture here, traditions that come from the land in front of me, from centuries of necessity and self-sufficiency. The same is true of the local community in Gageac.

They have almost grown out of the land, their lives dominated by the seasons. Before I came here to live and work I barely noticed the seasons. Now they are in my blood, as is Gageac with its rolling vines, its beautiful Romanesque church, its twin-towered fourteenth-century château and my simple farmhouse. What was so foreign to me when I arrived and which, at a given moment, I wanted to escape from is now so familiar I can't imagine ever leaving.

2

The traditions here endure through nature's cycles, through the changes the country has seen in its history the lives of people whose roots in the land have touched it. They are older than Gageac, older than the château; they have survived war and famine and plague. They mirror the passing of time with people in it changing or simply passing through.

It is 2003 and Pierre de la Verrie, the old *comte* from the château, has just passed away. Towards the end of his life he would walk slowly up the village road past my house for exercise, walking stick in hand and supported by his nurse. Paper-thin, his steps faltering and his pale face almost translucent with age, in his mind he carried a century of memories. His son Geoffroy is gone too. He took care of the château, he was my friend, he loved life and order around him. Now the plants in front of his house grow tall and wild. Time moves on. I think of them as I look down towards the vines and feel the stillness of the day, the turning of the season, the end of a cycle.

Seven years ago I stood in exactly this place wondering what the future held for me. The first two harvests since buying Gilles's vineyard had been gathered in and vinified and I was about to head into the third, having just planted two hectares of vine saplings, delicate and vulnerable.

It was the end of a cycle that had begun for me in 1990 when I moved here with my husband, James, and bought a small house with some vines attached. It was his dream to move to France, to have vines. I loved him, bought into the dream. In those days we were full of hope for our new life. Disaster struck with the first red wine harvest turning to vinegar and our savings soon gone. James fell ill and returned to England while I stayed behind reluctantly to work the vines and salvage something.

The initial feeling of abandonment, resentment and personal distress I felt then was rapidly replaced by the harsh reality of my situation. I could speak no French, knew nothing about wine or

3

winemaking and had no money. I learnt to drive tractors, speak French and make wine simultaneously, living from day to day.

In those days my sole purpose was to survive. I learnt to live on my own. I learnt to make wine as a woman in a man's world, discovering as I did so a friendship and community spirit among not just my neighbours but the winemaking community in general. It was to be my salvation. The help they gave me, the friendship they extended, the generosity of spirit they displayed was and is overwhelming.

My marriage foundered in the process with James's visits sporadic and difficult. He was no longer part of a dream; perhaps I wasn't either. The dream had become a harsh reality. He looked for work in England to get us out of our predicament. His visits became less frequent. He lost impetus as I gained it.

My life became more fulfilled without him, time and distance taking its toll. What had been a long but temporary separation had frozen into two different lives and eventually to divorce. His dream had become my reality. He was working again in England and had bought a house. He still lives there, but with someone else now.

As for me, I threw myself into work with a vengeance. It became my compensation, a displacement for the loneliness, grief and bitterness I felt at having been left in limbo; separated yet not divorced, hundreds of miles from my children and my grandchildren. Emptiness washed over me from time to time, immersion in work only masking an inner sadness. I had the compensation of my family but they were a long way away. And yet I did have a form of liberation and a realisation that I was moving on.

My Swedish friends, Pia and Ekan, were coming to dinner at my house one evening. An old friend of theirs had arrived unexpectedly for a short visit from Switzerland where he lived and they asked whether they could bring him along. Tall, slim and wearing a dark blue shirt and corduroy trousers, he stepped in through the door. Taking a stride towards me, he introduced himself, bowing slightly and taking my hand in his. He held my gaze with black, sparkling eyes. He smiled slowly, a wide smile.

I was taken aback. I'm not sure what I had been expecting, if anything, but the silent exchange between us was penetrating and slightly unnerving. 'Patricia! *Hej!*' boomed Ekan behind him, breaking the momentary silence and kissing me in greeting. Pia followed him. '*Hej*, Patricia,' she said as she kissed me. 'It's so kind of you to invite Fidde too.' 'Yes,' said Fidde, standing next to them, holding me still with searching eyes, 'thank you.' And then we moved into the salon where other guests were already gathered.

His laughter and deep voice were gentle, his gaze disquieting. I felt his eyes following me as I served dinner, as the evening passed. Each time he talked or laughed, a deep, resonant laugh, he looked at me. Every time I spoke, he listened with attention. He was amusing and interesting. After everyone had gone, I found myself wondering about him and his life, why he disturbed me, what he did, what made him. He was worldly yet reticent, confident yet shy, an observer of people.

A bright but cold spring day and I was working up and down the rows of vines on the tractor, mowing the grass. In the distance, at the bottom of the row of vines I was turning into, I saw Fidde waving and walking purposefully in my direction, his dark hair and suntanned face outlined by the sun as he strode through the vines towards me.

'*Hej*, Patricia!' he yelled as he reached me, shouting above the noise of the tractor. 'I wondered whether I could take you out to dinner tonight?' He put his hands to his ears. 'To thank you for the other evening!' he shouted. I switched off the engine and stepped down from the tractor, dishevelled and dusty from soil and grass cuttings. 'If you're free and have the time?' he continued.

I had wine vats to rack and barrels to fill that evening and I

5

hardly knew him, yet I contemplated declining for only a moment. 'I'd love to,' I laughed. 'Good! I'll pick you up at eight then,' he said with a smile and was gone.

His voice rang in my ears as I watched him climb into his car in the distance. He turned back towards me and waved. I waved back, standing stock still next to the tractor asking myself why I had only taken a second to accept his invitation; there had been hardly any delay or indecision on my part. I knew why. He had been on my mind since the evening he had come to dinner.

I was still standing next to the tractor as my closest neighbour and friend, Juliana, hurried up the road towards me, a baguette tucked under her arm. Small, Italian and in her fifties, she had moved to Gageac shortly after me with her French husband, Yves, and their Yorkshire terrier, Chloë.

Gageac is awakened each morning by the sound of her booming voice as she opens her bedroom shutters with gusto. She waves and shouts a greeting as each of three sets of shutters clatter open, followed by the front door, where Chloë is deposited in the garden for her morning pee. 'Chloë! *Tais-toi!*' I hear her bellow habitually when Chloë's insistent barking fills the air.

As Fidde's car disappeared round the corner heading for Saussignac, the sound of her voice echoed up the road. 'Patriciaaa!!' she yelled, marching up through the vines. '*Quel bel homme!*' she roared as she reached me, holding out her right hand and shaking it in appreciation. Her words reverberated around the vines. '*Oh là là*, Patricia! *Quel bel homme!*' she repeated with raucous laughter, handing me the baguette.

I looked at her for a moment in silence and at the car turning the corner at the top of the hill, disappearing out of sight. Then I laughed too. It was an undeniable fact that Fidde was '*un bel homme*'. 'And about time too!' she called as she walked back through the vines towards her house. '*Il faut un amant de temps en temps!*'

Chapter 1

'Oúi! Il faut quinze jours de gavage!'

I'M FEELING NAUSEOUS. GILLES HAS JUST EXPLAINED TO ME THE FINER points of force-feeding ducks in general and his in particular. We are in my kitchen having coffee and at Gilles's feet is a plastic bag. It is moving. In it are thirty or so live frogs fished out of the pond near one of my *parcelles* of vines not far from his old house, La Tabardy. Their legs will be removed and fried for tonight's dinner.

Gilles is one of my greatest friends. In the early days of my life here, when I had only four hectares of vines and knew nothing about the land or winemaking, he taught me to drive the tractor and work the vines. Short, dark-skinned and solid, he has a deep, resonant voice and vociferous opinions. He is fiery of nature and fierce, his solidity given life by the quickness of his emotions. He is a force of nature. Everything about him – his stature, strong facial expressions and classic shrug – epitomises a true Gascon. He hunts; he fishes. He grows vegetables. He force-feeds ducks, he strangles pheasants and he dismembers frogs.

He continues his discourse, unconcerned by the moving bag at his feet, and I just know that the vivid description of the methods used to inflict cirrhosis of the liver on his ducks will continue for some time. Force-fed, they are so full of soaked maize that after fifteen days they can no longer swallow.

Morning and evening for three weeks they are fed with maize grown by Gilles himself and, when the time is right, are killed and hung up '*par la tête et les pattes*' so that the fat can descend around the carefully fattened liver. The abdomen is then slit and gently pried open. The exterior fat around the liver is carefully gathered – '*on l'a garde pour les frites*' – exposing the foie gras which is delicately removed with the inner fat immediately surrounding it intact.

'*Et oui*; and our foies gras are richer and finer than other regions,' he says with obvious pride. 'Our maize is richer and deeper in colour, so our foies have better colour and a better taste.' I had to admit that they did taste utterly delicious, in spite of not wishing to know the intimate details. In fact, there was now little I didn't know.

Nothing is left of the ducks when he has finished with them, he explains. 'I like my foie gras *pur* – the way I like to cook them. Not surrounded by *saucisson* or any of the other rubbish you find these days! You must take out the veins, but carefully. *Il faut le sel et le poivre*, fill the jar to the top, surrounded only by the fat and cook for thirty minutes in the *bocal* – no more. It will shrink if it's overcooked . . . and dry out too.'

Then silence. 'So be careful!' he warns, emphasising the point and looking at me earnestly as though I might have the intention of personally throttling a duck, hanging it by its head and legs, ripping out its liver and cooking it. '*Et pour le reste . . .*' he smiles, sipping the last of his coffee. '*Il ne reste pas grand-chose*, not much is left by the time I've finished.'

The legs are taken off and salted for forty-eight hours, then cooked in an oven for two hours to make confits. '*Pas trop chaud, le four, attention!'* They are so rich in fat, he says, they have be cooked in the oven to take some of it away. The same for the *magret*, the breasts, *'sauf si je les cuit sur les braises de sarments'*, unless I grill them on vine embers.

The neck bone is kept for stock for soup. *'Oui!* If the neck is still full of maize in the morning,' he continues, returning to his force-feeding methods, 'the duck is made to eat and it's time to kill it.' He stands to leave, picking up the bag of frogs. 'Do you want some?' he enquires. I smile weakly, shaking my head. 'No, I don't think I like them and isn't it cruel to take their legs off?'

'Milledieux!' he shouts. 'Cruel? Cruel? You could say the same about anything! What about a lettuce? We pull it from the ground by its head! When you cut it, that's death, isn't it?' His voice is rising by decibels. I begin to wish I'd never mentioned cruelty as he shakes the bag of live frogs in his hand. Even worse, he seems about to open it.

He holds out a jar of foie gras, *'fait maison'*, made by him. 'Everything's cruel,' he continues, once more in control of his emotions. 'But you wouldn't spit out a nice breast of chicken, or a *gibier* just because they've been killed.' We look at each other. 'And I don't know many who would spit out a good foie gras either, do you?' he laughs, handing me the jar. With a broad smile, a kiss and a *'Salut'* he throws the wet, heaving bag into his van and is gone.

I love Gilles's visits and I love his approach to life, dismembered frogs nothwithstanding. His sense of identity with the climate and the landscape, his interaction with the land and the seasons impose an order on his life. I had felt a pang of sadness at his departure from Gageac five years earlier, along with a nagging worry that I might lose touch with him, even though he had only moved to Sigoulès, ten kilometres away. I needn't have worried. There had been a short gap in his visits while he put his new house in order, after which he settled back into the old routine.

9

The new house in question is very different from La Tabardy, where he had lived for forty-six years. Located next to the Cave Co-operative at Sigoulès, it is modern and three-storeyed, sitting on a small plateau at the side and above the main road. The two kitchens, one on the first floor and another at ground level, along with the salon and bedrooms make up the living quarters.

Below ground is the cellar and garage, home to Gilles's impressive collection of tools and sundry equipment, along with old pieces of iron and ancient, rusting tractor appendages that he had brought with him from La Tabardy, insisting he might find a use for in the future.

In his new cellar are serried ranks of stoneware jars in which sit *confits de canards*. Rows of glass containers stand beside them filled with foie gras. Others hold preserved vegetables, and yet more contain pheasant pâté and *rillettes*. Large baskets of walnuts sit beneath them on the floor, and above them drying onions and garlic hang on a washing line, fighting for space with two *jambons*.

The menagerie of ducks, geese, chickens, pheasants, hunt dogs and vegetables had moved with him from '*la campagne*' to the town. '*Bien sur je continue!*' he had replied when I had asked him on one of his visits whether he would continue to strangle pheasants, cook up the bones and necks of ducks and dismember frogs.

'*Bien sûr!*' he said, then a thoughtful silence, after which he looks at me earnestly. '*Mais, mes canards cette année; je ne peux pas les gaver avant Décembre! Ils sont trop petits!*' I can't start force-feeding my ducks before December this year; they're too small! 'Even the cows are lighter this year,' he continued, shaking his head in regret and incomprehension. 'It's the year; who knows why.'

He had bought his young *canards* at the market, taking care to look for the signs of a potentially good duck, not just for force-feeding but also for stews and sauces, confits, pâtés and breast fillets. I considered asking why he didn't save some of his own ducks to produce offspring. I wasn't sure I really wanted to know.

He had already described in vivid detail all other aspects of his ducks' existence.

'*Si tu es douée*,' if you're gifted, he had said, 'you can stuff the neck skin too. The carcass, *je la gratte*, I scrape off the meat to make a *pâté de canard*.' Some people, he claimed, put it on the grill then pick off the meat with their teeth. 'I add milk, eggs, *sel et poivre* to the meat scrapings, and perhaps some *échalottes* too, and make *pâté à ma façon*.'

'*Et, alors*, there's nothing left. The foie is cooked, the *magrets* and legs too for confit. The pâté finishes the rest . . . not forgetting the heart,' he added. 'Sauteed – delicious. Nor the gizzards either, for *salade de gésiers* . . . And of course, *la sanguette*!' He smiled broadly. 'The bones I give to the dogs. *Et voilà!*'

He had inherited pride at his lack of waste from his mother, Madame Cholet. I knew already from her that *la sanguette* consisted of duck blood coagulated into a round cake, fried in fat and served with garlic and parsley. She found *la sanguette* delicious, not only for its own sake but because she considered any waste sinful.

Stale bread that I gave to Eida, the horse which lives opposite my house, she would have used to thicken her soup. And wild lambs' lettuce which grew between the vines and which I mowed with my *girobroyeur*, she gathered in and mixed with nettles to make her legendary *mâche* and *ortie* salad. Wild sorrel she mixed with the white haricot beans grown in her garden to make *soupe à l'oseille*, and chestnuts from the tree at the bottom of my garden she gathered up, cleaned and grilled, then peeled and used.

Gilles had learnt how to make confits and pâtés from her. Once a year her earthenware jars, '*toupines*', were washed, cleaned and placed upside down in a neat row to dry in front of her house ready for the new season's confits and foies gras. She died three years ago, peacefully at home, aged ninety. Now her house is empty, about to be restored. I have bought it from Gilles. It sits among my vines, not far from La Tabardy. The wooden seat under the tree in front of the house where she used to sit is still there, as are a few of her *toupines*. The rest have been taken over to Sigoulès by Gilles.

Her vegetable garden is also empty now, save for the few rogue sorrel leaves that grow there still and the wild rambling rose that climbs up the side of the house. 'Will you save me those when the builder starts work on the house?' Gilles had asked, pointing at some asbestos sheets which were clinging forlornly to the edge of the crumbling roof, the old tiles covering them long ago fallen. Alarmed, I pointed out that they contained, indeed were, asbestos.

'Pah, it won't be a problem for what I want them for. You won't forget to keep them?' I made a mental note to remind the builder to keep them. At the same time, I wondered what his mother might have said about it had she still been alive. She was vehemently against him lifting heavy weights of any description.

'Madame. Those stones! He's lifting them again,' she had announced with displeasure when Gilles transported stones I had given him from the vineyard for building the wall around his new house. She was standing outside her front door, shaking her finger at us. Her words ring in my ears still.

Stones have overshadowed Gilles's life. Years of heaving them off his land and into trailers have weakened his spine, with operations on his back and neck to ease the pain having limited success. Indeed, stones are one of the reasons I now own his vines. He sold the vineyard to me as he could no longer continue lifting them off his land.

He has just collected another load, along with some old beams and gravel. Covered in white dust from them, he wipes his hands, spits on them and sets to lifting another huge boulder up into his trailer. Should he be heaving them up again, I ask him. What would his mother have said? '*Mais, ce n'est pas bien grave!*' he laughs. 'I'm used to them!' as he heaves the last few on to the trailer.

Even as a child stones dominated his life. Leaning on the now full trailer, arms folded, he recounts how when he was a boy the families in the village, in lieu of paying village taxes, had what was called a *prestation*, where work was done without payment. He points over towards the road then folds his arms again. 'See that section there? I laid that . . . from your house as far as the Mairie!' He continues. 'It wasn't only the children who worked on them – the parents did too. It was called '*la prestation de la commune*'. He articulates the words carefully, folding his arms higher on his chest.

Stones from his parents' land were transported by carts pulled by their cows and left by the side of the lane ready for breaking up. Those in the commune who didn't have stones of their own had them delivered to them. The village children were each given a hammer and a rucksack, their task after school being to break up the stones into rubble with the hammer and carry it to the road with their rucksacks, laying the base for what would become the village roads. 'After school and milking the cows, I had my *sac* and I broke stones – one wheelbarrow a day . . .' A silence, then he adds, 'Yes . . . when you had your *prestation*, you knew what you had to do.'

I am horrified. It was medieval, I tell him. He's only three years older than me and I can hardly believe that such a system operated. '*Oui!*' he boomed, laughing at my reaction. '*Je te jure! C'était comme ça!* Life was very different then!'

As well as collecting beams and gathering stones for his wall, Gilles has come round to fish for frogs in the small pond at Les Ruisseaux and to inspect La Tabardy, his old house. Now fully restored, it looks beautiful. We walk up to it from Madame Cholet's house. The grey cement facing on its exterior has been removed, revealing the original pale stone Gilles had told me about. The adjoining *chai*, wine cellar, has been integrated into the house. The old cement vats that filled what was a vast, dark cavern have been demolished and in their place is a large, airy and lime-beamed salon. Behind the house and replacing the small, damp

13

back rooms that were not worth keeping is a wide, open terrace running the length of the building.

'*Oui*,' says Gilles, approvingly. '*C'est bon. C'est très bien fait.*' We wander from room to room. What was his *salon* is now a bedroom and what was his *cave*, which had housed confits, pâtés and conserves, is a bathroom. 'I probably would have done the same had I stayed,' he said, nodding in appreciation of the mirrored walls and green glass basins.

We walk on down towards Les Ruisseaux and the frog pond, leaving behind La Tabardy and his trailer of stones and beams. The *parcelle* of vines in front of us creates a canopy of lush green, stretching away into the distant valley. '*Oui*,' murmurs Gilles, '*c'est joli ici.*' Suffused with morning sun, the valley shimmers. The sound of frogs leaping in and out of the pond next to us is restful as we gaze at the view in silence. '*Bon*,' he says, turning towards the pond and the unsuspecting frogs. '*Il faut au moins dix par personne!*' We need at least ten legs per person!

He catches them surprisingly quickly without a net, simply with his bare hands. He will take them home to Sigoulès, he says, and prepare them for this evening. One sharp stab through the head, a quick tug at their legs and it will only remain to rinse and fry them. The body he will throw away, he says, smiling and looking at me. I feel sick again. 'Eh?' he shrugs his shoulders, laughing, amused by my reaction. 'If you want the legs you gotta take them off!'

Leaving Gilles to his frog fishing, I walk back to Madame Cholet's house, then through the vines towards home. A sand and white stone wall borders the small courtyard with tamarisk trees and wisteria that houses the tasting room, office and depot. The red letters of Clos d'Yvigne, the name of my vineyard, are affixed to it. To the right of the buildings is my house and attached to it the *chai*, the working heart of the vineyard.

In the near distance the château of Gageac dominates the

landscape. Sunlight catches its richly coloured tiled roof, a contrast to the pale grey stone of its immense walls. Two towers, each with a weather vane, are silhouetted against the blue sky. The walls, surrounded by a wide moat, now grassed, lead to the main gate and courtyard within. The château is the nucleus of the village. It protects and guards Gageac. It is Gageac.

As are the cypress trees of the cemetery, peaceful, brooding, and the simple country church opposite my house with the war memorial in front of it. And the mission cross at the bottom of the road, and Eida in her field opposite the house. They are as familiar to me as the château, so much a part of my life here in the village. The sun's rays soak into the ancient stones of the church's Romanesque frontage, reflect back from its solitary bell.

On the distant horizon I can see the château of Saussignac, huge and barrack-like, its two towers tall and imposing. My friends Pia and Ekan live in one of them. Pia's family had always owned a property in France. She fell in love with the tower the moment she saw it when looking for a house in the area and bought it, in spite of it being a ruin and against the advice of her husband, Ekan, and most of her friends and family. Now it is restored and beautiful.

This year we have had the most extraordinarily hot summer and, secretly, I am expecting one of the best harvests ever from my vines. I already have massive concentrations of sugar and taste in the grapes. Only two days ago the vines looked stressed, with bunches of grapes shrunken from lack of water. A thunderstorm followed by gentle but persistent rain in the night has refreshed them greatly. At least three weeks in advance of the season, we will almost certainly have an early harvest.

It is hot. Concentrated heat burns down on my head and the vines as I walk through the rows. I look at the grapes through the glare of the sun. Bunches of them hang along the wooden *lattes* in abundance, the vines already de-leafed in preparation for the *vendange*. I inspect them more closely. They are beautiful. There is no rot, no disease. Only clusters of rich, ripe fruit.

Each year their beauty strikes me anew. Rows and rows of rich merlot grapes hang like precious jewels from the vines. '*La belle saison*,' as Gilles would say. All I need for a perfect harvest is rain to plump them out. I look at the deep blue sky, the shimmering rows of vines, the dark purple grapes and the hot sun. There's not going to be any rain today that's for sure.

La belle saison has been providing me with all manner of feasts for most of the summer. Reaching home, I find a basket of vegetables sitting outside the door. Michel Founaud has been. In his mid-to late fifties, he is the recently retired *cantonnier* of Gageac. Short and stocky like Gilles, he is a *chasseur*, an expert mushroom picker, a *pêcheur*, gardener, cook, general handyman and long-time friend of Gilles. He is also one of my firm friends. Along with Gilles, he helped me greatly with the vines during the early days of my life here.

I pick up the basket. Freshly picked red and green peppers spill out of it. Tomatoes, still warm from the sun of his garden and with their unmistakable aroma of tinny geraniums, vie with onions, the whiteness of their inner skins showing through the topaz outer layers. Small heads of white garlic peep through bunches of red radishes, soil still clinging to their root tips.

Potatoes and short, fat cucumbers sit in an old Clos d'Yvigne wine carton beside the basket. At the very bottom of the carton are some shrivelled, pale pods containing the white haricot beans that Michel grows. They are the main constituents of the *sobronade* soup he makes from them. I open one of the pods. The beans inside are moist and have a pearl-like translucence, contrasting with their dried outer exteriors.

I bite into one. It is delicious. Eida the horse looks at me from the field opposite and snorts, eager for something to eat. Taking

16

some bread from the kitchen, I feed her with it as I eat another haricot bean. I look at the beans in my hand. Their dessicated husks signal the end of the summer and the imminence of the *vendange*.

Chapter 2

A BAKING AUGUST MORNING AND THE GROUND IS PARCHED. IT IS hot and still as Eida canters over for her breakfast of stale bread. Her mane has tumbled down into her gentle brown eyes; large and bulky, she stands in anticipation. Bathed in the morning sun, the grass of her field reflects the golden brown colours of a dry, hot summer. I haven't time to go back into the kitchen for the bread.

We look at each other, then I capitulate and return to the house for her breakfast. She chomps and slowly masticates the stale baguette I feed her, gazing at me mutely as I throw the rest of it over the hedge, jump into the car and head for the lab.

The wine samples jiggle around in the basket on the floor of the front passenger seat as I hurtle down the hill en route for the laboratory. I eye the bottles as I take the corner at the bottom of the road. They deliberately, it seems to me, shift their weight to one side and the basket with them, teetering dangerously. One hand on the steering wheel and the other lurching towards the basket, I manoeuvre the corner and the bottles.

The fertile valley looks serene and calm as I drive along the road towards Bergerac. To the right, gentle slopes of vines run up to the ridge, interspersed with houses that rise up out of the land. The air is still, with the sun already high in the sky as I pass the village of St-Laurent-des-Vignes. It silhouettes the church, its rays shining directly through the bell tower, an intense and cloudless blue sky behind it. I continue along the valley road, the only car, and turn on to the main road and the lab. Dropping off the samples, I leave the car and walk up towards the centre of town.

Hot, noisy and bustling with activity, it is alive with conversation. It hums with life. It's market day in Bergerac. Surrounding the church of Notre Dame in the centre of town, and in the square in front of it, dozens of brightly coloured parasols have been erected. Spotlit by the sun, they jostle for space with each other. Some have fringes that complement their colours; others have long since lost them and their colours, bleached by the sun.

Beneath them, stallholders display their produce. An old farmer, flat-capped and sitting beside his wares, chatters to a customer, his large basket of fresh eggs and sheaves of sorrel deposited on the ground. Next to him, a trestle table is buckling under the weight of leeks, onions, cucumbers, charentais melons and plump, purple garlic.

In the old *quartier*, half-timbered houses and winding backstreets of medieval buildings surround the covered market. In the small square in front of it, stalls with breads of every description are for sale. Small baguettes sit next to huge brown loaves with shapes of every size and type piled high: white bread, brown, organic and walnut. Some of the larger loaves are cut in two. Thick, coarsely cut slices invite customers to taste.

Live ducks and chickens with geese and rabbits sit in cages or simply on the ground beside the traders. They blink occasionally, impervious to the noise and hubbub around them, awaiting their fate patiently. Customers haggle over the price and inspect them at closer quarters. Next to them on a trestle table birds, already slaughtered and trussed, are displayed for sale, their gizzards attached, their necks and heads neatly tucked into the cavity.

Beside them a woman laughs and chatters to her customers, her voice rising above the staccato quacking of the poultry and the noise of the crowds. She sells soft, fresh goats' cheeses. Moist, patted rounds wrapped in translucent paper, they look pure and succulent. Alongside them, dry, stronger-flavoured cheeses and half-dried creamy rounds sit in pyramids. People have come as much to talk to friends and neighbours as to buy and inspect.

Fish and meat, walnuts and mushrooms are for sale, along with nylon pinnies and pink, boned corsets. Leather belts, sunglasses and wallets sold by tall French Africans vie for space alongside flowers and plants, a riot of colour next to them.

The crowd hums and sways, moving from stall to stall. The buzz of conversation, the gossip, the smells and aromas merge into one. The crowd have come not only to buy but to look and to share in something which is as timeless as this part of France. It is simple and direct.

The old farmer next to the church with his sorrel and eggs lights a cigarette and hands over some sorrel to a customer, weighed on ancient hand scales. Next to the live poultry another old man slaps his thigh with merriment. His face has the dark, burnt brown of the sun and the seasons, his hands large and thick, the tell-tale signs of manual work. He pushes his hat back from his head.

Two old women standing next to him are laughing and chattering, their faces lit up by mirth, invigorated by each other's company. I hear words in English as a family wanders by to look at the ducks. A well-dressed French woman, chic and perfumed, glances disdainfully at the chickens as she hurries on, carrying a wrapped and ribboned carton of cakes from the *pâtisserie*.

I approach one of the vegetable stalls. Green courgettes, their flowers intact, their skins creamy speckled sit beside bulbous, outsized spring onions. Melons and strings of pale purple garlic mingle with fresh herbs: thyme, mint, basil and marjoram.

The air, redolent with garlic and mint, transports me suddenly and unexpectedly back to my childhood. I am lost in the past of sun and scent, three years old, somewhere in my own history, weightless. The sensation of transcience, of stepping out of time, stops me in my tracks. It's elusive, mysterious, and I can't quite capture it.

Like the culture here in this part of France. Like the landscape, timeless yet changing. Like this market where yesterday's world meets tomorrow's, the focal point of all the villages and farms of the undulating, fertile landscape. The sense of urgency I had this morning before I arrived at the market evaporates. I feel myself in an ancient land again. I feel part of its history, immersed in nature, in the season's cycles, in the passing of time.

I join the queue for some melons and listen to the gabble of the customers and the quips of the stallholders. I stand next to the old man. His accent of the south-west, full of warmth and sun, his large, working hands and his way of life epitomise this part of rural France. He is smiling, talking to one of his customers as he lights another cigarette and gesticulates. He points to the sorrel, shoves his hat further over his eyes and turns to his neighbour who also joins in the discussion, laughing and shouting while serving and taking his customers' money or handing out change.

I look at the live poultry, sitting next to the trussed ducks and chickens. Or the goats' cheeses. Here is the essence of France. Town and country meet and merge. The sight, the smell and the mood are intoxicating. Late strawberries and wild raspberries, brightly coloured pumpkins, some cut into wedges, showing off their rich, amber flesh. Bulbous onions, deep-purple aubergines and pale, golden grapes. Apricots, with their decadent colour and heady perfume, and the first of the rich, black and wrinkled prunes, displayed on triangular wickerwork trays or in large, shallow baskets.

The vendors chatter among themselves and to customers. '*Salut!*' shouts one stallholder to a woman opposite. She turns to him, smiling. '*Comment ça va?*' he continues. '*Et les enfants?*' She approaches the stall. '*Ça va très bien!*' she shouts. '*Et vous?*' They catch up on children, the weather, business, each other.

A small, thin man selling pumpkins looks thoughtfully at a large woman at the stall opposite. She is babbling and laughing, her ample form shaking with every peal of laughter. Beside her, a woman inspects melons, picking one up and sniffing it for confirmation of its ripeness.

Behind the market and hidden in the rue Ste Catherine is Monsieur Blanchard's cheese shop. The best in town, constant streams of customers come and go, his shop an essential and traditional part of the Saturday morning market experience. Monsieur Blanchard is small and dark with intelligent eyes and usually has a navy beret perched on his head; he is passionate about cheese and wine.

A small selection of wines is for sale in his shop, those he considers good accompaniments to his cheeses, an extraordinary array of which are displayed on traditional straw mats in a long counter of polished glass running the length of his shop. Goats' cheeses are grouped together in all stages of maturity, from fresh and young to *demi sec* and hard. Tiny rounds of Cabecous from Quercy sit beside ewes' milk cheeses from Corsica.

It's the season for them both and for Monsieur Blanchard the seasons are primordial. When the animals are outside and the new grass is growing, the cheeses are richer and more complex, he tells me. He points to a Castagniccia, rolled in chestnut, and next to it a Fio di Pastori, creamy and rich.

There is only a short period of time in the season when Corsican cheeses are available for him to buy, he explains. Thereafter the Corsicans guard them jealously for themselves. He kisses the air in appreciation of them, pointing out a Broccin *frais* with pride.

They look fresh and inviting, their delicate smell emitting the sweetness of babies, of fresh milk and curds.

Beside them are the hard cheeses of the south-west. Large truckles of Cantal are on display, from mild young cheeses through to medium and strong. The matured Cantal, already cut into, looks succulent. A dappled grey and white crust invades its deep yellow body, which looks rich and strong. A huge, imposing Salers sits next to it, its thick crust the result of long maturing.

Pungent Roqueforts made from the richest ewes' milk and aged in the limestone caves south of the Massif Central look inviting, their blue-green veins running through the gleaming ivory interiors. Fifteen litres of rich, unpasteurised milk are required for a three-kilo Roquefort, Monsieur Blanchard tells me with enthusiasm. Further along the cheese counter are Pays Basque mountain cheeses, slabs of fine butter and *saucisson*.

A huge Tomme de Chèvre with a delicate down of grey and white is lifted out from the display counter and on to the wooden shelf behind. Monsieur Blanchard sinks his knife into it and it cuts as if through butter. It emits a delicate, fruity perfume, white in its centre and pale cream near the skin. '*Oh, que c'est bon!*' Monsieur Blanchard declares. He points to a Cathare Toulousain, suggesting that his customer try that too. '*Faites-moi confiance,*' he smiles, his knife hovering over it. His laughing eyes and open smile seduce his customers.

His assistant, Caroline, tall with long, dark, auburn hair tied in a ponytail, wears a fresh white coat and washes the large cutting knives each time they are used by Monsieur Blanchard. She dries them with pristine white tea towels, placing them back on the wooden shelf behind the display counter. Monsieur Blanchard inspects his counters even as he serves his customers, pointing out to Caroline a Brebis *de la ferme* which needs to be replaced, or a gap into which a Trappe Echourgnac could be placed. It is made from winter milk, he points out, when the animals are stabled.

His customers listen and look. He picks up the ladle from a huge wooden bowl of *fromage frais* and lets the creamy white contents drop back into it. He shows us a large cheese from the north of France. It looks like a perfect round stone. Aged for eighteen months, with a natural rind, it is just the season to eat it, he tells us. I had heard that the rinds shouldn't be eaten. He looks surprised. Most of his customers love the rinds, he tells me.

'The rind from *un vieux* Salers tastes of walnuts. Eaten with grapes *ce n'est que du bonheur!*' he replies, waving his hand in the air. His customers listen. 'There are no rules – it depends on the individual.' He points out a Puant de Lille, 'a pure marvel', and a Sans Nom, a cheese that had disappeared, its recipe recently resurrected by a young couple from the Pas de Calais. 'It's a *délice*, with a *petit point* of *saveur* that's a real pleasure!' He kisses the air. His customers murmur approval. One has already tasted it, another will try some today.

Now is the moment to eat this one, he assures the general audience, pointing to a cheese with his knife. One of his customers asks for a '*petit bout*' of it as well as some of his Roquefort; it is not factory produced, he tells her, but a Roquefort *fermier*. '*Un Roquefort fermier, ce n'est que le bonheur!*' he reiterates. The *bonheur* of his cheeses figures largely in his shop, I decide. I tell him that I often drink my sweet wine with Roquefort on toast as an *apéritif*.

'But of course!' he replies, looking around the shop for general agreement. 'The saltiness of Roquefort with the sweetness of wine!' It might even have been the English who introduced the French to the notion of sweetness and saltiness, he muses, smiling. '*Mais non!*' exclaims a small, older woman next to me; she has a gentle voice and a lined, smiling face. 'I come from the north of France and we often have that mixture. Black pudding with apples, for instance,' she says, addressing us in general and her husband who stands behind her in particular.

'*Eh voilà,*' says Monsieur Blanchard, addressing her husband. '*Un monsieur* from the north. Taste the Sans Nom and see what you think.' We all taste it. It's perfumed, not strong, and very delicious. 'And what about apples with foie gras?' counters a younger woman from Bergerac at the other end of the shop. '*Eh oui!*' agrees Monsieur Blanchard. 'Every region has something to offer. Take my grandmother's choux farci for example!' He laughs. He remembers it, he says, as if it were yesterday. It had the most wonderful aromas and a taste that remains fixed in his memory. A murmur of approval ripples around the customers in the shop. 'Did she steam it or roast it?' asks one of them.

'How did she make the sauce?' asks another. Her mother used to serve it with a *poularde* made from a recipe her grandmother had. 'Mmm,' says another. '*Attention*, it's not a chicken,' corrects Monsieur Blanchard when I ask whether it was made from a *coq* or a hen. 'A *poularde* is much richer!' 'And what about *coq au Chambertin*?' counters someone else. 'A pure delight!' agrees Monsieur Blanchard.

All the customers have a view. They chatter excitedly together. One of them is making an Aligot with Tomme *fraîche* at midday. 'I hope you're serving it with grilled *saucisson* or tripe?' asks Monsieur Blanchard. '*Que c'est bon!*' he counters when she confirms the former. 'When you've eaten that, you know *le bonheur*,' he says, turning to me as he cuts a large chunk of Tomme for her.

The shop is now humming. Recipes are discussed and methods disputed, the men expressing their views as vociferously as their wives. The husband of the lady from the north of France insists that Roquefort is better than Gruyère with *crêpes*. The foie gras and apple lady is still describing her grandmother's method of *choux farci* that differs in subtle ways from that of Monsieur Blanchard's and the noise level as I leave is deafening.

At the vegetable stall it's my turn and I have smelt the melons, choosing two with the sweetest perfume. Firm yet ripe, they are perfect. 'Are they for *ce soir*?' asks the stallholder, also smelling them and gently pressing his thumb to one end, nodding in approval at my choice. We talk, discussing melons in general and my two in particular.

Further along, a stallholder is shaking hands with one of his customers, reaching over ripe Marmandais tomatoes to do so. The aroma of dried hams from the next stall mingles with the perfume of melons as flat-capped locals, hands tucked in pockets or gesticulating to make a point, catch up with local gossip.

One of them reminds me of Gilles. 'It's always been like that!' I hear him shout, laughing as he removes his hat. He shakes hands with the group and moves off. They laugh too. People move on from one stall to the next, their places instantly replaced by others; a slow dance. Jean Roland, the owner of l'Imparfait restaurant, waves from a distance and blows a kiss, part of the dance. He is carrying fresh bread and mushrooms. He holds up the bag of mushrooms, pungent with the powerful aromas of the earth. '*C'est la belle saison!*' he shouts.

The first evening Fidde and I had dinner together he picked me up exactly on time. I was only just ready, having mowed the *parcelle* of vines I was working on for the rest of the day and hurriedly filled some of the barrels in the *chai* with wine to give me a head start the following morning. The headlights of his car shone in through the kitchen window as he manoeuvred the turning and the cross at the top of the road. He approached the door. '*Hej*, Patricia,' he said with a smile as he opened it.

The car was silent and silky after the roar of the tractor's engine that had assaulted my eardrums for most of the day. Fidde's voice was deep and melodious over it, his Swedish accent giving a lilt to his voice as though he had some secret to impart.

As we sped along the valley road towards the restaurant he recounted some of his life. 'Ekan and I have been friends since we were at university together in Fribourg,' he said, turning to look at me from time to time and smiling. 'He left after graduating, and I stayed on.' He had been involved in a printing company there after university, he continued, then bought an ink supplying business which led to a paint business, which led him to build houses in Abu Dhabi before he created his golf club in Fribourg. 'Yes,' he smiled, looking at me for a moment as he parked the car. 'Such was my dynamism, I never really left Fribourg!' He laughed a deep laugh, full of life and optimism. It resonated around the car.

At the table, the bubbles from my glass of champagne gave off a faint scent of rose petals as I sipped it. Once we had ordered, both of us enticed by meat sizzling on the open fire next to us, Fidde settled down to the evening. His company was both stimulating and interesting. The oysters I started with were delicious, lean and salty with a taste of the sea. 'Are they good?' he asked me, looking at them and me. They were. Would he like one? I asked him.

No, he said, smiling. He no longer ate oysters. When he first met and fell in love with his wife he ordered them when he took her out to dinner. He knew they were considered aphrodisiacs, ate thirty-four and was taken to hospital with food poisoning where he stayed for three days. 'I wanted to impress her,' he laughed. 'She wasn't at all impressed.'

He told me about his life. He was divorced with two grown-up children: a daughter, Ebba, who worked in London and was dynamic and successful, and a son, Gustaf, who was working with him temporarily at the golf club in Fribourg before starting his own business in Spain, where his ex-wife, Carola, lived.

'So, Patricia!' he said, smiling, his Swedish accent accentuated by the conspiratorial tone in his voice. 'I'm doing all the talking here! And now you know all about me . . .' We laughed. 'I want to know more about you.' I smiled, guessing he would have interrogated Pia and Ekan before now and that he probably knew quite a bit about me already. He looked at me with a broad grin, reading my thoughts. His eyes glittered, the glow of the burning fire next to us reflected in them. 'How long have you been driving tractors, Patricia?' he asked. 'And making wine?' He paused. 'And why are you living on your own? Where are your children?'

He listened as I told him of my hand-to-mouth existence in the early days. Like any peasant farmer, I told him, I was at the mercy of nature and the elements. If the vines didn't produce a good harvest, if the tractor broke down, if the business failed, I did too. He was attentive, interested. 'I admire farmers,' he said. He understood about land, he added, about the harshness of the elements, the ripening of crops.

He loved nature, loved being in it. He skied, rode horses, skated over the lakes in Sweden, he played golf. Scrutinising my face, he laughed as he read my thoughts again. His laugh was infectious, deep and resonant, inviting a form of complicity. 'It's not quite the same as being on a tractor, I know!' he rejoined self-deprecatingly.

I studied Fidde as he talked. He was certainly 'un bel homme' as Juliana had said. His eyes were dark brown, almost black, with laughter lines around them. His mouth was wide and full, his teeth white and uniform. Occasionally he sucked the inside of his cheek, displaying a slightly crooked smile. He had dark-brown hair, his face tanned and rugged looking, yet with smooth skin. His style of dress was casual but studied. His hands were neat; on his left he wore a blue signet ring which he touched from time to time.

He was exciting to be with. Masculine yet with a gentleness of manner, he was knowing. Behind a jovial, light-hearted appearance, he was perceptive, determined and confident. We talked and laughed. The wine was rich and delicious. I told him about my children only in a superficial way. I told him how proud I was of them, how beautiful my grandchildren were. I didn't tell him of the emptiness that came from my separation from them in the early days of my life in France. Part of the reason for throwing myself into work was not only the loss of James, but of them.

Chantal, my daughter, had two daughters of her own, the eldest born only a year after I had moved to France. Phone calls weren't enough. I had felt impotent, unable to help her, guilty at having to be in France working rather than being with her. As for John, he was living in Thailand, thousands of miles away in another country, another place.

'And your husband, Patricia,' he smiled. 'Why isn't he here with you? Why are you working here on your own?' We looked at each other. I felt myself blush, from the wine, from the open fire, from his question. He took from his inside jacket pocket a cigar holder. 'May

I?' he asked and removed half a cigar from it, which he lit. He took only two puffs then returned it carefully to its tin case. 'I like to smoke,' he said. 'But only a little,' he laughed. 'Now and again.' He smiled as he sipped his wine and looked at me, waiting patiently and studying my face.

I told him of James's illness, his return to England and the eventual disintegration of our lives together. He stared at me intently as I talked. His direct questions, his perceptive character, his insight, calmly extracted from me more than I expected to divulge. He looked down occasionally, then back into my eyes. 'I don't think I want to talk about it any more,' I said and he changed the subject instantly.

'When do you take your holidays?' he said. I laughed. 'You mean you don't have them?' he continued, laughing with me, scrutinising me. No, I said, I don't play golf or ride horses or skate over lakes, not for the moment. 'You should!' he laughed. '*Skol*, Patricia!' and he raised his glass.

'Do you know how to *skol* properly?' he asked me, smiling. 'It's a Swedish tradition. You raise your glass and look into the eyes of the person you want to *skol*, then you take a sip from it, holding their gaze.' He fixed me with his black eyes as he drank. 'Then you raise your glass slightly again – always holding their gaze.' He looked at me intently. I looked back at him, at his dark eyes, sparkling, intelligent and knowing. 'Can I take you out again?' he said quietly.

I am, in fact, quite ready for an early *vendange* this year. The *chai* is clean, the press is ready, the vats are shining and I am impatient to start. I have my very own '*maître de chais/chef de culture*', cellar-master and vineyard manager. Benjamin, who has been with me since April, worked previously in the Loire Valley for a vineyard producing white wine. He had a baptism of fire from his first day here due to an unusually precocious year in the vines followed by a very hot summer.

With Benjamin I now have two employees in the vines. Alain was employed shortly after I bought Gilles's vines. It was clear after a year that it simply wasn't possible to work the vines effect-ively with only Alain and me. As a result of Benjamin's arrival, life is easier. I no longer need to spend my days driving tractors, or pulling wood from the vines, or pruning or cutting off shoots.

The forecasted early harvest has already arrived for some wine-makers who have begun picking their white grapes. Michel Founaud picked his nine rows of red grapes some days ago. He came round the morning after his harvest to ask for two of my old barrels to put the juice in to and also to invite me to dinner tonight.

The *cicadelles*, in full throat as they have been for weeks, reach a crescendo as I climb into the car to drive down the road to Michel's and dinner. They seem to sing louder the hotter it gets. It is certainly hot tonight. The sound is supersonic; in Eida's field, in my garden, down the road towards my neighbour Juliana, in the hedging, over towards the church. As I drive down the hill I see a *vendange* machine heading into the vines of my neighbour, Jean de la Verrie, son of Pierre, the old count. He waves from a distance. His *vendange* is beginning.

Michel and his wife, Monique, live on the edge of Gageac, towards La Ferrière. Their house is simple, situated on the corner of a country road. A small wisteria-covered terrace leads from the kitchen to the garden, which is bordered by lilac trees. To one side of the terrace is a makeshift barbecue and across the road is Michel's vegetable patch, along with his nine rows of vines.

Michel raises his hand in welcome as I park the car next to his house. He is crossing the road from his vegetable garden. The basket in his hand holds three large tomatoes, some onions, a head of garlic and the shrivelled pods of white haricot beans, the constituent parts of *sobrouade* soup. Monique is seated at the terrace table picking over some *haricots verts*. '*Salut!*' she calls as she walks towards me with her wide smile.

The tomatoes are warm to the touch. Gilles and Pamela, his wife, have arrived too and we are all sitting around the table under the shade of the wisteria. Michel slices some bread from a baguette lying on the table and with the small knife he always carries with him cuts open a clove of garlic and rubs it on to the bread. He adds some of his home-made pâté. '*Tiens*. Here you are,' he smiles and hands me the slice. The *sanglier* pâté is strong, unctuous and delicious.

Michel deftly skins the tomatoes while we de-stalk haricot beans into a bowl and chatter around the table. It's an impossibly hot evening and we are drinking some of my rosé, fresh and cool. Everybody is talking at once. Michel throws the vegetables into a pot on the stove in the kitchen and rejoins us. He hasn't ever really left us as the terrace is simply an extension of the kitchen. Aromas of fresh garlic and tomatoes send sinuous trails that follow him back to the table.

We talk of Gilles and Pamela's new home, their wall, my forthcoming *vendange*, the last wild boar that Michel shot, the tiny ruin of a house at the bottom of my garden that I now own and have done nothing to. It has a roof and walls but not much else. The evening races on, helped by the rosé, the heat and the headiness of friendship. The *sobronade* is just as good as I remembered it from last year. We sip the first spoonfuls in silence. Greater than the sum of its parts, the sensation of fresh vegetables, married with the richness of pork rind is luxurious. The fresh, crusty bread intensifies the taste. '*Que c'est bon*,' says Gilles. We all tacitly agree.

My *vendange* has begun in earnest. The memory of last night's *sobronade*, followed by barbecued chicken kebabs and *haricots verts*, has all but disappeared. It has rained during the day, giving me much-needed water to plump out the grapes. We pick dry white sauvignon grapes in the coolness of the night rather than the heat of the day to ensure that the grapes come in at a low temperature and don't start their fermentation during maceration.

We have already worked through the vines removing leaves and any substandard grapes. The *vendange* machine lumbers up and down the rows, two powerful headlights pointing the way. It looks like some prehistoric monster. Higher than a double-decker bus, it straddles a row of vines, the narrow aperture in its middle containing rubberised handles that gently massage the grapes from the vine.

Temporarily stashed away deep in the machine's belly, the grapes are periodically disgorged from it into trailers driven by tractors, which wait patiently beside the *parcelles* of vines for a load. They bounce down the rows on their journey back to the *chai*, beaming headlights sending light flickering up and down through the black night like shooting stars. The tractors and trailers bring in heavy loads of clean, golden sauvignon grapes, depositing them in the de-stemming machine and on into vats where they will macerate for eight hours. The juice from them tastes fresh and clean.

A week of pressing, cooling and barrelling propels us onwards and into the other white grape picks of sémillon and muscadelle, both early in the morning and in the cool of the night. *Vendange* machines arrive at four in the morning or sometimes at midnight, and I wonder whether the villagers of Gageac stir in their dreams at the whirring sound of the great machine working up and down the vines.

Alain, Benjamin and I work late into the night and early in the mornings. Sleep is a rare commodity but the adrenalin of the moment and the culmination of the year's work in the vines drives us all on. Pipes, pumps and vats full of different white grape juices fill the *chai*, along with the heady aromas of fruit from the newly fermenting vats.

The reds follow: ripe merlot grapes, then cabernet sauvignons and cabernet francs. The *vendange* machine picks well into the night, lumbering up and down the vines, once again its powerful headlights shining out in the darkness like two large, luminous eyes.

Days run into nights in the *chai* with, for once, no anxious calls to the weather centre before harvesting. Just hard slog with full vats of fermenting juices emitting wondrous fruit aromas and the *chai* a mass of pipes, pumps, buckets, yeasts and grape skins. I am at one with myself, exhausted but alive, in the moment; the past is irrelevant. The future is sitting right there in the vats.

My harvest has been a good one, lower in yield because of the hot summer, but high in quality. I hardly felt the time pass. Worries then about non-fermenting vats or overheated grape juices are now gone, although not yet the obligatory stress spots on my scalp that arrive without fail each *vendange*. The vats of fermenting grape juice are now transformed into wine. The fruit aromas in the *chai* are heady: raspberries and strawberries from the rosé vat, citrus fruits and melon from the whites and cherries and ripe blackcurrants from the reds.

Autumn is here with its morning mists and hot afternoon sun, both of which are helping to transform the ripe sémillon grapes still sitting on my vines into botrytised ones which will make my sweet wine. Benjamin and I inspect them. Some of their skins are brown and golden, others a pale and beautiful violet with the soft, white down of noble rot, botrytis.

Picking noble rot requires patience, nerves of steel, skilled pickers and faith. Patience to wait until the grapes have the botrytis that gives up sweet, shrivelled grapes. Nerves of steel to wait for enough of them to justify a pick. Skilled pickers to know the difference between botrytis rot and other rot and faith that rain won't fall before they can be gathered in, saturating their porous skins and diluting their concentration. The renewed sun and drying wind needed to dehydrate them again after rain is never guaranteed at this time of year. As we walk back from the vines, I will them to produce luscious, shrivelled, pale-purple noble rot grapes quickly and easily.

Another two days and I know I will have enough to make the first pick viable. I have been picking noble rot grapes for fourteen years now. You would think that I could stop worrying about them. I can't. I can't because the grapes are still sitting out there at the mercy of nature. I can't because the morning mists, the afternoon sun, the wonderful evolution of luscious noble rot on my grapes that I have at this moment could be eradicated by one heavy downfall.

Chapter 3

IT IS MID-OCTOBER AND *LA CHASSE* HAS BEEN OPEN FOR SOME weeks. We hear the echo of shots and see pheasants, rabbits and occasionally magnificent hares racing through the rows of vines as we pick the late noble rot grapes. They rush this way and that in a frantic attempt to escape the guns of the *chasseurs* as we pick. '*Vite! Vite!*' shouts Juliana, one of my pickers. 'Hide! Run!' as a hare leaps in the air and bounds out of sight. Partridges still sit calmly in my trees in the garden and on the telephone wires above the church, unaware of their impending fate.

The countryside is ravishing. The vine leaves have turned colour, either to a rich, deep red or a pale, golden yellow. The noble rot grapes are now purple, shrouded with the delicate white down of botrytis. Those that are still in their evolutionary stage are golden and pink but already with the beginnings of botrytis. Their perfume is delicate and the sugar in them concentrated. It sticks to our fingers, luscious and rich as we pick in the afternoons when the mists have dispersed and the sun shines down, hot and intense.

*

'Huh!' Gilles ridicules the notion of mass slaughter. He is here to invite me along to hunt on Sunday and is sitting in my kitchen. It is more than a week since my last noble rot pick. Feeling buoyant, heady with the pleasure of having most of my harvest in, delighted at the quality generally in the *chai* and eager to finish, my scalp no longer itches and I listen to Gilles attentively.

'Don't think you can just catch them like that, *les gibiers*. *Milledieux*, they're crafty!' Gilles booms, nodding his head and smiling, probably remembering past shoots or particularly crafty *gibiers*. 'But in comparison to the tame pheasants we set free to shoot . . .' he shifts his chair to face mine and looks at me earnestly. '*Il faut les sauvages pour une bonne bouffe*' – you need wild game for a good feast. 'They may be tougher, but they're sweeter. They've eaten in the wild, they've lived in the wild and we shoot them in the wild.' Describing the feeling of satisfaction after a successful day's shooting, he insists, 'It's a test of skill! And at least they've had a life in the wild, those *gibiers*, not like the factory-farmed chickens you buy at supermarkets!'

His voice reverberates around the kitchen. My already weak moral stance on behalf of hunted wildfowl has crumbled at the thought of countless incarcerated chickens and ducks leading miserable lives in innumerable factory farms. The undeniable reality of my consumption of *gibiers*, pheasants, wild boar and venison, regularly consumed with Gilles, Pamela, Michel and Monique, does not help my cause. They were all, without exception, succulent and tasty.

'Yes, when all's said and done, the wildfowl, are the *plus jolis*. Much more interesting to kill and to eat.' He shakes his head to emphasise the point. 'No comparison . . .' and I just know he is about to launch into the finer details of *la chasse*.

He raises his pheasants in the run made for them. 'Some stakes, some wire pulled tightly round the base and the top and some chicken fencing', in effect a ground cage. It is three hundred metres long. 'So they can run!' And three metres high. 'And fly!' he tells me. He sets them free two days before a shoot or some-times even on the same day. '*Oui*', he continues, '*mais les vrai sauvages* are much more interesting to *chasse* than my tame pheasants. They just stand in the road waiting for you. Where's the fun in that?'

I point out that the beautiful brace of pheasant he deposited on my table at the beginning of the last *chasse* weren't hunted at all. They were still warm, newly dead, their plumage a brilliant blue and rose pearl against the pale wood of the table. It had been my present from the *chasse* for allowing them to continue to hunt on my land after Gilles had sold it to me. 'Well, we didn't want you to have shot in yours, so we chose the best two and wrung their necks instead,' he said in justification.

Gilles's *chasse* includes one of his sons, his brother-in-law, some nephews and various friends. 'And don't forget either, we can't start before 8 am and we can only *chasse* until sunset.' This I already am aware of by the cacophony of sound that always heralds its onset at 8 am on each of the Wednesday and Sunday *chasse* days and, more frenetic, the approach of 6 pm, with guns going off in all directions. I inevitably worry about my cats as I guess that anything that moves is a potential target in the *chasseurs*' frenzy to bag a few more birds, rabbits, pheasants or hares before close of play.

Pheasants can only be hunted for five months of the year. Some even escaped death, Gilles insisted, reproducing and becoming '*sauvage*', much more interesting for *la chasse et la bouffe*. Yes, he says with faint disgust, returning to the subject of pheasants that are kept in his run, released and shot the same day. They are virtu-ally tame. 'Why would you expect them to run away? Where's the pleasure in shooting such a bird?'

I wondered whether the pheasants which escaped death the previous season became as crafty as the other *gibiers*. '*Non*, not exactly,' replies Gilles, a slow smile spreading over his face. 'I wouldn't call pheasants crafty, exactly. But, all the same, they're not bad . . . at least they give us a run for our money. And they do taste sweeter.' He rises to leave. 'Of course, if you'd come on a *chasse* with me a couple of years ago before my back problems, you would never have been able to keep up with me! *Bon*. See you Sunday,' and he's gone.

The last pick of botrytised grapes and we pick everything that the birds haven't already taken. Each year the birds and I wait for the last of the noble rot to appear on the grapes. They sit on the telephone wires waiting and watching, like me. Each year they steal at least half of them before we can gather them in. Alain suggests a system of ball trap explosions to frighten them away. Benjamin thinks the neighbours' chickens might be frightened away if we use them. I think the neighbours will frighten me away if we do.

Clouds of white botrytis powder rose up from the press as we tipped the grapes into the *presse* and unctious juice fell into the tray underneath the *presse* as the grapes gave forth their juice. Transferred to a vat overnight to settle, it was then racked, had yeast added to it and was put straight into barrels, where it now sits slowly fermenting. Aromas of apricots and honey rise up from them.

It is Sunday, 6.30 am and still dark as Eida snorts gently and stamps her foot for breakfast. Gilles is here to pick me up. We are going to set free some pheasants from his brother-in-law, Monsieur Jean-Lis Bichon's property. There are eight of them for today's shoot. Dawn has not yet broken as we climb into his van. Prune, his black Labrador, barks in the back. She knows we are going to *chasse*.

Jean-Lis's house sits on the highest ridge in Gageac, overlooking the valley of Cunèges, La Bastide and beyond towards Sigoulès. To the side and behind his house are woods, fields and vines. A solitary light shines from the kitchen like a beacon as we drive up the hill to his house and the smell of freshly brewing coffee beckons us in as we approach the back door. We are still sleepy and the peace of half-light softens our voices and quietens our thoughts.

We drink our coffee at the table with Jean-Lis. It's the first time I have been inside his house and I'm surprised at how large the kitchen is, how ordered and clean the house is. The tiled floor in the kitchen shines, the table tops are clean and devoid of anything other than a kettle and bread board. Long divorced from his wife, Josianne, Jean-Lis lives here with his son and Gilles's favourite nephew, Emanuel — Manu.

Manu is twenty-four. He has been a *chasseur* since, as a child of four, he followed Gilles and his group on their weekend *chasses*. When I first moved to Gageac he was ten years old and almost the only child in the village. With large eyes and a gentle demeanour, he was much loved by Gilles, his wife Pamela and everyone in the village. Now he is grown tall and large and works with his father who has a vineyard of thirty hectares. He drives huge tractors, he works the vines, he gathers in the hay. He hunts. Unlike Gilles, who hunts only *gibiers*, he also hunts wild boar (*sangliers*) and deer (*chevreuils*).

Manu appears in the kitchen. He wipes sleep from his eyes as Gilles's son Sébastien arrives, along with Jean-François, a friend who has driven over from Souillac, some forty minutes away, where he is a butcher. '*Bon. On y va?*' asks Gilles and we step back outside. Gilles takes from his van two large boxes and gives one to Jean-François. We descend towards the woods in the half-light. Carefully sliding open the top of the box, he pulls out a *coq* pheasant by its feet and one wing. He tucks in the wing, holds the bird firmly in his hands and heads for the bracken on the edge of the wood to set it free.

The silence of the morning is broken by its piercing squawk. The flapping of its wings sends leaves dancing into the air as the pheasant half-flies, half-runs into the wood. Gilles and Jean-François release the others one by one into woods and hedges, then we head back to the house where Sébastien is on the terrace pulling on his boots and Manu, standing beside him, is calmly smoking. All of them wear khaki gilets festooned with variously coloured cartridges placed in loops designed for that purpose.

Gilles's black Labrador, Prune, descends from the *camionette*. Two other dogs rush around in front of the terrace, excited and energetic. They are eager to be off. One is Manu's English setter, the other, with a bell attached to his collar, is Jean-François's spaniel, Cécile. Both are bitches with shining coats; both are pedigrees.

Sébastien is resting on his gun, smoking a cigarette. Lean and tall, his body curves into the gun and seems almost part of it. Manu, large and standing full square on the terrace, legs slightly apart, has his gun by his side. He picks it up, positions it over his shoulder and steps down from the terrace, flicking away his cigarette end and repositioning his hat firmly on his head.

At the stroke of eight o'clock we set off down the hill, the valley spread out before us. A mist hangs over the distant horizon. Dawn has broken and we can *chasse*. '*Bon. On commence dans le bois,*' says Gilles, pointing to some woods to the left.

With a slight nod, Manu heads straight on towards a field below in search of hares. He doesn't hunt pheasants; his forté is *les gibiers nobles*. We watch as he strides down the sloping meadow, gun slung over his large shoulders. Sébastien, Jean-François, Gilles and I walk towards the woods.

Gilles directs us. Jean-François will cover the far edge of the wood, he and I the near side and Sébastien will walk through it. 'Stand behind me,' he advises as we set off. 'It's dangerous to be walking by my side with my gun loaded.' I do as I'm told, half-walking, half-running. Gilles strides along, looking into the wood, occasionally calling to the other two *chasseurs*. He needs to know

42

where they are in the wood for safety reasons. Three shots suddenly break the silence. I cover my ears as the sound, shocking and violent, echoes around the valley. 'He missed,' announces Gilles calmly.

We enter the oak and chestnut wood. Fallen leaves create a carpet of gold and copper. The trees are delicate and upright, reaching skywards and spreading their branches out into a canopy. Above us, the dark rust colour of drying oak leaves and the pale yellow of large chestnut leaves that still remain on the trees appear translucent and magical against the sky which seeps in through the branches.

The snuffling of dogs, the crackle of leaves and twigs as we tread on them and the muffled tone of the bell collar around Cécile's neck are the only audible sounds. Gilles crouches suddenly, turns his gun towards the sky outside the wood and fires one shot. It happens in an instant. The sound of the shot echoes through the wood. A pheasant in flight is frozen momentarily in mid-air, then falls heavily to the ground.

Gilles turns slowly towards me as he disengages his gun. 'Prune! Fetch!' he shouts and Prune, scrambling through undergrowth, appears on the other side of the wood and retrieves the pheasant. It is stone dead. 'Did you get it?' Jean-François's voice echoes through the woods. 'Did you get it?'

Prune's tail stands to attention as she walks towards us, holding the pheasant gently in her mouth. She parades up and down with it until Gilles commands, 'Gently, give.' A red *coq* with a white collar and gleaming nut-brown feathers is placed at his feet. It is beautiful. I gaze at it for a moment in horror and admiration, before Gilles picks it up and tucks it into an open-ended pouch at the back of his waistcoat.

We set off again. I walk behind him, the pheasant's claws and long, elegant tail protruding from one end of his back pouch, its beak from the other. Another two shots echo through the woods.

'Missed again,' says Gilles calmly as we leave the woods and head towards a thicket.

As we walk, Gilles muttering that raised pheasants aren't nearly so interesting to *chasse*, he stops sharply and points to what look like small and pale oval stones on the ground in front of us. 'Hare droppings,' he explains. 'Always two, sometimes three with hares ... look at the rabbit droppings.' I peer at a mound of much smaller and darker round droppings nearby.

He points out a hare's imprint in the soil. It is small, delicate and hardly noticeable to an untutored eye. A pale yellow leaf masks it slightly. 'It's fresh,' he says, quickening his step. He knows it's fresh as the leaf stuck to the imprint hasn't yet blown away. He pulls out some cartridges from his gilet to change the shot in his gun as we walk with quickened pace towards a bare, recently ploughed field. We need different types of cartridges for different types of animals, he explains.

With the new cartridge still in his hand, the old one unchanged, he cocks his gun upwards. I look at him then at the sky. A single shot and a small bird is dead and falling from the sky. He smiles broadly. 'Prune! Fetch!' He turns to me. '*Une grive*,' he pronounces with pride. '*Le vrai sauvage*.' Prune retrieves a large thrush. Gilles tucks it into the pouch behind his back with the pheasant and changes the cartridges as we head towards the field.

The dogs are beside us suddenly, running backwards and forwards, sniffing the ground with tails up. Manu is already at the far end of the field, a solitary figure, large and imposing with shoulders slightly hunched and gun to the fore. We have long ago left behind Jean-François and Sébastien. They're obsessed by the pheasants, Gilles remarks. Occasionally we hear shots. 'Missed again,' he says.

Manu's English setter, Julie, is running up and down the edges of the field while Prune is circling the outer perimeter. 'They've found a scent ...' says Gilles, '... but the hare isn't stupid.' Manu

44

looks up at us momentarily. He is walking slowly and with measured steps, peering into the bare, finely tilled field. We walk into it. It is flat and exposed. Even a leaf would be visible I say. There can't be a hare in it. 'Ah,' says Gilles quietly, looking from right to left. 'He's here all right.'

Gilles's comportment has changed, his enthusiasm is different. He no longer looks at me as he talks, but scans the field. 'He sees us and hears us,' he continues. '*Ah oui*. He knows. He's not stupid,' he repeats as we walk slowly through the field, looking at the bare earth. 'It's dry. He likes dryness. Don't want to be wet, do you?' He addresses the hare, looking around as we walk, his gun now in front of him, as is Manu's who is also walking through the field, five metres or so away from us. We are parallel, the dogs still circling the outskirts of the field.

'*Non*, he's not stupid. He circuits the field three or four times before he decides to make a form for himself. He'll have at least three of them here. Once he's left traces round the field in ever-decreasing circles, he bounds from one of his resting places to another . . . so that the dogs won't pick up the freshest scent.' I'm fascinated and full of admiration for the hare. I look over to the dogs still rushing up and down the outskirts of the field, unaware that the scent is cold, outwitted by the hare's supreme cunning.

Manu says nothing, concentrating instead on the ploughed field. He walks slowly with measured step, a hunter. 'You can pass within half a metre of him and not see him,' Gilles continues. We walk on. 'He lets us pass.' I look around as we walk, an affiliated hunter myself now. 'He's silent. And he's *beau*.' My eyes scan the field. 'Yes, he's crafty,' he continues. 'He stops breathing so we can't smell him and he lies perfectly still so we can't see him.'

Distant shots, three of them, and we see a pheasant flying high towards Saussignac. 'And he waits until you're behind him before he runs,' he says quietly, ignoring the gunshots and with only a desultory glance up at the pheasant, 'so you should look back every twenty metres or so.' He wheels round, cocks his gun, aims and hits a hare as it bounds over the field, a good sixty metres from us.

Another shot rends the air, then another as Manu aims at a second hare. Its white inner thigh flashes, unnaturally angled as it bounds off at incredible speed, leaving the field behind and coursing through a *parcelle* of vines. 'You caught its leg!' shouts Gilles. 'It's going to run and run!' Jean-François and Sébastien appear. 'Did you get it?' they shout, breathless. 'We must find it!' bellows Gilles. Their dogs rush off in the direction of the vines and the now vanished hare. 'Prune! Fetch!' shouts Gilles and Prune rushes to retrieve the dead hare.

We rush to the vines and, spreading out, look down the rows. 'Either he'll run until he slows down with a haemorrhage, or he's not too badly hurt,' says Gilles, scanning the vines. He turns towards Manu. 'We need the other dogs.' Manu has already turned back towards home to get them. 'We'll wait here!' shouts Gilles.

'*Doucement, très doucement*,' says Gilles to Prune as she stands before us with the dead hare. It is, as Gilles had pronounced before he even saw it, *beau*. It weighs a good six kilos and it's a male, for which Gilles is pleased. He knew it was anyway, he said, as it ran off with its ears up, always a sign of a male. The females run with their ears down. That he had time to notice anything about the hare, such was the speed at which it ran, I find extraordinary. I look at it. It is handsome, magnificent. At least it died in an instant.

'*Oui, c'est très dommage*,' says Gilles of the wounded hare. 'That's not what the *chasse* is about. We're not here to wound them . . . we're here to kill them.' He stands in front of me, hands in pockets, his broken gun resting behind his neck and over his shoulders. 'Often they come back to where they started from,' he says quietly. 'But I doubt this one will.'

The hares have been reproducing since March, each leveret born outside and left to fend for itself from the outset, fed only once a day when its mother returns at night. Hardly moving from the small indentation in the soil where it was born and is left, only one in five survive, having no defence for the first three months of their lives, at the mercy of buzzards or foxes or cats and dogs or even the tractor. '*C'est beau à voir . . . très, très beau à voir*,' says Gilles, his eyes lighting up as he describes one. '*Petit*, with a curly, rust-coloured coat and black eyes — beautiful to look at.' After three months they bound off. '*Après, ils galopent!*' says Gilles with a smile.

The smell of cordite is still in the air. He takes a packet of cigarettes out of his pocket and lights one up. I ask him what dogs Manu has gone to get. 'We had the bird dogs,' he says calmly. 'We need something else.' As he speaks, Manu appears, Sébastien and Jean-François trailing behind him.

With Manu are two bloodhounds, unlike any I've ever seen before. They are enormous and terrifying, ranging in front and around us now with large paws and long legs. Almost a metre in height, their bodies have dark coats speckled with white. Their faces are long with white beards and their eyes dark, full of intelligence and intent. They dwarf both Manu's English setter and Jean-François's spaniel. Manu, in addition to the dogs by his side, has a large copper horn on a leather handle hanging around his chest.

We set off. Gilles looks over towards another *parcelle* of vines and a small wood. 'That's where he will have gone,' he says, pointing towards them. I look at the large form of Manu in front of us, silent, pensive, stalking slowly. His dogs range around him, then break away and bound off into the woods. It's a shame for the hare to die in the vines or the wood, Gilles is muttering. If badly wounded, loss of blood will have slowed him down by now.

Silence, then a low, disturbing howl emanates from Manu's dogs deep within the wood. '*Sangliers*,' pronounces Manu calmly. My heart skips a beat. Gilles has told me how dangerous they are. Manu looks at Gilles, then at me silently for a moment. He turns away from the wood towards a lower *parcelle* of vines. The distant howl of the dogs pales into insignificance as the air is shattered by the sound of Manu's horn calling them to heel. My heart is still pounding as they lope towards us, huge and magnificent.

Manu will not be with us for long. He will be hunting *sangliers* in half an hour or so, Gilles tells me as we walk on down towards another wood. Last night, with the aid of his dogs he had followed the telltale signs of a *sanglier*'s feeding route and traced its den. Boars come out at night to eat then hide themselves deep inside brambles and bracken thickets during the day. Where you have one, you often have two, three, five.

It starts to rain, fine but persistent as we approach the wood. The amber colours of the trees contrast against dull, grey clouds. Gilles's gun is on his shoulder now as we bypass the wood and head down into a gently undulating meadow.

The boars feed on acorns, wild fruit and the roots of brambles, he tells me. Why the roots, I ask. Because bramble tubers don't ferment in their stomachs as cabbage or wild swede do, he replies, surprised at the absence of such elementary knowledge of bramble tubers. They like maize too. If they chance upon a field of it they head for the middle to feed. 'For security, of course!' he says, responding to the question I haven't yet asked.

Gilles doesn't *chasse* either *sangliers* or deer. 'Their smell is strong and they're dirty,' he pronounces with distaste. 'We didn't have them here until relatively recently, even as recently as ten years ago. They came from the great forests, first one then two and now we're overrun with them!

'I first saw them here with Manu some eleven or so years ago. One by one they crept in and now they're a menace. Even in our countryside of vines we're authorised to shoot them, there are so many. They crossed the Dordogne one night and came. Same with the deer — we didn't have them before either.' I imagine troops of wild boar and deer advancing at dead of night towards one of the bridges that cross the Dordogne, looking to right and left to make sure the coast is clear, then skipping across. Or waiting until the tide is low and wading through to the other side, droves of wild pigs and deer.

I look ahead towards Manu striding along, his gun also over his shoulder. I remember the wild boar I saw one evening whilst driving back home at night some years ago. It careered across the road in front of me, a wild, prehistoric looking pig with a powerful body, sturdy legs and a huge snout.

The thought of three or five of them together in a pack is a sobering thought, I tell Gilles. He laughs loudly, announcing with gusto that they can run in packs of thirty or more: three or four mothers and several generations of the same family, or even two families together. They stay together until the boar become adults and reach a certain weight, between thirty and sixty kilos, when the males become solitary. During the rutting season they run sometimes fifty kilometres a night to find a sow or food. They have degenerated somewhat since they were first sighted here due to interbreeding, says Gilles, and a huge *sanglier* is now no longer common. To my mind, a sixty-kilo *sanglier* is more than big enough.

Our gentle *chasse* of birds and rabbits is in sharp contrast to that of *sangliers* and *chevreuils*. Manu and his *chasseurs* will hunt '*en battus*', with not less than five *chasseurs* to a hunt, each one positioned in his given place in the wood, relative to the *sanglier*'s den. They will send in the dogs, this time *chiens de pousses* rather than *chiens de pieds*, to root out the *sanglier*. 'What's the difference?' I ask.

'And when he goes, he goes!' warns Gilles, ignoring my question. 'Believe me, he moves fast, a *sanglier*!' One or two *chasseurs* enter the wood with their dogs to root out and shoot the boar while the others hold their positions around the outskirts of it in case the boar escapes. All have guns, all of which are loaded with bullets rather than the birdshot Gilles and his *chasseurs* use. 'You aim for the heart or the lungs,' says Gilles. 'If you do manage to

hit him, he can still run for forty metres or so before he drops.'
He looks at me for a moment. 'Of course,' he continues, 'if he's
coming straight at you, you just aim wherever you can.'

It is clear that we are not going to find the wounded hare. The
fine rain is dampening the terrain, Manu's huge dogs are used to
sanglier and *chevreuil*, not hares and pheasants and, in any event, its
real scent will have been masked by both the rain and its blood.
We regroup and they all discuss the shame of not catching it. The
shame that it will die in the vines; the shame that it will run and
run until loss of blood slows it down; the shame that another
chasseur might find it, that they have caused it to suffer and not
die cleanly. But mostly the shame that they won't be eating it
themselves.

Manu looks at me and points to the ground nonchalantly. 'A
lièvre's form', his bed for the night. I look at a shallow indentation
in the soil. 'He lay this way,' he explains, pointing to it. 'Always
facing the wind so it doesn't ruffle his fur — keeps him warm and
hides his scent.' He breaks his gun, throws away his cigarette end
then reaches for his mobile phone which is ringing from a pocket
in his gilet. He speaks three words, then turns to us. '*Bon. A toute
à l'heure.*' And he's gone — to hunt *sangliers*.

A sound from the wood stops any desultory conversation and
galvanises everyone into action. It is the coc-coc-coc of a pheasant.
Prune has chanced upon one and disturbed its hiding place. We
are back to two dogs and without Manu. It is now wet. Gilles mutters that it will make the hunt much more difficult as pheasants
don't fly when it's wet. Like hares, they don't like the rain. We
head back into the wood towards a winding path of golden leaves,
then on through brambles and ivy peppered with rust-coloured
oak leaves. Sébastien and Jean-François walk behind Gilles then
spread out, creating a line, and descend through the other side
and towards a smaller wood.

At its outer edges, damp leaves fall from the canopy of branches as Gilles cocks his gun the same moment a pheasant rises into the sky, contradicting the general view expressed only seconds ago. The time it takes for Sébastien and Jean-François to raise their guns and the bird hangs frozen in the air, a black form against the dark, brooding sky before it falls, Prune racing off to retrieve it.

We leave the wood as another pheasant rises into the sky and flies off into the distance, eighty metres or so away. It flies just above the roof of a house on the horizon as we leave the wood. Gilles aims, slightly higher than both the bird and the house. The pheasant descends slowly and majestically in the distance, wounded but not dead. 'Bah!' he shouts. 'I couldn't hit the roof and I thought the pheasant would reach the shot.'

We descend a gentle slope towards the house then turn into a dense thicket three metres high with long red shoots of *alisier*, in search of it. Mossy and uneven underfoot, spiked, thorned shoots catch my coat and just miss my face as I follow Gilles through the dense foliage. *Cardons* three metres high and brambles creating lethal foot traps in the ground slow our progress and make for treacherous terrain. I think of the wild boar Gilles has described and hope desperately that none of them are lodging here this morning. Panic rises. We seem to have been in there forever.

Suddenly we exit. Yellow swathes of wild turnip blossom border the edge of a *parcelle* of vines. Denuded of leaves they are beautiful and familiar after the thorned shoots and its attendant panic. A plantation of pines grows nearby, tall and dense. 'Prune! *Avant! Avant!*' Gilles shouts, then '*Doucement!*' as we reach the edge of yet another wood, scrabbling through more brambles and undergrowth, tripping over their shoots. Gilles charges on in front as I battle against ivy, oak stumps, brambles and my over-fertile imagination.

To no avail, he calls to Sébastien and Jean-François. 'They don't reply, *les morpions!*' he shouts at me. 'They don't even hear me!

What sort of a *chasse* is this with only two dogs and the *chasseurs* not together as a team? Prune! *Cherche! Cherche!*' Prune enters the wood, then exits again towards me. '*Et si tu ressors chaque fois!*' he bellows. '*Avance!*' She circles, searching, sniffing the ground.

I escape the thick undergrowth with rising terror of wild boars as we advance back down towards some vines already pruned. Piles of branches lie between the rows of bare vines. 'He's probably hiding in the *sarments*,' says Gilles decisively pointing to the branches. 'They like them; they can hide in them.'

The landscape is ravishing. Rays of sun pierce through the grey clouds as we leave behind the thicket. Raindrops on the vines and their canopy wires glisten like crystal. The black vines, bare in form, are gnarled and beautiful, stretching away into the distance. The sun spreads slowly over the valley. Patches of green with swathes of rust are highlighted one by one up to the bare outline of tall trees on the near horizon. The distant horizon is still shrouded in grey mist, cloud to the right and sun to the left. Even the telegraph wires look congruous, loosely draped over the landscape, stretching out over gentle slopes then disappearing into distant dells.

To my immediate left is Jean-Lis's garden. I feel disoriented from forays into woods and thickets and am surprised to find myself here. It is bare but for a recently planted row of cherry trees and a neat line of silver-grey artichoke plants, adding a splash of colour to the ploughed earth. Along the edge of it, the stunted forms of small nectarine trees, bare of leaves and washed with the blue gun-grey of copper sulphate delineate the line between them and a *parcelle* of vines.

Gilles has gone. Jean-François appears. '*Con! Ils sont piette!*' he shouts, running past me, gun to the fore. What's that, I ask? Walkers is the response. Walking pheasants. A grey hen pheasant flies up and is dead in an instant. The sound from Jean-François's gun resounds in my ears, as Gilles shouts, '*On arrête! On mange!*'

We walk towards Jean-Lis's house as they discuss their morning's shoot. The last pheasant shot by Jean-François was an undernourished grey hen. We look at it and Gilles pronounces it small, thin and miserable. It will only give dry meat. It's the one he winged over the roof of the house, he says. He knew it was wounded as he had seen a flurry of feathers before he entered the thicket, he tells the others. I saw nothing. They chatter as we march along, Sébastien's voice gentle and quiet, Gilles's deep and booming and Jean-François's incongruous, a light, half-broken lilt. They calculate how many pheasants they have killed. One was wild, so there are still six left. Gilles points to where he shot the other grey hen. 'It was right here!' he shouts.

I watch them. Gilles is describing how he shot it, gesticulating in explanation. They all describe where they were, what the dogs did, who went where in which woods, vines, fields. They break their guns as we approach Jean-Lis's house, removing cartridges and replacing them in their gilets. Arriving at the cars, they remove their booty from the pouches behind their gilets and inspect them. I look at them too.

They are lying in a neat row in the boot of the *camionette*. All of them have their eyes shut. The pheasants with their long tails and colourful feathers are as still as the hare. The large thrush now seems minute in comparison, its dark grey feathers still puffed out. The hare is lying on its side. Large, with soft, pale brown fur and a white underside, its long back legs are elegant, its body elongated, its feet and claws strangely delicate. It was once swift and fleet and powerful and now it is still. They are all still. They are all beautiful. They are dead.

We take off our boots and enter the kitchen. Inside, Jean-Lis is placing bottles on the table for the obligatory *apéritif* before lunch. Delicious aromas of roasting chicken, onions and butter attack our nostrils as we sit down at the table for our *apéritifs*, reminding us how hungry we are. 'Ouioo! We've walked at least twenty kilometres this morning!' laughs Gilles. We all look windswept, healthy, happy. '*C'était bien?*' Jean-Lis asks and a cacophony of sound hits my ears as everyone gabbles at once to recount the events of the morning. '*Tenez*, Patricia,' and Jean-Lis hands me a glass. He fills it with his '*blanc doux*', run off from one of his vats this morning. Pamela, Gilles's wife, here to cook lunch, kisses me in greeting. She laughs, raising her eyes upwards at the babble of noise.

We *trinque* our glasses and they continue their discourse. No conversation is ever far away from food or wine. Jean-Lis is describing the taste of the *bécasse*, woodcock, that Manu shot recently. He cooked it over the embers, he said. Everyone nods; it's obviously the way to cook them. Attached by its head, it hung on a string over the fire in the chimney, Manu on bended knee in front of it. It was cooked slowly for around an hour and turned every so often by tweaking the string to which it was attached. Jean-Lis demonstrates with an imaginary string over the fireplace. It was a fat bird with a rich, strong taste. A plate was carefully positioned to catch and save the excrement and intestines which fell through its body. Gilles looks at me. 'It's delicious!' he assures me. 'Almost the best bit! Not to everyone's taste, but delicious on toast.'

They all agree that *bécasse* is truly delicious. With aromas of chicken and soup permeating the kitchen our taste buds are super-receptive. You need one per person, they say. Even I begin to think that excrement and intestines probably taste just as good as they say, even that one *bécasse* might possibly not be enough. I nod my head in approval along with the rest. Gilles reiterates that they are indeed as delicious as Jean-Lis has described. They don't bear comparison with pheasants, and certainly not the one that Jean-François has just bagged. In fact — Gilles throws his cards on the table — in general, pheasant is simply a dry chicken and only good for pâté or, occasionally, cooked on the embers of the fire, cut in two. Unless it's a wild pheasant, of course. A murmur of agreement ripples around the room.

It's time to eat. In an instant, the table is transformed. Gone are the *apéritif* bottles and in their place is a plate, bowl, knife and fork for each person. A steaming pot is placed on the table. In it is tourain soup, made from onions and garlic with beaten egg whites stirred in at the last minute. A fat loaf of bread sits next to the soup pot, half-cut up into large, crusty slices. Served my soup first, only an act of extreme self-control stops me from plunging my soup spoon into the bowl in front of me before everyone else is served.

Soup never tasted better. For a minute or so there is silence while the first few spoonfuls are savoured. Almost white in colour, it is satiny and delicate in texture with not only the taste of sweet garlic and onions, but a light flavour of duck. The bread is crusty and full of taste. Gilles places his slice directly into his bowl of soup. He eats at least two baguettes a day himself, he informs us. He even has bread with chips or pasta. We listen as we eat our soup. Yes, he says, a restaurant with no bread, like the Chinese he was taken to last year, is not to be considered. 'If there's no bread, I don't eat there!' he shouts. 'I want to eat good food.'

We are eating good food. Gilles's pheasant pâté follows, along with his recipe for it. 'Yes, it's true that it's the fat you add that makes the meat tender in pheasant pâté!' shouts Jean-François over the general noise. He is a butcher in his father's shop at Souillac. '*Tiens,*' he turns to me. 'Do you know those English that live just outside Souillac?' I don't. 'You'll never believe it. They want a twenty-four-kilo turkey for Christmas! Stuffed with exotic fruits!' Everyone laughs. 'That I can do, I said to her. Stuffing it is no problem, Madame. But when she gave me the weight I told her it wasn't possible. Two birds yes, two at seven to eight kilos each. No, they said, they wanted only one.' He looks around the room at all of us in disbelief. 'They don't exist, I told them.'

'Oh yes they do!' retorts Gilles. A special breed of them indeed exists. He himself buys two a year and they always reach that weight. 'That I must see!' says Jean-François. 'Well . . . let's say twenty-two kilos,' qualifies Gilles, specifying downwards. 'And furthermore . . .' he continues, looking around the room, '. . . they are as tender as the rose.' Jean-François looks at Gilles with incredulity. 'Yes,' insists Gilles, shaking his head. 'They are.' He buys them at two months old, around a kilo each, when they are just beginning to have their combs. Bought any younger, and the first *maladie* that comes along kills them off.

In addition to the two giant turkeys, each year he buys thirty *poulets*, ten *canards* to force-feed, six *pintades* and two geese. 'I give them only maize and corn,' he insists. He buys the turkeys small and with their wings already cut. If not, they fly off. '*Oui!*' he says, returning to the pheasants. 'Pheasant meat is a mere *morceau du charbon*, with no fat.' Gilles mixes either pork or duck fat with all his pheasant pâtés, and milk and eggs to make the pâté moist and rich. Once it's made, the older the pâté is, the better. What we're eating is two years old, he announces with pride. It is delicious.

We wipe our knives on our bread as the roasted chickens are placed on the table. Already cut into pieces, they are golden in colour with crisp, gleaming skins. They smell of what they are: Gilles's home-reared chickens fed on maize, corn and milk and cooked to perfection by Pamela. The first mouthful explodes with flavour in my mouth, succulent and tender. *Pommes sarladaises*, thinly sliced potatoes baked in the oven with goose fat, garlic and parsley, dissolve sensuously in my mouth with it, the crunchy browned potatoes on top contrasting exquisitely with the soft, luxurious slices on the bottom.

Gilles returns to the subject of turkeys. 'Yes, they make a big beast.' He gesticulates. Almost the size of a *sanglier* it would seem. 'But they are gentle.' They eat from his hand — even a leaf of *salade* if he offers it. '*Ah là là!*' says Jean-François, winking and laughing. 'That I really must see.' '*Oui!*' recounts Gilles. 'It's true! And they're so big you need two large *bocaux* to make pâté from just a single wing!'

Conversation moves on to Manu and the *sangliers*. I ask whether Manu will be back for something to eat. '*Milledieux!*' says Gilles, turning to me. 'No way.' The overnight den of the *sangliers* would by now have been tracked by Manu and rooted out by his dogs, *les chiens courants* and *chiens de pousses*, says Gilles.

I am thoroughly confused with the dog classifications. There are *chiens de pieds*, *chiens de pousses*, *chiens de sangs*, *chiens courants*, *chiens d'arrêts*, *chiens à plumes*, *chiens de poils* — there can't be that many varieties of dogs in the *département*, I say. A silence as they all look at me in surprise. Each dog has its role, explains Gilles patiently. Some are used to retrieve, some are used to root out, some are blood dogs. What sort of dogs are Manu's, I ask. '*Chien de pousse*,' says Gilles. '*Chien courant*,' says Sebastien. '*Les Griffons Bleu de Gascogne*,' says Jean-Lis.

'You can't imagine how much a well-trained *chien de pied* or *chien de pousse* would cost,' says Jean-François, addressing me. 'Pah!' retorts Gilles. 'How can you put a price on them? Who in their right mind would sell them once they'd trained them?' They all agree. 'All the same,' interjects Jean-Lis, 'for all their training, many a dog has been pierced by the horns of a *sanglier* and had to be shot dead on the spot.' Jean-Lis walks over to a drawer and returns with four boar's tusks. Two of them are seven inches long, thick, curled and violent looking. He places them on the table with the two smaller tusks. Manu had successfully *chass*ed the *sanglier* they once belonged to. 'A hundred and thirty kilos it weighed! A big pig,' says Jean- Lis with pride.

'Michel and I made *saucisson* the other week,' says Gilles, broadening the subject. '*Oui*, three and a half kilos makes a *joli saucisson*. You need elastic and a skin from the butcher's. You fill it with the pork meat, wrap the elastic around it then hang it up, pricking it every day or so for the air to escape.'

Jean-Lis asks me about my wine harvest. What did I think of it? What was the sugar content? What was the yield? His yield was much reduced this year as a result of the impossibly hot summer and lack of rain. And his acidity was way down too. He had to add some. He shakes his head in regret for the loss of countless hectolitres of potential income.

'What you've done over there at Tabardy,' he says, nodding his head and gesticulating towards the back of the kitchen, '*chapeau*.' He's referring to my two recently planted *parcelles* of vines, narrow rows planted near La Tabardy and pruned short. 'You've made something there!' he continues. 'And it's well kept too.' I can't help feeling proud and pleased at his compliment.

A plate of cheeses arrives on the table; a Cabecou goats' cheese, dry and strong in flavour, with a Comte and a creamy and rich Monsalvat from the Auvergne. The conversation has moved on to Monsieur Bellegrue who used to own my house many years ago. He kept a pig, like most of the villagers, and had ducks, geese and oxen. They laugh uncontrollably as they recount how he used to wash himself by the well in the garden each Sunday in full view of the church opposite the house and the church-goers who gathered outside it after the service.

'*Oui! Torse nu!* In front of the whole congregation!' Gilles wipes a tear from his eye. Monsieur Bellegrue used oxen to till his vines and was drunk in charge of them every Saturday night and still suffering from the after-effects each Sunday morning when he doused himself in cold water from the well in front of the house. 'He did it on purpose,' declares Jean-Lis. '*Oui*,' says Gilles, touching his nose. '*Il était quand même rude.*' He was uncouth.

It's three o clock by the time we drain our glasses. Without exception a certain restraint was evident during the meal as far as wine was concerned. My conception of drunken *chasseurs* each *chasse*-day afternoon was quite unfair, certainly in the case of Gilles and his group. '*Bon. On y va,*' he says. '*On continue.*' We file to the terrace in search of boots and coats and set off again.

We head back towards a *parcelle* of vines. They belong to Jean-Lis. Wide rows devoid of grass, they have been systemically weeded both under the vines and between the rows. 'Barren *comme la table,*' pronounces Gilles. Why don't his *chasse* group release pheasants into *la nature* at the end of the season rather than on the day, I ask, especially as he prefers *le vrai sauvage.* 'Huh!' he waves his hand dismissively towards the vines we are walking through. They used to, he said, but it proved to be a waste of time, effort and money. Either the weedkiller or the fox got them.

There used to be a polyculture in the area, he said, with each farm having some wheat, some beetroot, a few vines and some cows. It was diverse. Jean-Lis's farm no longer has anything but vines now, and, furthermore, vines with no grass. What grass does grow and is eaten by the pheasants or hares either kills them or makes them sterile. The same with rabbits. As a result there are fewer and fewer of them, he says. I make an instant decision to stop weeding systemically underneath my vines. I had been considering it for some time. Restricted by the cost of the new equipment needed and the increased workload it would involve, I had decided to leave it for another year. Until now.

'And the fox is even worse,' Gilles is saying. 'He's as much a menace to the countryside as the *chevreuils* and the *sangliers.*' I sense a grievance coming as Gilles's voice begins to rise. The foxes had multiplied to alarming proportions as the ecologists – who know nothing about the countryside as they live in cities and are only interested in the politics of ecology – had earmarked them as a protected species. 'Why don't they ask the people who know about the countryside?' he is shouting. 'Who live in it? Who work the land and *chasse*?' I listen, silenced by the onslaught against the ecologists. 'It's the same with the *chevreuils* and *sangliers*!'

We are striding towards a large field of dry grass bordered with wild turnip. Jean-François and Sébastien nod in approval, listening intently. Even Prune appears to be listening. Yes, expounds Gilles. And the Comité de Chasse is just as bad, charging more and more money for a permit each year. In five years, the *chasse* will all be over such are the restrictions from them and the ecologists, he shouts. 'They're already saying we won't be able to shoot on a Sunday afternoon. And why? Because people want to walk in the woods!' We have stopped walking and listen as he shouts at us. 'Walk in the woods? The woods don't belong to them and it's not their land! They haven't paid to come on to it like me! And it's my land to boot!' He explodes. 'I've got to pay to *chasse* on my own land!' he yells then corrects himself, turning momentarily to me. 'Well, yours actually.'

'But they didn't pay us when they sent out an edict for us to kill all the foxes because they were sick did they?' Jean-François and Sébastien concur. 'And they don't pay us to kill the *sangliers* and the *chevreuils* now that we're overrun with them.' He turns to me again. 'Do you know that in your woods alone at Les Bûchères you have at least ten *sangliers* and fifteen *chevreuils*?' I am astonished. Les Bûchères is one of my *parcelles* of vines which has a wood next to it. There would hardly be room for them all it's such a small wood. 'And each year they change their minds, *les écologistes*! Two years ago foxes were protected. Now we can shoot them again, because they're full of diseases and we're overrun with them!' It's true that when driving back up the hill towards Gageac at night, I often see foxes. 'And next season there'll be something else.'

We are all silent, each of us with our thoughts. Mine veer from sympathy with the ecologists who must surely know what they are doing and sympathy for Gilles and the other farmers who definitely know what goes on in the soil, on their land, in their woods. They all three light cigarettes and blow out smoke from their mouths meaningfully and I sense that this is a subject that has a regular airing. '*Regarde*,' says Gilles and points out the imprints of *chevreuils* as we stride along over a path and into another field. I wonder how I have managed to spend fourteen years here working outside in my vines and on my land and not ever noticed hare *gîtes*, rabbit droppings and deer imprints.

The opening of the partridge *chasse* is next week, remarks Sébastien. Gilles saw at least five the other day, he tells them. Their discussion turns from them back to pheasants. 'Bah!' comments Gilles. 'They're smaller this year – and they don't sing.' Do they often sing, I ask. 'They always sing!' retorts Gilles. 'Coc-coc-coc,' he imitates, the sound we all heard this morning near the wood. Prune rushes off suddenly. Gilles cocks his gun as a pheasant rises high in the sky. Both Sébastien and Gilles shoot and it falls.

'*Oh, que c'est beau*!' Gilles exclaims as Prune deposits it at our feet. And indeed it is, a beautiful red *coq*. The feathers around its eyes are deep, scarlet-red, its neck pearl-blue and green with a snowy white collar. Its body is plump, covered with rose-coloured feathers changing subtly to brown, tapering down to a long speckled tail, magnificent and elegant. '*Le vrai sauvage*,' Gilles announces quietly with pride. He picks it up and we all admire it. It is tucked away behind his back and we continue towards a smallholding. I walk behind Gilles, feathers and claws protruding from the back pocket of his gilet once more.

The earlier conversation and attendant grievances are forgotten with the pleasure of the *vrai sauvage*, the countryside and the day. The dogs rush around relishing their freedom and sniffing the ground happily. They run in and out of woods, along rows of vines and into copses as we wander through another field of dry grass bordered with wild turnip that leads down into a dell. Prune leaps into a large, green pond as we pass by a single row of vines trained in a fashion none of us has ever seen before. The vines are as tall as I've seen, with twisting, elongated trunks and long *lattes*. In fact, they look more like trees than vines.

'*Oui*, maybe it's a new method of pruning!' booms Gilles with a broad grin on his face. We are all laughing. '*Oui*,' splutters Sébastien as we walk by. 'It's so they don't have to bend their backs to gather in the grapes!' Laughter erupts on all sides. I ask who they belong to. 'Don't know him,' replies Gilles. 'He's the son of Père Bouche.'

The delapidated land and property of the son of Père Bouche is in sharp contrast to the beauty of the woods and surrounding vines. Old tractor tyres and a rusty stepladder lie beside the green pond. Dirty white plastic covers litter the landscape with rolls of old wire and discoloured, ugly coils of immense yellow tubes. Nearby, a corrugated, sheeted barn is half-rusted. Next to it, three large oil drums stand half-full of dirty water. Discarded steel poles with bits of ragged cloth attached to their ends lie on the ground next to them.

'*C'est une petite exploitation*,' says Sébastien with an apologetic smile as I gaze at the raw and savage sight. I lost my sense of direction some time ago and have no idea where we are, but this is the first time I have ever been here. No time to reflect as we march on towards another *parcelle* of vines and a road. A small plantation of pines is enclosed by electric tape, no doubt to keep the *chevreuils* and *sangliers* out or even in. Two huge and bare willow bushes grow alongside the edge of the *parcelle*, splashes of deep ochre stems against the black, gnarled vines.

The dogs rush off again, suddenly excited, and up goes a pheasant. Up goes Gilles's gun, a second before Jean-François and at the same time as Sébastien. Only Sébastien shoots and down it falls, retrieved by Cécile, Jean-François's dog. We wander on, through woods, back to vines and over ploughed fields. Sometimes, all three *chasseurs* have their guns over their shoulders, trigger guard upwards and barrels in the air. Or sometimes through the crooks of their arms with barrels pointing at the ground. Or sometimes held by the barrels with the butt over their shoulder.

A fresh breeze is blowing and the tops of the trees of the nearby wood begin to sway. 'Not good,' says Gilles, looking up at them. 'The pheasants will be helped by the wind.' As we speak one flies up. Gilles aims and shoots as it rises high in the sky, gaining momentum with the wind. It falls with a flurry of wings and feathers. Prune retrieves it and places it at Gilles's feet, still alive but badly injured. Gilles picks it up and raps its neck on the gun barrel. He turns to look at me as I look away.

We are all noticeably slowing down. My legs are beginning to feel heavy and I guess that the guns Gilles and his group are carrying are too. Gilles is walking with a more measured step and stooping slightly. 'It's the *coq*,' he says. 'It's heavy.'

Dusk is falling as we walk slowly back up the hill towards Jean-Lis's house. I carry Gilles's gun for the last half-mile or so as his back is aching. Gilles heaves the pheasant out from behind his gilet and throws it into the back of his van. Cartridges are removed from guns and replaced in appropriate pockets; cigarettes are lit. Manu is not back, they remark. He's sure to be out until nightfall.

We look at the day's shoot. In the back of Gilles's *camionette* is an array of pheasants, a hare and a *grive*. The *vrai sauvage* pheasant is magnificent and dazzling to look at set against the rest, the hare too. A gentleness surrounds their dead forms, a quietness, and I'm taken aback by the confusion of feelings as I look at them. I have seen nature today, and power and violence along with seduction, beauty and, ultimately, death.

Primitive feelings fill my mind as I gaze at them, the age old link between death and life and the ritual of killing to eat. We kill to live. Ancient peoples worshipped that which they planned to destroy, venerated what they ate. I visited the prehistoric caves, only an hour's drive from me, when I first came to live here and saw the wonderful wall paintings of bison and *sangliers* drawn by earliest man who shared the forests with mammoths, bears, wild boars and bison. Light flickering over the paintings on the walls of the dark caves gave the impression that the animals were alive and running.

The pleasure of today's *chasse* was not just for the kill. It was a link to the earth, to nature and its food scource. Their hunters gave the animals a respect. They didn't want them to suffer. A respect was given too, for the land and its beauty. The inextricable link between the two and the food value of the wildlife for the *chasseurs* was evident.

Gilles drives me back home. I clamber out of the *camionette* with stiffening limbs, the sight of my front door and the prospect of a long, hot bath more welcoming than I could have imagined. Eida peers at us over the fence as Gilles hands me the magnificent *vrai sauvage* pheasant, kisses me goodbye and is gone.

Fidde came to see me the morning after our dinner together to buy some wine and to say goodbye. I was in the kitchen standing next to the wood stove to warm up, hours of racking the two vats of wine in the *chai* plus barrel-filling having turned my hands and feet to blocks of ice.

'*Hej*, Patricia!' he said, smiling as he opened the door, his voice lilting and deep. 'Can I come in?' I was astonished and delighted to see him, hadn't been expecting him. 'I tried to call you,' he said. 'To see if I could come and see you. But there was no reply, so thought I'd try anyway in case you were around.' We stood in silence for a moment. 'And you are!' He laughed. 'I've come to see your *chai*,' he said. 'And taste your wine again.'

He was leaving for Switzerland later in the day. Dinner with him the night before had passed quickly. I lay in bed that night feeling a mixture of exhilaration and trepidation. It had been a wonderful evening. There was no doubt that he was exciting to be with. He was intelligent, attentive and appreciative as well as handsome. But the way he looked into me was unnerving and the way he drew things out of me made me more aware of myself somehow. Even as I crystallised my thoughts, I chased them away, telling myself how ridiculous it was to be indulging in this form of self-analysis.

I didn't think about how I looked, only how pleased I was to see him standing in front of me. The contrast between my appearance the previous night and what faced him then couldn't have been greater. With wet hair and clothes, a dripping nose and blue hands, I took him into the *chai* and showed him round. He looked at the ordered rows of barrels in the *chai à barriques*. 'It's like horses' stables in here,' he said with appreciation, touching a barrel. He ran his hand over it. 'It's so clean – and it smells so good.'

I felt a surge of pride as I looked at the *chai* with him, saw it through his eyes. It was clean and ordered and pleasing to look at, the rows of crafted barrels objects of beauty in themselves. They stretched from one end of the cellar to the other in perfect symmetry. Aromas of cherries and ripe fruit from the wine I had just put into barrels hung in the air, the floor still glistening with water from its washing down after racking the vats.

We tasted wines from vats and barrels. He moved from foot to foot, the coldness of the *chai* floor seeping into him. Returning to the warmth of the kitchen he said, 'OK, I'd like twelve cases of your Saussignac sweet wine and twelve of your red.' I was amazed that he wanted so much, assuming he would take only the three bottles you would normally be allowed on the aeroplane.

'Oh yes, and three bottles of red to take back with me,' he laughed, amused by my reaction. 'It's great wine, Patricia!' he added. The cases could stay at Pia and Ekan's, he said, as he had other wines stored there for the moment. 'And I'll be back soon. Can I call you beforehand?'

As Fidde and I reached his car, Juliana's voice echoed up the road. '*Bonjour, Monsieur!*' Her small figure advanced towards us. '*Vous allez bien, Monsieur?*' she asked, smiling and shaking his hand. She peered up at him, her eyes alight with interest, turned to me then back to Fidde. Eida's head stretched over the hedge. She gazed at our group inquisitively.

'*Attention à ma soeur, Monsieur!*' Juliana shouted, nodding her head and shaking a finger at him. Be careful how you treat my sister. '*C'est ma soeur!*' she reiterated, diamond rings flashing, gesticulating with her finger from her breast to mine.

Fidde looked at her uncomprehendingly for a moment, then burst into laughter. She laughed too, a loud raucous laugh. As his car disappeared down the road, she turned to me. '*Oh là là, Patricia!*' she said, head bent, a grave expression on her face, eyes looking up at mine. '*Quel bel homme!*' She shook her right hand again to signify appreciation. Eida stamped her foot. '*Et quelle classe!*' she added.

He did call, only days later. He and Ekan had a business together, a factory in Paris. He would be visiting it with him, after which he would be coming to Saussignac for the weekend, staying with Pia and Ekan. Could I have dinner with them on the night of his arrival? And could he take me out the following night?

It was the beginning of a deep attachment for both of us. Something inexplicable was happening. I wasn't expecting it, wasn't expecting to be entrapped by his eyes which looked into me with insight. Wasn't expecting to find him peeling away the layers of protection I had carefully given myself. Wasn't expecting him to sweep into my life and touch my loneliness and my independence. I loved his visits, waited for them. And he loved coming. He would call from Fribourg or Sweden or Paris, wherever he happened to be. '*Hej, Patricia!*' he would say in his slow voice and I could almost see his smile as he spoke the words.

'And I'm doing all the talking again here!' he chuckled as we sat sipping wine one night after dinner. He had recounted stories of his schooldays. Deep in the forest in the north-west of Sweden, his school set great store by sport. The children went home only once every two months and were expected to excel, not just academically but in as many outdoor pursuits as possible. Almost all spare time was spent in open-air training.

He loved his school, eventually sent his children there and suggested that Pia and Ekan sent theirs too. Most of Fidde's friends from his schooldays remained so in his adult life. As a result of its rigorous training, he was as good at skiing down dangerous slopes and ice-skating over frozen lakes as he was at climbing mountains or riding or playing golf and certainly at playing bandy.

'You never heard of bandy?' he replied incredulously when I asked him about it. 'Patriciaa!' he exclaimed and he laughed uproariously. He took his half-cigar out of its holder and lit it carefully. 'It's a form of tennis, Patricia,' he said. He took a puff on his cigar. 'But you need a frozen lake instead of a tennis court and a crooked club instead of a racket. Like ice hockey.' Laughter bubbled up in his voice as he returned his cigar to its box. 'I thought everyone knew that!'

He related more stories of his childhood, always with humour. His face broke into wide smiles at a remembrance of some schoolfriend's adventure in which he was embroiled, laughter erupted from deep within his stomach at a recollection of some buffoonery. Life and the sheer pleasure of it burst out of him.

Chapter 4

MID-DECEMBER, AND THE DAYS ARE CRISP AND COLD. EIDA BLOWS clouds of steam through her nostrils and into the air as I feed her the previous night's stale bread. The down around her mouth glistens with frost. The countryside is bare and the sound of the sharp crack of vines being pruned echoes through the *parcelles* like the shots from Gilles's gun during the *chasse*. Benjamin and Alain can be seen in the distance, moving slowly and methodically up two of the rows with Madame Cholet's house behind them, solitary and beautiful.

Juliana's voice fills the air as she strides towards me, waving. *'Coucou!! Patriiciiaaaa!'* Her booming voice and infectious laughter resound regularly around Gageac. I hear them if she is out and about in the village, which she invariably is. In winter, she gathers in the *sarments* and vine stumps from my vines to keep for barbecues. In spring she picks the wild flowers growing among the vines and gathers in dandelions or *mâche* and the nettles that grow there for salads.

She pulls up the wild turnip that seeds itself in the vines for soups or gathers lilac from the field around the church opposite and in summer she picks cherries from my trees and wild raspberries from the hedgerow around Eida's field. In autumn she gathers mushrooms from the woods. She used to feed my dogs, Sam and Luke, when they were alive and still feeds Lulu, my cat, when I'm not here. She waters my plants. She leaves me morcels of food she has cooked. She guards my house. She is generous. She is vibrant and alive. She is loud.

Now her voice echoes over the village again. It bounces off the road and around Eida's field. Eida looks up in alarm then gallops off to the other end of it. '*Comment tu vas?*' she bellows, even though she is standing next to me. My eardrums vibrate as we cross the road and hurry into the warmth of the kitchen. Closing the door, she drops Chloë on to the floor where she deposits a small, yellow puddle.

Juliana is dressed in black velvet Chanel leggings and a large red jumper. She wears a heavy, gold necklace, pearl and gold earrings and diamond rings on her fingers. '*Tiens!*' she smiles, depositing a porcelain bowl containing a generous helping of still-steaming lasagne on to the table. '*Et quoi de neuf?*' she asks. What's new? She saw Michel the other day, she said, and he told her he had shot a *sanglier*. Have I been on a *sanglier chasse* yet? She scoops up Chloë from the floor. And how is Gilles's back and how many pheasant did he catch on his last *chasse*?

What's going on in the *chai* and is everything now in order? And what about the sweet wine? Is it doing what it should? And how are the children? Does Amy have her uniform yet? Has John started his new job? 'I'm gathering vine stumps this morning,' she announces. 'Do you want some?'

She leaves the house and heads towards the vines. 'Don't forget to eat the lasagne!' she bellows. 'You're too thin, *ma soeur!*' and she's gone, a lone figure making her way up the row of vines towards Alain and Benjamin.

I have not been on a *sanglier chasse* yet. It's fair to say I have chickened out for this year. The fact that Gilles doesn't like it, that the *sanglier* squeals, that real bullets are used and that it's a much bigger animal than the *gibiers* we hunted on Gilles's *chasse* have somewhat dampened any enthusiasm I may have had. The *sanglier* bleeds and dies in front of you. In any event, both the *sanglier* and deer *chasse* are now closed until next year. Manu says he'll call me when he next goes on one.

Oenology is the science of wine and an *oenologue* is a wine scientist. Everyone who makes wine, from Monsieur Paysan to Monsieur Rothschild, needs one, wants one, has one. During the *vendange*, they visit, usually twice a week. They give advice on the grapes you pick. They take samples of the resultant juice from them. They transport it to the laboratory for analysis. They supply a support system should you need it.

Bruno Bilancini was my *oenologue* until he bought his own vineyard. He was also one of my first friends here, along with his wife, the beautiful Claudie. They now have their own vineyard of thirteen hectares and make a sweet Monbazillac wine. The obligatory morning mists and afternoon sun needed for the evolution of noble rot appear with ease on their slopes, which are steep and well-aired. And the gentle winds needed to dry and shrivel the grapes after the mist and sun have done their work run up and down their terrain, aerating and developing noble rot with ease. I know the vines well as I used to help pick grapes for them at *vendange* time, as they did for me.

They, too, have had a good year in the vines and a relatively easy picking season. The birds were kinder to them than to me on their last pick. Their barrels of noble rot, like mine, are gently fermenting at their own speed in the *chai*. In fact, relative calm has been restored both there and in the vines after the inevitable chaos of the *vendange* and, pruning, wood-pulling and replacing pickets apart, things are under control.

A grey Monday morning in December and Bruno and I are going to the truffle market. We approach Ste Alvère through the rain. Silhouetted against a dark grey sky, a ray of winter sun strikes the stone of the thirteenth-century tower that dominates the small town of 750 inhabitants, situated in a triangle between Bergerac, Sarlat and Périgueux. In the square the church bell strikes ten as a small crowd waits outside the *salle de truffe* for the opening of the *marché*. The doors are opened dramatically at the last strike of the bell, the air filled suddenly with the earthy aroma of truffles.

Inside, men in flat caps or berets and women in overcoats and aprons stand behind long tables displaying their wares. Unlike the fruit and vegetable markets of summer where tabletops groaned under the weight of produce, here there is plenty of room for the small quantities of produce on sale. Long tables, arranged in a U shape and covered in white cloths that reach the ground, have a scattering of small baskets of truffles sitting on them. Some truffles are not even in baskets but spread out on coloured napkins, each truffle a different shape and size. The powerful bouquet penetrates the hall and my nostrils. We join the queue as people shuffle round the hall slowly, moving from table to table inspecting the wares on sale.

Covered in tiny wart-like protrusions, the truffles are mesmerising to look at. Their blackness is intense and they gleam slightly, like exquisite black marcasite. Against the whiteness of the tablecloths they look like jewels. '*Ah oui, Madame,*' says a vendor, nodding and smiling, reading my mind as I gaze in fascination at them. '*Ce sont les diamonds noirs du Périgord*', the black diamonds of Périgord.

Even in antiquity, truffles were well known in France. In the Middle Ages they had a satanic image because of their black colour, their carbuncled skin and the fact that they grew under the ground. During the Rennaisance François Ier, who first tried them in Spain where he was held captive, fell in love with the taste and introduced them as a regular dish for his banquets when he returned to France. I wonder how long the black diamonds of Périgord have existed here in the Ste Alvère area. The square in which the *salle* is housed is named Le Marché aux Truffes and Bruno has told me the Ste Alvère region, with its limestone slopes, is the natural home of the truffle.

There are two categories of truffles on sale today, plus the 'extra'. Some are *melanos*, the renowned *tuber melanosporum*, and the others *brumales*, a truffle of lesser quality but with a fine aroma. In front of each basket or napkin of truffles a certificate lists the category and type, plus the price. The *brumales* today cost around 600 euros a kilo and the *melanos* 1100, with an 'extra' at 1600.

Bruno and I shuffle round with the onlookers, inspecting the truffles, feeling part of some country ritual. The simply dressed people talk softly among themselves, truffles the only subject of conversation. At one of the tables a man next to us, small and dark and wearing a flat cap, shakes my hand. He nods in the direction of the truffles on the table. A perfect truffle should be firm, have a good aroma and lots of taste, he tells me with a smile. If they are too ripe they are soggy. If they are too hard they are woody.

He points to one of the truffles in the basket in front of us. It shouldn't be gnawed by insects either, he says, and the best way of buying them is by smell. A truffle breathes and lives after it has been lifted from the ground, then after a while loses its aroma so once it is ripe it should be eaten as soon as possible. He smiles at me. I am fascinated by him as well as by the truffles, by his laughing face, brown and lined by the sun, his black, intelligent eyes, his accent of the south-west, full of sun and friendship and song; his enthusiasm for and knowledge of the black truffles of Périgord.

As I peer at the basket of black and gleaming *melanos* in front of us, leaning over them, like him, to inhale their aroma, the vendor folds over them the cloth on which they sit. He addresses us with a smile: 'Sold,' he says. A chef from Paris has bought his entire basket. We move on, a slow dance with heads dipping occasionally to smell truffles, or a step to the side to greet someone, or a backward glance to the last table then a step forward to the next.

Each truffle on display has a different shape. Some are large knuckle-like forms, others small currant shapes and others walnut-like; knubbles of black aromatic gastronomic diamonds. One of the vendors explains that the tables are sparsely filled because there are fewer truffles to be found this year. The dryness of the summer has proved to be catastrophic for them, excessive heat delaying their ripening process.

Jacques Lambert, a pharmacist friend of mine and another passionate truffle enthusiast, told me that even disregarding the heat of this summer there are fewer truffles to be found in France generally. At the beginning of the century, such was their abundance, country people here ate them as a vegetable. The war and lack of maintenance of the oaks and their habitat radically reduced their availability and sent the truffle trade into a decline.

Today, technicians are studying ways of reviving their growth, trying to reproduce truffle mycelium on to the roots of trees. Yet the mycelium itself is quite difficult to kill off, surviving sometimes a hundred years. 'It's not a very exact science . . . simply the fruit of a very complex alchemy; a mystery!' Jacques had laughed. I had told him I would be going to the market today. His friend, Gilbert, has a truffle wood. 'I'll take you next time we go truffle hunting.'

'Yes, there are many fewer truffles this year,' the vendor is saying, shaking his head. He turns a truffle over. 'Here, have a look.' He hands one to me. I hardly dare take it, having assumed we were forbidden to touch, simply to inspect from a distance. I hold it in both hands.

It is firm like a nut. I put it to my nose. It emits a penetrating bouquet of the earth. Of roasted dry fruits and nuts. '*Très belle melano*,' he confirms. 'A miracle of nature.' Taking a small, sharp knife he cuts a sliver from the truffle. Its interior is beautiful, a deep, marbled brown with cream and white veins, like the deep chocolate colour of marble of prothyra.

The vendor's name is Edward and, like Jacques's friend Gilbert, he has his own truffle wood. His father, along with four or five of his friends, revived the '*culture de la truffe*' in his region twenty years ago. Edward is now passionate about them too and since his father's retirement has taken over the business. He asks where we come from and as we explain he pronounces with delight that we live very close to a truffle-growing area.

'On the *côte*! The *grand côtes*, before Rouffignac . . . heading towards Sigoulès!' he declares excitedly. 'You go up the hill, over and along on the left. Do you know where I mean? *On peut ramasser les truffes là! Je vous jure!*' He gesticulates wildly. His friend who lives there, Père Lascelles, had cried with joy when he found them, he tells me. He spreads his arms as he speaks, the palms of his hands open towards us.

Fired with passion and wearing a wide smile, his enthusiasm for truffles bursts out of him. 'Did you know,' he exclaims, 'that the gestation period for a truffle is nine months, just like us?' He turns to me, picking up one of his *melano* truffles. He holds it in his open hand. 'I had some with *oeufs à la cocotte* last night.' He blows a kiss into the air. 'The *vapeur*! The aromas! The taste! *Magnifique!*'

His enthusiasm is infectious. We both laugh and he hands me the truffle. Bruno tells him that Ulma, their pointer puppy, is a natural truffle hunter. She brought them summer truffles dug up from their own garden. 'Don't let her eat them!' he exclaims. 'They're delicious *en salade* with some *pain grillé* and olive oil dribbled over them.' Edward holds up another truffle, proffering it to us to smell.

I ask him to choose me two. As he selects them by smell, I too put the assorted truffles to my nose. All smell of the warmth of the earth, some of sugar with a hint of hazelnuts, some more acid, some of celery and nuts but all with a mystery, an unfathomable earthy *odeur* of something lost in my subconscious. I buy the two chosen by Edward and Bruno does the same. We look up and see that in the twenty minutes or so since we arrived almost all the truffles have gone, sold to chefs and Parisians, their rarity and value creating a demand impossible to meet.

The crowd has thinned; the dance is over. I look at the other vendors, some talking quietly together, hands in pockets, others gathering up their empty napkins, their produce sold. Outside, it's raining hard as we run back to the car, our precious purchases safely tucked away in our pockets. Claudie is awaiting our return with hot coffee. 'Eh?' she enquires with a smile. We lay the truffles on the table. 'Mmmm . . .' she murmurs, leaning over the table to inspect them and breathing in the earthy perfume. The tasselled violet scarf wrapped round her neck hangs down towards the black truffles on the table, its rich velvet colour complimenting their own.

Bruno toasts three small rounds of bread as we drink our coffee, then dribbles olive oil over them before slicing one of the truffles with a mandolin. He lays delicate slivers of marbled truffle on to the toast, then adds more oil and some coarse salt. He hands one to each of us. The toast is still warm, the truffle slightly melted. Bruno and Claudie's puppy, Ulma, puts her front paws on my shoulders as I put the toast and truffles to my mouth. Her nose follows its perfume as I bite into it.

Rich and dry, still with that taste of the earth, of fruits of the wood, of hazelnuts and mystery, of velvet and cream, it is truly divine. Ulma looks at the toast then and me. '*Oui*,' says Claudie, laughing. '*Elle aime les truffes!*'

Bruno repeats Edward Aynaud's recipe for *oeufs à la cocotte* to

Claudie. The simpler the recipe, the better it is for the truffle, he says. We discuss recipes for them. Francis Miquel, my barrel vendor friend and sommelier, loves *lièvre à la royale*, hare stuffed with foie gras and truffles. Bruno favours a capon with cream, or a good roast farm chicken with truffles stuffed under the skin. Claudie suggests an *omelette baveuse* or scrambled eggs with shavings of truffles and I suggest fresh pasta tossed in olive oil, butter and *brunoise* of truffles.

The truffle is a queen says Bruno, laughing. She needs to be put on her throne to show her off. 'It's a shame it's become such a luxury,' says Claudie. 'Like foie gras or caviar, it's the rarity that creates the demand.' She asks how much they cost this year and whistles when we tell her. Still, we don't always have them in our hands, she says with a smile. So we should profit from them while we do. *'Tout le monde peut se faire plaisir avec une petite truffe'*, everyone should be able to enjoy some truffle. We laugh and arrange to have supper together on Thursday to eat them. *'A la truffe!'* says Bruno.

The sun is shining weakly as Jacques, Marie-Christelle Lambert and I head to Gilbert and Andrea's. Truffle hunters who have their own truffle wood, they walk towards us as we park our car in their courtyard. A cinnamon coloured, mostly Labrador, dog runs to greet us. 'Cannelle!' shouts Andrea as Cannelle jumps up at me. Cannelle is the real truffle hunter and she is eager to be off.

Andrea carries a small basket lined with kitchen paper similar to those I saw at the truffle market. In it is a plastic bag containing tiny cubes of cheese. A quiet, discreet woman, tall and in her early sixties, she wears a pale orange jacket buttoned up against the cold with black trousers and sensible boots. She has short hair and sunglasses and holds her basket delicately in front of her with both hands, as if it is a posey of flowers. 'To thank Cannelle when she finds a truffle,' she explains. Cannelle has been trained to hunt them. She learnt quickly. Small cubes of cheese were hidden in the house for her to search out when she was still a puppy. Rewarded with more cubes when she found them, she progressed from cheese cubes to cheese cubes coated with truffle oil and finally to cheese with particles of real truffle in a pierced plastic box buried in the garden. Now she is fully trained and invaluable.

Gilbert's *truffière* is five kilometres or so out of town. A truffle needs an oak or hazelnut tree, a precise climate, mycelia, white filaments that spread like a spider's web on and underneath the roots of the tree, and some luck, Gilbert explains. '*Et voilà,*' laughs Jacques. 'Like I told you, it's not an exact science, but *la magie, le mystère!*'

Gilbert's wood consists of almost an hectare of planted oaks and hazelnuts, enclosed in wire and secured with a huge lock and chain. We park the car and walk through a small pine plantation to reach it. Winter sun shines through the clusters of pine needles above us. They cascade outwards and downwards like falling stars.

A large, grassed avenue leads us up towards the gate. Gilbert unlocks it as Cannelle rushes in. The sun penetrates less easily the oaks and hazelnut trees, small, stunted and covered with lichen. Cold underfoot and damp, the ground, according to Gilbert, is perfect for truffles in that it is chalk and stone, the soil rather poor. I look at the ground.

Covered mostly in moss, dried, pearly oak leaves lie everywhere but under the trees where the earth is devoid of any growth or debris and looks slightly burnt. This, claims Gilbert, is a very good sign and means that the mycelium of the truffle has colonised the ground, preventing other weeds and grasses from growing there. Truffles need light and warmth to develop, then some cold weather to mature.

He planted all his trees, a hundred of them at the same time, fifteen years ago. Half are pubescent and green oaks, the rest Japanese hazelnuts, planted in two separate blocks. He wishes now he had mixed them together in two or three plantings or even planted two-third green oaks rather than half and half as the oaks tend to give him more truffles than his hazelnuts. Whether or not they yield truffles depends on the year. '*Elles sont très capricieuse, les truffes,*' he smiles. Although the season begins towards the end of November it's not until January that they reach real ripeness and give off their heady perfume. By the end of February, their season is all but over.

'Wait for us!' commands Gilbert as Cannelle rushes over to the foot of a tree and starts to scratch excitedly at the soil. 'Stop!' he shouts as we all rush to the tree. Gilbert kneels down and with a fine, long screwdriver turns over the soil delicately. Truffles don't like to be disturbed, he says quietly as he searches carefully, sifting through the earth. He gently pushes Cannelle's nose out of the soil.

The pungent perfume of a truffle is evident even before he has removed a clump of earth from around the walnut-shaped form. The speed and precision with which Cannelle found it inspires deep admiration on the part of Jacques, Marie-Christelle and especially me. We inspect the truffle, crowding round Gilbert in excitement. '*Une brumale,*' he says, turning it over in his hand, scraping it with his thumbnail and removing particles of soil from it delicately. How does he know, I ask. If you scrape it you can peel to a white skin, he answers. A *melano* doesn't peel at all.

I put the truffle to my nose. It smells of the earth and of celery, slightly acid, enticing. Cannelle, meanwhile, is sitting to attention, looking up at Andrea expectantly, who removes with care one small cube of cheese from her basket and gives it to the dog. She devours it, then rushes over to another tree.

'*Doucement,*' says Gilbert, then 'Stop!' as she scratches the carpet of moss beneath the tree. 'Stop!' he repeats and inspects with his screwdriver the soil she has turned over. He points out to us delicate truffle-root filaments and then scoops a clump of mud the size of a tennis *balle* out of the earth. '*Oh là! Celle-là, elle est belle!*' he exclaims. '*Celle-là, elle est très belle!*' It is a *melano*. 'This oak always gives *melanos*,' he says, evidently delighted and patting Cannelle's head in appreciation while turning the truffle over and over in his hand. He passes it to me.

I feel as though I've been handed a precious jewel. Firm to the touch, its skin is harder and blacker than the *brumale*, with smaller warts. I look at it closely. It is truly beautiful, emitting its perfume to the small group gathered around it in admiration. Cupping it in both hands, I put it to my nose. The aromas from it are rich and pungent, peppery with a powerful bouquet of nuts, earth and forest. Endless nuances permeate from it. It is the very essence of nature, concentrated and powerful.

Cannelle appears nonchalant about her precious find. She has already rushed onwards to another oak. Inspecting the soil she has disturbed, Gilbert finds a very small *melano* that is white and soft and has never ripened. He crushes it in his fingers and puts it back into the earth to encourage more spores before covering it up with care.

A robin has been accompanying us through the wood. Every so often, Cannelle rushes towards it. It hops and scurries away for two or three steps then stops to look back, unconcerned by her presence. Cannelle loses interest in her and returns to scratch at the base of another oak. Gilbert removes from the soil a smaller, walnut-sized *melano*, much sought-after by the grand chefs for its uniformity of shape and ease of shaving.

He replaces the earth again carefully as Cannelle waits for her reward. The roots mustn't be disturbed too much, he says. We all watch and listen as Andrea gives Cannelle a lump of cheese. She swallows it whole and looks at Gilbert. She appears to be listening too, then rushes off in search of a squirrel rather than a truffle. It sees her, scurries up a tree and is gone.

Gilbert decided reluctantly to fence in his *truffière*, he tells us, as the local *chasseurs* kept tramping through it and disturbing the flora. He sighs. Being a *chasseur* himself, it was a difficult decision to make. They didn't need to tramp through in search of *gibiers*, he said. It was perfectly easy to see if there were any from the edges of the wood. He had warned them a number of times that if they didn't respect the area he would close it off. Rabbits were also a nuisance. They dug for truffles too and disturbed the root filaments. 'So, now it's enclosed for good,' he pronounces with finality.

Last year, five or six of the hazelnut trees yielded *melanos*, but so far this year there are none, he tells us. I ask if the truffle fungus moves from year to year. They are not always in exactly the same place, he replies. When it's hot they need shade and when it's cold they need some sun to penetrate the wood, though not too much or they burn. In the more humid spots, he has noticed, one is likely to find *brumales* rather than *melanos*.

Andrea remarks that if it rains in August they tend to have a good harvest of truffles. She points in the direction of the robin, which appears to be listening, and a small tree where Cannelle found a huge *melano* last year. The tree is only five years old so when Cannelle started to scratch there, she and Gilbert were convinced she was mistaken. According to the technicians who now advise them on trufficulture, trees don't begin to give truffles before ten to twelve years. Even then it's by no means certain they will yield anything.

We move out of the oak plantation and towards the hazelnut trees. Catkins hang from them in pale-cream fronds. Shoots that have spurted from their bases and have grown up and around them like a bouquet of flowers are almost as high as the stunted tops of the trees. 'Cannelle,' says Gilbert gently. She is sitting at his feet, looking up at him. 'I'm not happy. You've found nothing here.' She looks at him. Her concentration is lost since chasing the squirrel. She stands and wags her tail.

'Sit,' he says and she does so immediately. He takes her head in his hands and looks into her eyes. 'Show me where they are.' She gazes at him. 'I don't see any.' She jumps up and heads towards a tree, scratching again under its branches. Gilbert looks at the soil and inspects it with his screwdriver. Cannelle rushes to Andrea and looks up at her. '*Non, non*,' she says quietly. 'You haven't found anything.' Returning to the patch, Cannelle continues to scratch. 'Ah!' says Gilbert, as he scoops up another truffle and Cannelle gobbles down another cube of cheese.

Before Cannelle was trained, he tells us, he and Andrea found their truffles by sunlight. Swarms of golden flies often cluster around truffle spots. The sunlight highlights them. It's not the truffles the flies are attracted to, says Gilbert. A small insect lays its eggs in the truffle. When the eggs hatch into worms the flies arrive in search of them. My passion for truffles diminishes briefly. '*Mais non*,' says Gilbert, laughing, one hand on his hip, the other caressing Cannelle. 'The wormy truffles have the best flavour and the truffles are soaked in water to clean them so any residual worms will be expelled.'

Cannelle is definitely losing concentration. Three quarters of an hour is the maximum she can work, says Gilbert. It's tiring for her to concentrate. I say she has worked very well so far. Gilbert laughs. 'Yes, but not enough! *Elle gagne pas sa vie!*' She's not earning her keep! He turns to her, the cold winter sun behind them as he looks down at her and strokes her head. 'And if you have to find me one last one?' he asks. She looks at him. 'Show me, Cannelle! Come. Find me one.'

Five now cold and damp onlookers watch as Cannelle circles the trees. The temperature has dropped considerably since our arrival. Marie-Christelle's hands are dug deep in her pockets against the cold. Her grandmother used to love truffles, she says as she watches Cannelle in a desultory fashion. Her preferred dish was scrambled eggs with cream and truffles. She also made *terrine*

82

de foie adding cognac impregnated with truffle. Gilbert laughs. In his view, he says, one taste destroys the other. 'Not if the raw truffles are preserved in it,' insists Marie-Christelle. Andrea says she's heard that *lièvre à la royale* is magnificent, but very complicated to make. It is, however, stuffed with the two great luxuries of the south-west, truffles and foie gras, she says with pride.

We stop as Cannelle finds another truffle, a *melano*. It is round and black and aromatic. She remains seated after her reward. '*Elle est fatiguée*,' says Gilbert, looking down at her gently. '*Elle ne cherche plus*.' Cannelle and our party walk back through the oaks towards the gate. Gilbert points to a small, stumped, seemingly dead oak, no higher than Cannelle. Last year, he said, it gave him a *melano* of 740 grammes. He points to two other trees with nothing around the base for a circumference of a metre or so; they give summer truffles, he adds.

We return to the cars via the wide avenue and the pine plantation. As we turn off, Gilbert points out two peach trees standing on the edge of the pine plantation. They give wondrous peaches, deep yellow with a red blush, he tells us. Last summer, they forgot to gather them in before they left for their annual holiday in Arcachon and when they returned scores of peach stones on the ground were the only evidence that they had existed after the squirrels had feasted on them. We reach the cars. As I shake their hands to say goodbye, Gilbert hands me two truffles. 'Soak them in cold water for five minutes, then scrub off the mud and leave them to dry on kitchen paper.'

'You have them too. Over at Les Bûchères,' says Gilles calmly when I show him my truffles the next day. Les Bûchères is one of my *parcelles* of vines bordered by a small copse of trees. 'The small oak on the left-hand side that doesn't grow,' he continues. 'The one that looks dead with two branches sticking out in an odd way.' I know exactly the tree he is talking about. In fact, I would hardly call it a tree, more a stunted bush. Bramble and bracken surround it.

'Every year we used to dig up one or two – they were the size of tennis balls.' I think of the magnificent *melano* truffle that Gilbert harvested and which he was so pleased with. Gilles's truffles at Les Bûchères were '*chassées à la mouche*' too, he recounts. He and his father, like Gilbert and Andrea before Cannelle, looked for the tell-tale golden flies around the base of the dead oak tree, always around one o'clock when the sun was high.

'And then people got to know about them.' He sighs. 'They need silence, *les truffes*.' The villagers came to hunt them for themselves. They dug up the ground around the base of the tree, leaving holes and breaking the precious filaments on which the truffles grew. The truffles were lost.

Yes, Gageac is definitely truffle land, he pronounces. Manu has planted ten or so truffle oaks in front of Jean-Lis's house, Francis Queyrou too. 'But if everyone does it, it will end in tears . . . Mark my words!' He looks at me earnestly. 'It should be natural. Manu wants to do it because he likes the taste and it's interesting – not for the revenue. If everyone does it, they won't be worth anything . . . like wine!' I feel a grudge coming and I'm not wrong.

When Gilles was young, all the farms in Gageac had cows and some wheat and beetroot fields with only a few hectares of vines for home consumption. Everyone in this area got rid of their cows as well as their wheat and beetroot and planted vines instead, thinking they would become rich on it. Like Jean-Lis. 'And now there's too much wine and not enough milk!' he shouts.

As an eight-year-old Gilles had to be up at five each morning to milk by hand the fifteen cows his parents owned. They were milked twice, once before school and in preparation for the milk lorry that called at 7 am and again in the evenings. And in summer after school, in addition to building the roads of Gageac, he would walk two of his parents' cows on a lead along the verges in Gageac.

They fed on the grass there which saved on stocks of wheat and beetroot. It was only in 1976 when Gilles took over the property that they sold the cows and planted vines. His parents wanted to continue with the cows, but Gilles had had enough. 'You keep cows, I'll plant vines,' he had told them.

'And do you know, when we stopped the milk in '76 we were paid only one franc a litre? He still calculates in francs even after more than two years of euros. I do too and feel vaguely ashamed of it. 'Even now it's only two francs!' he is shouting. 'The *agriculteurs* have only just doubled their income in the last thirty years.' He looks at me earnestly. 'And the *fonctionnaires*? They have multiplied theirs by twenty!'

I have somewhat lost the thread of the conversation. Is Gilles in favour of milk or vines? I know he is not in favour of *fonctionnaires*. Is the price of milk now going up because there isn't enough milk, I ask, unaware until now that such a scarcity exists in France. Like truffles? We return to the relative safety of truffles as the subject of conversation, then quickly move back to vines.

'Like the different *cépages*!' he says. 'Sauvignon became the mode so everyone pulled up their merlot; *rouge* became the mode so everyone pulled up the *blanc* and planted red again. The price fell and we had to pull them all up!' I am horrified. It takes five years for a vine to begin to yield a reasonable harvest. 'Same with walnuts!' he continues in full spate. 'Or chestnuts! No one bothers about them now but everyone planted them at the time thinking they would become rich on them!'

A silence as he looks at me. The kitchen is ringing with the sound of his voice. 'We should plant what corresponds to the region and the land and not dream of riches,' he says more calmly. He rises to leave. '*Salut!*' and with a kiss he's gone.

I think about his argument. It's true I haven't seen any rich walnut sellers around the place, or chestnut sellers, come to that. In the market at Bergerac in autumn walnuts are sold by the majority of local producers. Bruno told me there is a wholesale market of them in Belvès, an hour upriver from Bergerac under the old covered market there. The prices are not so good now due to the influx of cheaper but lesser quality walnuts from other parts of the world, but it was one of the more important crops among the peasant families in earlier times and Belvès was an important market for them.

Almost every house in Gageac has at least one walnut tree. Madame Cholet even had her own mallet and board to crack them with. She knew exactly where on the nut to tap in order the extract the nut whole, she once told me with pride. And the shells were not wasted either, she said, as she burnt them on the fire. And did I know that walnuts from the Dordogne were the very best in France, possibly the world?

Just up the road next to my neighbours Roger and Pepita Merlos's house is a grove of them. Roger and Pepita have two themselves. Even here at Clos d'Yvigne there are six. Juliana makes an *apéritif*, alcoholic and probably illegal, from the walnuts and their leaves that I often find left in the fridge for me after one of her visits.

During the *vendange* when Juliana and I return from the vines in the evenings, we gather some of those that have fallen from the trees near the chai. We usually step on them as we pass by the trees, the familiar crunch a prelude to discovering one, then five, then fifty. Like mushrooms, she says, you have to have an eye for them as they often hide under leaves or camouflage themselves as one.

We crack one or two and eat them sitting beneath the tree, leaning against the trunk in the late afternoon sun, a welcome resting place for our backs after a day of harvesting grapes. They taste young and moist and delicious. Only gather those that have fallen to the ground, Juliana counsels. Any that are still on the tree or you shake down from it will always be green, damp and inedible.

She usually gathers the remainder after I have left her and disappeared into the *chai* to start the vinification. Each year she leaves half her crop for me on the step next to the house, carefully spread out on flat cardboard to dry. And each year I trip over them on my way to bed after a long night in the *chai*, sending them scattering into the house and down the driveway and causing the owl who lives there to screech loudly at the disturbance.

It's dark and windy as I drive up the hill to Bruno and Claudie's house at Monbazillac. It's Thursday and the promised truffle evening is here. Ulma's welcome is unusually vociferous and a blazing fire is as welcome a sight as the three champagne glasses on the table next to it. I have lots to tell them, having been on my truffle hunt since last seeing them.

Bruno, Claudie and I started making wine and owning vineyards around the same time. They rented their vineyard after years of expertise in winemaking and with a definite idea of what they wanted from their vines. Hard work and sustained effort have reaped their rewards and their vineyard is now a huge success. They make Monbazillac sweet wine, a dry white and have recently bought half an hectare of vines in Pomerol for a red.

I found myself with my vines fourteen years ago, not knowing anything about wine or winemaking and with no idea how to drive a tractor, make wine or speak French. I learnt on the job. Bruno was still working at the laboratory in those days and was my *oenologue*. He was kind and generous with his help and advice. When I think back to those times, it's always with deep gratitude. Gratitude to them, to Gilles, Michel and so many others whose generosity of spirit carried me forward.

We chatter and catch up on life while drinking a glass of champagne and eating *rillettes de porc* spread on warm toast and cut into bite-size pieces. Wine sales are slower generally this year and we commiserate. Bruno and Claudie's main market is in the States where the euro is very strong against the dollar. The fact that there is lots of wine around, and some very good New World wines, doesn't help either. They are proving to be a problem to French wines, undercutting the prices of the French *négociants*.

Those wines are not really a threat to us, Bruno says, laughing and grimacing in mock dismissiveness. '*Non, non, non!*' he continues, shaking his head. 'They still lack the finesse and elegance of French wines — even though they are entirely drinkable,' he adds. We laugh. The last time we were all together we had a bottle of New World wine that was so good it could have been a *grand cru classé*.

In the dining room, Claudie has placed boiled eggs in black egg cups before us, their newly opened tops with a delicate mound of minutely diced morcels of dark, marbled truffles on them. The deep ochre yolks look rich and luxurious, encased in their bright, dazzling whites. Grains of coarse sea salt are scattered over the plate.

Bruno opens a bottle of Côte Rôtie and fills each of our glasses. Ulma's head appears under my arm, her nostrils quivering, eyes fixed on my spoonful of egg and truffles. The richness of egg yoke with the dryness of the truffle is a sublime combination. No one speaks while we eat. The 1987 Côte Rôtie is round and fruity and without any aggressive tannins, perfect with the texture of the egg. '*Mmm — la vie est belle, n'est-ce pas?*' says Claudie, savouring the taste.

Every drip of egg yolk and piece of truffle on my plate is devoured. Claudie disappears into the kitchen as Bruno opens another bottle of wine. '*Oh là,*' he laughs. 'You don't need truffles for strong aromas. Smell the *bouchon*.' He hands part of the cork from the bottle to me. The other half remains firmly in the neck. '*C'est un bouchon d'un certain âge,*' he smiles, removing the rest of it from the bottle in pieces. '*Avec la patience!*' Claudie calls from the kitchen. 'What is it?' I ask of the wine. 'Tell you later,' he replies. 'Or you can guess.' He pours it carefully into a decanter.

The intense aroma of truffles accompanies Claudie as she brings in hot dishes of *pâte aux truffes*. Made with fresh tagliatelle, pepper, *crème fraîche* and finely grated truffle, it is simplicity itself. The texture in our mouths is different from that of the eggs and the taste also has a subtle difference, mysterious, velvet and creamy. Ulma has her head tucked underneath my arm again.

The wine Bruno has decanted is a 1949 Cos d'Estournel from Ste Estèphe. As he pours it into our glasses, we see the tell-tale brown rim of aged wine. We taste it. Filling my mouth with roundness and elegance, it is altogether remarkable. I feel privileged to be drinking it, fifty-five years of life and time captured in a bottle and poured out into a different age. I look at the bottle. The white and grey label, its lettering blurred from dust and age and almost illegible, contrasts with the vibrant red of the lead capsule.

We sip the wine. Bruno had hesitated to open it earlier because of its age. In fact, it is opening out and changing as it rests in the decanter, becoming more concentrated, with a note of spices. We still have the remains of the Côte Rôtie in our other glasses and try it next to the Cos d'Estournel. It is much less complex in contrast, two completely different styles.

The *foie gras poêllé* with thin *lamelles* of truffle shaved over it tastes of heaven. The juice from the pan in which the foie was cooked has been dribbled over four brussels sprouts, the only other accompaniment. I'm surprised to see them with foie gras. They go very well together, says Claudie, slightly undercooked and crunchy to add freshness to the richness of the foie.

The dish is voluptuous. The dry and concentrated truffle complements the rich foie and the sprouts really do add freshness. The Cos d'Estournel is opening out, becoming more complex with notes of walnuts and spices. We drain our glasses, wiping up the last of the juice from our plates with bread.

The wine is obviously having an effect on me. The table of cherry wood looks as dark and rich as the truffles, and even the marble of the fireplace, dark red and brown with cream and white filaments, is truffle-like, it seems to me. On the mantelpiece, seven decanters, some modern, some made from old glass, look beautiful, a painting above them in an ebony frame contrasting against a yellow wall enhanced by soft lights.

Bruno and Claudie's Cuvée Madame Monbazillac that we drink with the Roquefort is rich and honeyed, an explosion of apricots and spicy orange in my mouth, accompanied by *les petites nonnettes de Dijon*, spicy bread pudding rounds with a nugget of marmalade in their centre. The recipe is at least four hundred years old Claudie tells me, originating from a convent in Dijon. The cognac on the table is a mere fifty. '*Il ne faut pas se priver*,' laughs Claudie. '*Quelques grammes de truffe pour les tonnes de plaisir. C'est sympa, le jeudi soir!*' One mustn't deprive oneself. A few grammes of truffles for tons of pleasure.

I have been to see my truffle tree on my own. I displace the soil from around its base with care, like Gilbert. Kneeling on the ground, I search for the delicate filaments that might give up a truffle. My nose too is searching for the unmistakable aroma of truffles. The season for them is gone, I know, but I had somehow hoped for a miracle. It was not to be. There were no signs of any. At least the base around the tree is relatively free from grass and weeds, a good sign for next season.

 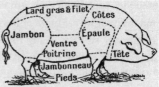

Chapter 5

MID-FEBRUARY, AND THE DAYS ARE CLEAR AND CRISP WITH A quality of light that heralds a change in the season. Pruning continued through December and January followed by wood-pulling, which is now the main task in the vines. Spring is on its way. I know this, as the roads are full of hordes of brightly dressed racing cyclists, all with dark sunglasses and long limbs and dreams of the Tour de France. They seem to have burst out of the ground like the swathes of daffodils along the roadside and the first cherry blossom in the trees.

Gageac is waking up. The cypress trees look dark against the wall of the cemetery, spring sun casting light on to it. The grass around the church looks greener. The château's dimensions seem more imposing with bright, clear sun reflecting from its walls down into the courtyard within, its gated arch now open as an invitation to spring.

Eida rushes around her field like a pony. Her ears prick up when she hears the sound of my bedroom shutters opening each morning. She turns slowly, gazing towards me, then tosses her mane and gallops over from the other side of the field.

In the vines, *piquets* and broken wires are being replaced on the canopies in preparation for tying in the *lattes*. Last year's chaos brought about by an early growing season is just a bad memory and this year we are more or less up to date in the vines. The buds are already swollen, ready to burst into delicate leaf — slightly worrying as we are still at risk of frost.

In the *chai*, the grapes that were harvested are now transformed into wine, ageing in oak barrels. I taste them often, both with Benjamin during the day but mostly on my own in the evening when the working day is over. I find the silence of the *chai* peaceful and calming; even the low temperature there is somehow pleasing, adding to the general tranquillity.

The new barrels are soaking up copious quantities of wine and need topping up each week, the wine in them changing subtly with tart, aromatic and young merlot flavours in the reds. Its *évolution* in barrels is well under way, already impregnated with tannins and vanilla from them. The minute amounts of oxygen ingested through the barrels is helping the wine mature, softening the taste and deepening its colour.

The barrelled white wines of sauvignon, sémillon and muscadelle are not yet blended with the very pronounced characteristics of each grape variety identifiable in each of the barrels. They are still on their lees, stirred each week to extract complexity and freshness with rich and aromatic flavours from the sémillon and sauvignon and a discreet perfume from the muscadelle. The unbarrelled vats of dry white are fresh and alive with grassy, flinty flavours. Almost ready for bottling, I draw some wine from one of the vats and taste, running it over my tongue. Clean and refreshing, wakes up my taste buds with notes of flowers, spices and fruits.

The rosé vat is bursting with aromas of raspberries and strawberries, spectacular and showy. Apart from a racking, it has had no filtering. Its colour is brilliant and flashy and it tastes clean and fruity, looking and smelling positively decadent.

The barrels of sweet wine made from pure, nobly rotted grapes are the only ones still fermenting. They do so gently, emitting aromas of apricots and honey. I close the door behind me as I leave, breathing a sigh of relief that the harvest is over and we are under control again in the *chai*.

Odile Lugagne is one of my greatest friends. In her late fifties, with a deep voice, the result of years of heavy smoking, she lives eleven kilometres away in Ste-Foy-la-Grande. She is tall and beautiful and I have known her almost since my arrival in France. My French improved in the early days here partly thanks to her. Concentration was required then to follow her conversation, such was the speed with which she rattled off words. Now I speak at the same speed.

She is here for an aperitif, dinner and to inspect the newly laid terracotta tiles on the floor of Gilles's old house, La Tabardy. We are drinking her preferred aperitif '*un petit blanc cassis*' and eating foie gras that she has brought with her. Spread on warm toast, it is delicious. I have related Gilles's duck-feeding methods and she has just given an eloquent defence for their fattened livers, gently ridiculing the notion that the ducks might have suffered.

'*Mais non, mais non!*' she laughs. 'They quickly learn to love it. Her neighbour also has ducks and geese and she has seen it done. 'And they queue up to be fed! They don't suffer as you imagine,' she says, laughing and coughing simultaneously. 'If they were wild, they would normally stuff themselves for the winter migration anyway!' Her voice is deep and loud. Wisps of smoke escaping from her cigarette as she speaks are hurriedly drawn back from the air and inhaled. She returns to the subject of her neighbour. 'This is her home-made foie gras. It's *délicieux, n'est-ce pas?* Like her *miques*.' What are her *miques*, I ask.

'You don't know what *miques* are?' she asks incredulously when I admit to never having heard of them. *Miques*, she explains, lighting another cigarette and inhaling deeply, then taking a sip of her *petit blanc cassis*, are leavened dumplings, very much a feature of peasant cooking in the Dordogne.

Usually simmered in a cast-iron kettle filled with vegetable and bacon soup, they are made from basic dough enriched with eggs and with duck fat replacing butter. Left to rise in front of the fire for a few hours, they are then placed carefully in the broth where they simmer gently. 'The stock mustn't boil and you must pierce the *mique* with a knife to release the steam after you remove it from the soup and before you cut it.' It is served with either the soup or the main course. '*Souvent*, you have it for breakfast as a *tartine*.' She pauses, inhaling any stray wisps of smoke from her cigarette and swallowing them. 'Even if it doesn't look so good' she adds, '*c'est délicieux*.'

We walk towards La Tabardy through the vines where their *lattes* stick up in the air, replete with delicate, swollen buds positioned along their length and occasional minute leaf-burst from one of them. Soon they will be tied down to their wire supports. The rhythm of nature is moving on. '*Oh là!*' says Odile, peering at them with me as I inspect them. 'Are they supposed to be so far forward?'

At the bottom of the small, country lane leading to La Tabardy we stop at Madame Cholet's house. Its restoration has already begun. Gone now is the miscellaneous corrugated sheeting clinging forlornly to the rooftop, gone is the hangar barely attached to the house. Gone, too, is the wooden shed next to it and the plastic sheeting on the roof which kept the rain out, along with the oak beam jammed in at an angle to keep it in place. The outhouses that were falling down of their own volition did fall down. And the woodshed kept up by breezeblocks and old vine *piquets* has gone too.

The exterior with its pale stone walls now looks beautiful, as does the solitary mulberry tree in front of it. Inside, the kitchen and the thin, dark corridor leading to two small bedrooms have disappeared as have the ceilings separating the loft from the living areas. In their place is one large room, opening out the house and giving it dimensions that I could not have imagined.

The roof is also gone. The old tiles from it have been carefully stacked, ready for reuse. The beams, most of which are rotten are all that remain. An old stone sink juts out at right angles from one of the walls. Built with the original house it is firmly embedded there, suspended a metre high from the floor. Outside, Madame Cholet's wooden seat still sits under the mulberry tree.

'It's beautiful,' says Odile, looking upwards and taking a deep drag on her cigarette. Then, looking around at the mud floor, the gravity-defying sink and the rotten beams, she adds, '*Mais, quel travail, ma cocotte!*' We walk up the *allée* to La Tabardy and the inspection of the floor tiles. '*Ah . . .*' she says. '*Voilà une maison finie et magnifique!*'

Gilles continued to live in La Tabardy for two years after I bought it from him. He was still there when Fidde first saw the house one spring afternoon. Just back from Switzerland, he came in search of me in the vines next to Madame Cholet's house. 'Patricia!' he shouted from a distance. I looked up, watched him advancing towards me in long strides, behind him the silhouette of Pia's tower at Saussignac. '*Hej!*' he said as he reached me, kissing me and taking both my hands in his. 'I'm back.' He smiled, dark eyes looking out at me from a tanned face, healthy and rugged. He looked up towards La Tabardy. 'Whose is that house?' he asked in surprise. 'It's beautiful!'

Madame Cholet appeared at her front door and stood next to the mulberry tree. '*Bonjour, Monsieur!*' she said, looking at Fidde with deep suspicion. I kissed her and introduced Fidde. '*Bonjour, Monsieur!*' she repeated drily, shaking his hand. Tabardy looked very beautiful, I told her, in this afternoon light. '*Oui*,' she said, peering still at Fidde. 'A very beautiful house,' he said, looking over at La Tabardy as Gilles sauntered down towards us in his shorts, espadrilles and cap. He turned to her. 'But so is yours, Madame.'

They looked at each other. Madame Cholet regarded him intently, inspecting, interrogating, judging. Fidde returned her gaze, open and smiling. He sucked the inside of his cheek for a second as a slow smile spread across her face. '*Merci, Monsieur*,' she replied, bowing slightly, her face lighting up.

'*Salut!*' said Gilles in greeting, kissing me. '*Bonjour, Monsieur*,' he said gruffly, taking Fidde's hand and nodding to him. Madame Cholet continued to look at Fidde with interest. After microscopic scrutiny, he had passed the test, I could see; Gilles was reserving judgement. 'See you tonight, Patricia,' said Fidde with a kiss and was gone. We watched him stride away down a row of vines, a last wave to me before disappearing. '*Qui c'est?*' asked Gilles, nodding at Fidde's retreating figure and looking from him to me with shrewd eyes. He smiled broadly.

Fidde's children, Ebba and Gustaf, arrived in Saussignac later in the day and I met them at dinner that evening. They were staying the weekend at Pia and Ekan's, whom they had known since childhood; Ekan was Ebba's godfather and the children of both families were firm friends. '*Hej*, Patricia!' shouted Ekan in welcome as I descended the stone staircase leading to the *salon*. All Swedes say '*Hej*' or, more emphatically, '*Hej Hej*'. Even I started to say it in greeting. A huge fire was burning in the hearth with everyone seated around it. Fidde leapt up to greet me with a smile and a kiss, then introduced his children.

Ebba was dark-haired like her father, with porcelain skin and delicate features, Gustaf tall and fair-haired with intelligent eyes and a lean body. '*Hej*,' they said, smiling, inspecting me more discreetly than Madame Cholet had Fidde. Fidde was smiling too, happy to have his family there, delighted to introduce them to me. '*Hej*, Patricia!' said Pia, her arms opened to greet me. 'We've been waiting for you.' She put a glass in my hand and filled it. Fidde spoke in Swedish to Ebba. 'You gotta learn Swedish, Patricia!' boomed Ekan.

The evening passed quickly as we sat around the fire and talked. Fidde's children were intelligent and interesting. I studied Fidde as he talked to them and us, his deep voice always with a hint of laughter in it, his handsome face without guile. I wondered when it was that he had taken such a large place in my life.

I only saw him for any time in the evenings when he was here, as my days were still taken up with work in the vines or the *chai*. I wasn't prepared for the rush of feelings that always accompanied his visits. Still enveloping myself in layers of protection, although I was separated from James and had been for some time, nevertheless I was stubbornly not accepting that my marriage was over.

I told myself that I couldn't allow Fidde to take over every waking moment, yet he swept into my life, then out of it at will, with not a wit of respect for my barriers; they came tumbling down the moment he touched them.

Eida's field is awash with young dandelions and a scattering of the long-stemmed yellow blossom of wild turnip. Beyond her field and on the gentle slopes leading up to the ridge, the paths between the vines there are studded with them. They sway gently, glittering and heralding spring. The trees on the horizon and not yet in leaf look elegant and beautiful behind them, their bare forms about to be transformed.

Early spring has also brought out the first delicate *pissenlit*, nettles and *mâche* that grow in between the rows of vines. Young, tender and as yet untouched by sprays or weedkillers, they are perfect for gathering: Juliana wanders through my vines collecting them daily for fresh salads, a wave from her in the distance and the sound of her voice in greeting carried on the air. Madame Briand, another neighbour, also picks them. Her chickens have begun laying again and freshly laid eggs, still warm when I collect them, are once again available. With deep ochre yolks and brilliant whites, they taste as good as they look.

Today Juliana — dressed in a yellow Chanel T-shirt with black leggings and a large gold necklace — is picking *mâche*. Pearl earrings and an array of diamond and gold rings complete her ensemble. '*Coucou! Patricciiaaaa!*' she bellows as she opens the kitchen door. She has a basketful of fresh *mâche* and nettles on one arm, Chloë on the other. '*Comment tu vas?*' she shouts as she gives me a kiss. '*Et quoi de neuf?*' she asks, depositing Chloë on the ground and the basket on the table. She is positively bursting with life and energy, in keeping with the bright spring day. '*Oh, que c'est bon!*' she shouts, 'to have bright days again, to wash off the sombre winter, to find the land alive and replenishing itself with good things!'

Would I not like some of the *mâche* and nettles she has gathered from among my vines? Have I not finished replacing the stakes among the vines yet? And did I see Jean Brun perched on one of them right next to the house the other day? Jean Brun is the name given to the large brown buzzards that either hover in the sky over Gageac or perch on vine posts surveying the land in search of prey at this time of year.

She deposits half her harvest of *mâche* and nettles on the table for me and scoops up Chloë. She is off to Bergerac, she says. To buy fish. The trout season has just opened and if she gets to the bridge in time she can buy some from one of the fishermen there. Do I need anything? Can she bring me a trout back? How was Odile? Can she deliver the wine samples to the lab for me to save me going to Bergerac too? Isn't life good? With a kiss she is gone, the kitchen still vibrating with the sound of her voice.

I can hardly remember what life was like before Juliana. She is so much a part of the village, part of my life here. With her jewellery, her sense of humour and her raucous laughter, she brings the commune alive. Gageac is her fiefdom. She knows where to find mushrooms. She understands nature. She loves gossip. She is as vibrant and alive as the spring day, bursting with energy and promise.

Next to the laboratory and alongside the old bridge in Bergerac, long fishing rods arc gracefully from the embankment above the river, their lines stretching down into the water. The sun glints on them and the river, sending prisms of light along its surface. Old and young fishermen chatter among themselves and talk to passers-by who come to watch the spectacle. It's the season for trout.

It's the season for pork too. In the charcuteries and supermarkets, it is everywhere. Fresh in aspect and pink in colour, extra counters are installed and given over entirely to pork. Whole sides, along with chops and sausages, sit in rows. Beside them legs of *jambon* hang in their dozens with *saucissons* of different shapes and sizes piled high. On the hardware shelves sterilising kits, huge pans, preserving jars and *toupines* are on sale for those who still kill and preserve their own pigs.

Madame Cholet used to keep a pig as well as ducks and geese, as did most of the villagers. The ceremonial slaughter of it took place either in winter or in early spring. The Fête du Cochon in Gageac following it was an annual feast, a celebration of the filling up of larders. As with Gilles's ducks and geese, nothing was wasted.

Tripe and offal, feet, liver and brains as well as fillets and sides, sausages and hearts were retrieved and portioned out. Blood gathering preceded it. Gilles held the cauldron that caught the blood from the newly slaughtered pig. Once it was full he carried it to the fireplace to keep it warm, stirring so that the blood didn't coagulate. Some of it was later mixed with puréed chestnuts or potatoes to make *boudin noir*. Madame Cholet also made *sanguette* from it, using the same method as her duck *sanguettes*. Ears, tails, muzzle and feet along with other unidentifiable bits of guts, skin and gristle were neither forgotten nor wasted.

Neither was *jambon de campagne*. Her hams were heavily salted, spiced with pepper, wrapped in muslin and left hanging from the beams of her attic to dry. Monsieur Bellegrue must have salted and dried *jambons* when he lived here as one of my kitchen walls is impregnated with saltpetre, impossible to eradicate. Small bubbles of it occasionally burst from the wall sending white paint flaking to the ground.

We no longer have a real Fête de Cochon in Gageac. It simply disappeared, Gilles told me, shrugging when I asked why. Probably because people have more money now, he decided. 'We're less poor, we don't need pigs to live and we've got freezers.' He never liked pork much anyway, he continues, having had too much of it as a child. And he never liked the killing of the pig and the fetching and carrying of buckets of warm blood to the fireplace.

He is sitting in my kitchen now. If I want to, he says, looking at me, I could always go and watch Monsieur La Force killing his pig. He still uses the old methods, he says. I decline hurriedly. The *chasse* is one thing, but killing and dissecting a pig quite another,

I say. I have agreed to go on Manu's *sanglier* hunt when it opens in mid-August and that's more than enough for me. '*Eh, les sangliers?*' bellows Gilles, laughing. 'What do you think they are?'

'*Coucou! Patriciiiaaa!*' Juliana's voice resounds around the kitchen. She has come for an espresso coffee, she says, before taking Chloë to the vet. '*Salut*, Gilles!' she bellows and kisses him in greeting. Chloë is getting on in years, she says. Her breath is beginning to smell and her coat is no longer shining. Her morning and afternoon walks with Yves no longer last very long as she tires so easily. Mostly Yves has to pick her up and carry her home.

'It's really Yves that needs exercising, so she must keep having her walk!' Yves is older than Juliana. '*C'est ma femme!*' she laughs, referring to him and gesticulating with her thumb in the direction of her house. He takes an age over his *toilette* in the mornings and when he does appear he is immaculately dressed and smelling of cologne, she says. Chloë deposits a puddle on the floor. 'Chloë!' shouts Juliana, scooping her up.

Yves is in real need of a walk today, she continues, as they went to the Repas de Cochon in Gageac last night. Not the same as a Fête du Cochon, but all the same . . . 'Of course they didn't kill the pig here, but "*que c'était bon!*",' she shouts. They started with a Jambourra, a soup of vegetables cooked in the stock that the black pudding was boiled in. It still had *morceaux* of black pudding in it that had burst during cooking, she said.

It was followed by a *fricassée* that simply melted in the mouth. The meat was tender, cooked slowly with onions and carrots all day. It was hardly meat at all, she said. 'Then we had the *grillade!*' she exclaims. '*Très copieux!*' There were chops, there were fillets, *saucissons* and *boudin noir*, all cooked outside on the huge iron grill. The salad, cheese and dessert were lost on her, she said, although, of course, Yves managed all of them.

Even if I hadn't already known from Juliana that the Repas de Cochon was taking place at the Mairie, the sound of cars passing and people laughing would have told me something was happening there. Eighty or so people, some from further afield than Gageac, had attended and it was generally agreed, said Juliana, that it was a *bonne bouffe*. '*Alors, t'as besoin de quelque chose?*' she shouts as she leaves, turning back into the kitchen, Chloë under her arm. She's in a hurry, she says, and hopes that Yves is now ready. 'I told you; *c'est ma femme!*' she yells, raising her eyes to the ceiling and kissing us goodbye.

Gilles is leaving too, to buy today's bread. I know that a day without bread would be unthinkable for him, I tell him. He looks at me. '*Tu parles!*' he shouts. 'Of course it would be unthinkable!' His soups need bread in them, his pâté has to be spread on something, what would he wipe his knife on if he didn't have any and his *gibiers* wouldn't taste the same without it. A house without bread, he shouts, isn't a house! '*Salut!*' and he is gone, the kitchen and my ears resounding to the sound of his voice.

Benoît and Caroline who own the bakery in Gardonne live five kilometres from Gageac. Relative newcomers to the area, queues for bread in their shop are testament to the quality of their produce. The aroma of freshly baked bread and buttery, warm croissants that you know will melt in your mouth or *pains au chocolat* tempt you as you open their shop door. On weekdays, small queues form just before midday for their baguettes and *pain de campagne* and on Sunday mornings, when Gardonne has a small market in its square, the shop is crammed with people queueing for bread, croissants and their Sunday *gâteaux*.

I open the back door of the bakery to the smell of freshly baking bread. Benoît is standing next to a huge oven with a large, long table before it. Benoît's apprentice, Sébastien, a young, dark-haired youth of eighteen, stands in front of it. He offers a forearm in greeting, hands covered in flour, a light dusting on his face and hair. Dressed in a short-sleeved T-shirt, he wears a white sheet wrapped round his waist.

A bell from the oven rings and he opens its door, reaching with a long, wooden paddle deep into its heart. He removes hot, golden breads. Benoît picks one of them up and taps its underside to ensure it's cooked to his satisfaction as Sébastien piles the rest into long wicker baskets behind him. Round, large *boules de campagne* removed from the oven follow the baguettes into similar baskets.

Beside Sébastien are scores of uncooked baguettes, sitting in neat rows on dark linen cloths and separated from each other by a pleat. Holding the fabric with one hand and a shorter wooden paddle with the other, Sébastien pulls the cloth towards him, gently scooping up one of the baguettes. His hand touches it deftly for a second, guiding it on to the paddle then over to the long table in front of the oven where he rolls it on to its top. He taps the dough lightly on its side with the paddle, perfecting its shape and repositioning it slightly. Turning back to the cloth he repeats the process, pleat after pleat, until each baguette is transferred to the tabletop. Rolling up the empty cloth, he throws it into a long basket which contains thirty or so others; dark in colour and made from thick Irish linen, they look like rolls of parchment.

Making three cuts on the surface of each loaf, he touches a button on the side of the table, raising it up to the level of the oven. As the door opens, a blast of steam simultaneously hits the bread and Sébastien sends the entire batch speeding into the heat of the oven, the door slamming shut behind them. Benoît watches calmly, master guiding apprentice. The breads that are baking this morning in the oven were made yesterday and stored in a large, walk-in fridge.

A mixer nearby, its huge arm rotating slowly, churns flour and water, together with yeast, for tomorrow's bread. Sébastien pushes down the mix then turns the speed to rapid, introducing more air. A large bubble appears and is dispersed by him. The air from it hits my face for a second. It smells clean yet unperfumed. 'It's in the fermentation that the perfumes rise,' says Benoît as the machine is turned off, restoring silence to the bakery. 'Seems stupid to say, but you must let it live on its own. The less you mix the more you develop the aromas. They mustn't develop too much, or it becomes acid.' I look at the dough, fascinated at the similarity with wine. It, too, only develops perfumes with its fermentation. It, too, can become too acid.

Aromas of sweet vanilla and butter hit my nostrils as I enter the croissant room, along with the strains of a 10CC song on the radio: 'I'm not in love . . .' I hear as a mixer making *pain au levain* churns round, Sébastien next to it, his head nodding in response to the music. A huge marble table dominates the room. On it are *gâteaux* awaiting chocolate or fruit fillings, slabs of butter, flour and sugar bags along with spatulas, bowls, rolling pins and spoons.

Croissants are baking in a small, compact oven. Beside the oven are *pains au chocolat, pains aux raisins* and *choco suisses* fresh from the heat of the oven, gentle wisps of steam rising from them. Benoît makes croissants speedily on the marble table, folding over thin layer upon layer of pastry which he cuts diagonally into small sections. Curling each end of each section slightly to make the delicate crescent shapes of croissants, he passes them to Sébastien who paints egg yolk on them and sends them into the oven. Baked quickly, croissants and *pains au chocolat* are shuffled out as new batches are sent in.

Caroline appears and with her the unmistakable aroma of hot coffee. Dressed in a pale blue jumper that matches her eyes, she has dark, exotic hair cut short and coiffured in spikes. She looks fresh and awake and alive. It's Tuesday morning and yesterday was chaos, she tells me. There was no time to put things into the shop as she had only two helpers. 'Help yourself,' she says as she points to the croissants, pouring out coffee for all. Taking a hot croissant fresh from the oven, I bite into its buttery flakes of pastry. Sébastien, too, eats one. I sip my coffee in silence, experiencing the taste sensations of both and the sheer pleasure of such luxury.

Sébastien, working methodically and silently now, makes baguettes and *pain de campagne* for tomorrow's batch. He cuts chunks of dough into rounds of six and throws each of them into small linen hammocks hanging above his work space. They swing gently as the dough lands softly on them, small puffs of flour rising above each one.

Retrieving them from the hammocks one by one, he kneads them swiftly on the wooden board in front of him. Reaching behind him to the long basket of rolled-up linen cloths, he rolls one out on to a tray next to him, pulling a section of it towards him to recreate a pleat in the fabric. With a rolling pin, the dough in front of him is transformed speedily into a baguette and placed on the cloth. A second pleat, a roll of dough transformed into a baguette and a rhythm is formed. He works quietly and quickly with the slim rolls, one per pleat and twelve per cloth.

The marble table in the croissant room is suddenly empty, washed clean with a hot cloth. It shines in the morning sun. A large sink filled with hot, soapy water holds the spoons, spatulas, rolling pins and containers of the morning. Various machines, mixers and ovens are turned off, the only sound now the shop bell echoing in the bakery.

The bright morning sun blazes through the windscreen of the car and on to my face as I drive out of Gardonne and back towards home. Next to me on the seat is one of Benoît's *pains, une vigneronne*. Made from walnuts, raisins and his black sarrasin flour, it is still warm. The vines on the hillside in the distance seem to ripple with life, their black forms soaking up the energy of this morning's sun. Soon they will burst into leaf. Another growing cycle has already begun.

The château *pigeonnier* looks serene and perfectly proportioned standing in the sloping meadow in front of the château as I climb the hill to Gageac. The sun shines on its round turret and its pale stone walls. Only one of the château's towers is visible, the rest hidden by a row of tall trees. I pass the *pigeonnier* and the long, low barn on my right as the château appears gradually through trees, resplendent with its near tower and its walls overwhelmingly beautiful. I never tire of it, always look forward in anticipation to the sight of it as I pass the low barn. Today its pale grey stone is soaked with bright light, the weathervanes on its towers glinting in the sun.

<hr />

Fidde loved the château of Gageac. He loved its proportions, its simplicity and its elegance. The first time he saw it he wanted to buy it. I laughed; it wasn't for sale I told him, and, anyway, were it to be, he would have to join the ever increasing queue of people who had put their names down. 'But I would appreciate it more!' he said, laughing with me.

'*Bonjour, Monsieur!*' boomed Juliana's voice, her small figure suddenly beside us. She shook Fidde's hand. '*Vous allez bien, Monsieur?*' she asked, smiling up at him. He shook her hand and bowed slightly. She glanced at me with knowing eyes and a wink, then turned back to him. 'I see you like the château,' she continued. At her feet, Chloë barked insistently at Fidde, stretching her small neck to look up at him. '*Tais-toi!*' she shouted, scooping her up.

'*Aah, Monsieur . . .*' she said, stroking Chloë. '*C'est vrai que c'est joli.*' We looked back at the château. '*Très joli,*' she repeated. Sunlight glinted on its roof, the pale grey stones of its towers magnificent and awesome. '*Mais, vous savez, Monsieur,*' she continued, '*si jamais c'est à vendre . . .*' She paused, looking at him intently. '*. . . Ça sera Patricia qui l'achètera!*' she announced, laughter in her eyes.

She glanced at us both, then back at Fidde. '*Sauf, bien sûr, si c'est vous qui l'achètera pour elle!*' She nudged him and laughed raucously. As she left us she turned back to Fidde. '*Et n'oubliez pas, Monsieur,*' she warned, wagging her finger at him. '*Faites attention à ma soeur!*'

Fidde's form striding towards me in the vines, his smile and '*Hej,* Patricia!' in his slow voice were part of my life. I loved his forthright approach to everything, loved his sense of humour. He was impetuous, generous and adventurous. On one of his visits he rang to say he was driving from Fribourg with Gustaf who was moving back to Spain and would be calling via Gageac. Or he would ring up from the airport: 'I've just made a smart decision and decided to come and see you, Patricia!'

On another of his visits he met Michel for the first time. My tractor was parked next to the outside tap at the side of the house, its motor running. The water hose was open and directed into the spraying machine behind it as Michel climbed out of his van. A basket with fresh vegetables from his garden was in his hand. 'I knew you'd be spraying,' he said, looking up at the sky. 'I'm going home to do the same.' He glanced over towards the church as Fidde parked his car there and strode towards us.

'*Hej,* Patricia,' he said with a smile, greeting me then Michel, who shook his hand and blushed slightly, his nut-brown face taking on a ruddy glow. He looked down at the ground for a second, touched his nose and looked back at us again shyly. 'This is Michel,' I said, introducing him. He took off his cap, shuffled his feet a little. Fidde looked at the vegetables and murmured appreciation. Michel smiled.

He had been up since before dawn, he said, fishing, then working around the *commune* cutting the hedges. He had slipped back home to gather some vegetables before calling here to collect some spray for his vines. '*Et dis-donc*,' he said, looking at me and laughing, less shy now he had broken the ice with Fidde. '*Tu es devenue bleu!*' The blue copper sulphate powder was not only in the spraying machine.

We talked together in a desultory fashion until the machine was full. '*Eh bien*,' said Michel, picking up the bucket of copper sulphate I had put aside for him and with a '*Salut!*' he was gone. I told Fidde who he was, how much he had helped me in the early days, how he lived his life by the seasons, how much I valued his friendship. He listened. 'He's a rich man,' he said.

Fiddle had invited his sisters to stay at the nearby golf club, Château de Vigiers, for the weekend. I had heard a lot about them. Two of them and a brother lived in Sweden, another sister and an elder brother in America. We had dinner together at Pia and Ekan's on their first night. As I arrived and descended the stone staircase, Fidde leapt up to greet me, putting his cigar back into its holder.

He kissed me and fixed me with penetrating, gentle eyes and his smile. He took both my hands and held them up. The room seemed to fade into the background for an instant, along with his sisters and Pia and Ekan smiling behind him, waiting patiently. He held my hand as he introduced me to them. '*Hej*, Patricia,' said Pia with a smile, kissing me. 'Patricia!' said Ekan, '*Hej!*'

His sisters were as curious to meet me as I was to

meet them. Fidde had told them all about me, they said, looking from him to me. 'You're being inspected, Patricia!' he announced. I laughed; I was. Agneta was over from America, where she lived. Tall, fair-haired and with a wide smile like Fidde, she, along with her sisters, Regina and Ika, had the same porcelain complexion as Ebba, a gentle manner and a soft, lilting voice.

'Patricia!' boomed Ekan as he raised a glass at dinner. 'You really gotta learn Swedish now! *Skol!*' Pia laughed. 'I'll bring you back a dictionary next summer from Sweden, I promise.' Fidde's sisters laughed too. Fidde was sitting at my side, attentive, demonstrative. He looked deeply into me at that moment. I saw him do it. He saw in me something he wanted. He wanted me.

Fidde's friends began to visit periodically from Sweden or Switzerland to play golf at Château de Vigiers and became my friends too. Château de Vigiers was owned mostly by Scandinavians. Another Swede, Lars Urban Petersson, and his wife, Elizabeth, had come to France in the early '90s from England where they were living and discovered the then dilapidated and burnt-out shell of what is now the golf course and hotel. They found investors for it and made it the huge success it is today. One of the investors was Fidde's cousin, Svante, and another his closest friend, Tom.

Fidde loved involving everyone, loved having his friends together. He drew people to him. 'You know, Patricia,' said Tom, who was over from America, as we were all having dinner together one evening after a golf tournament, 'the Swedish language is so word-poor, Fidde would have to be pretty dumb not to teach it to you in a week or so! *Skol!*' he laughed, holding up his glass.

I had already decided that I would learn the language. Often, I was the only non-Swedish speaker in the room and it seemed unfair that they should all have to speak English for me. 'You would speak it well, Patricia. I feel it!' replied Tom, raising his glass again. 'I'll help you!' said Fidde. 'You've got six days,' said Tom and a peal of laughter accompanied the *skol* as we drank to my future mastery of their language.

Surprisingly, I knew no Swedes at all before moving to France, or golfers, come to that. It seemed bizarre to have met so many since coming to live here, a concentrated group of them in my small rural world that consisted mainly of French. 'Ah, but it's only a certain type of Swede, you know,' Fidde had said when I told him. 'The best!' and he laughed uproariously.

The investors of Vigiers, along with friends of Lars Urban and Elizabeth, including Pia, Ekan, Fidde and I, were invited to the black-tie dinner given in celebration of Lars Urban's sixtieth birthday. As I stepped out of my car at Château de Vigiers I heard Fidde's voice. 'Patricia!' he shouted as he walked towards me through the black night and firmly took my hand.

'*Hej*, Patricia' he repeated softly as he kissed me. Stars hung in the sky like sparkling diamonds and the moon was bright and luminous. We hurried into the warmth of the château. Every room was lit by candles. Glasses of champagne greeted us. Hundreds of people milled around drinking *apéritifs* before dinner, moving from room to room.

The round dining tables looked magnificent, white linen tablecloths sweeping down to the floor, each table dressed with candelabra, flowers and place names. Guests gathered in the dining room, having been called to dinner and searched for their places on the noticeboard at the entrance.

'But I don't want to sit there!' said Fidde firmly to Elizabeth. They spoke to each other in Swedish, after which Fidde marched purposefully over to the table with his place name and removed it. He took me to my table, placed his name card next to mine and pulled out the chair for me, handing the spare place name to one of the waiters with instructions to put it on the table without one. 'Patricia!' he said. 'Let me help you,' and he laughed, seating me, then placing himself firmly next to me.

Chapter 6

IT'S MAY AND THE YOUNG DANDELIONS AND WILD TURNIP IN EIDA'S field have gone. She is knee-deep in ochre-coloured buttercups. She looks comical, like a pantomime horse, her legs cut off at the knee by swathes of yellow. I have never seen such elongated buttercups. Juliana says that's because they are not buttercups but wild celery flowers. Eida snorts at me, waiting for titbits.

The wisteria in the courtyard is in full blossom, dazzling against the delicate sprays of pale pink flowers in the tamarisk trees. Beneath them, lilies of the valley send out their perfume. Nature is bursting out, vibrant and ebullient. The grass between the vines has already been mown twice and is growing again, the acacia trees are in full leaf and the hedging around the house is sprouting upwards and outwards at an alarming rate.

Inside the courtyard of the château the wisteria is more dazzling still than mine. Vivid mauve blossoms cascade down the wall, millions of petals shimmering in the sun. They contrast with the pale grey stone of the walls and the deep, varied colours of its roof.

Green and white asparagus are on sale in the shops and

markets, with fresh young spinach and artichokes. The first shoots of fresh garlic, '*aillet*', are everywhere, among my vines as well as in the shops. Resembling slim spring onions, they have a delicate taste, something between garlic and onion, and when served in an omelette made with fresh eggs are '*que du bonheur!*', as Monsieur Blanchard would say.

Traditionally, they are served on 1 May, the day lilies of the valley are offered to wives, sweethearts and mothers. I have already had my first '*omelette à l'aillet*' of the season, made by Juliana on the day in question. It was succulent and rich with eggs from Madame Briand's chickens and my own *aillet* growing between the vines.

Jean, who lives at the bottom of the hill of Gageac in La Ferrière with his wife, Annie, has also left the obligatory lily of the valley outside my kitchen door. I am not alone in receiving one from him. As well as Annie and me, a fair number of the women in Gageac are recipients. I often wonder what Annie thinks about this and once asked her. She doesn't seem to mind at all.

The buds on the vines have opened out and are now incontestably leaves. I inspect those at Les Bûchères, near La Tabardy, where the growing pattern is always slightly ahead of the others. Large and fresh, they send out their shoots, some of which are already working their way up to the second wire on the *palissage*. Embryos of grapes push upwards towards the sun, enveloped by small, curling and rose-hued leaves with no hint of disease on them. The rose bushes at the end of the rows of vines, their deep red leaves a contrast to the pale green of the vines, reflect the same growing pattern, buds pushing upwards, their outer layer of leaves concealing flowers within.

Walking back through the vines towards Madame Cholet's, I see that work on the house is progressing with a roof already in place. I think of Madame Cholet with fondness. She knitted me toe socks to keep my feet warm in winter while pruning. She used to bring me sprigs of mimosa at this time of year, great sprays of delicate canary-yellow flowers, a prelude to the flowering season. She used to walk through the vines daily on her way to the cemetery with flowers for her husband's grave and gather in *mâche* for her salads among the rows of vines. I wonder what she would think of her house were she to see it now.

Fidde didn't buy the château at Gageac but he did buy a house here. We were sitting on a wall outside the restaurant where we had just eaten when he told me he was going to look for one in the area. He took his cigar end from its holder and lit it. 'I've decided. I want to be here, Patricia,' he said, turning to me. He looked at me searchingly. 'What do you think about that?' I looked back at him, then at my feet, a rush of conflicting feelings washing over me.

My heart leapt and sank at the same time. In a way his decision felt like a natural progression, an inevitability, and yet I was resisting, stepping back, apprehensive of something. Afraid of commitment, a little afraid of Fidde, I could feel him looking at me, smiling. He laughed gently. 'Patricia,' he said, 'I feel you thinking!' I looked back at him, at his gentle eyes. 'I'm a patient man, you know.' He laughed again, softly.

In the spring and summer of 1998 he found his house, stone-built in the style of Madame Cholet's and, like hers, a ruin. Unlike Madame Cholet's, it was a manor house, large and sprawling with huge rooms leading into one another on the ground floor and a large, uninhabited space on the first floor. A garden and expansive sloping lawns leading down to a river lined with poplars bordered one side of the house, with a courtyard and *pigeonnier* on the other.

It had taken some time to find it. His architect cousin, Arvid, came over frequently from Stockholm whenever Fidde saw something he felt might have potential. Tall, slim and gentle, he too became part of my life along with his wife, Shirstin. He only ever spent a day or two at most on each of his visits. 'How's the Swedish coming along, Patricia?' he would ask with a laugh each time we met.

Pia had taken him to see endless châteaux, manor houses and *chartreuses* in his search for one that suited him. 'Why can't you come along, Patricia?' he asked. I couldn't as I had spraying to do, or wood-pulling or mowing, I told him. I had taken him to more than a few, including the beautiful château de la Jaubertie nearby and one on the hill of Rouillac, next to Gageac. 'When I see the house I want, I'll know it,' he would say.

A beautiful house near Villeneuve de Duras, it was hidden from the small country road on which it was situated. You would not know it was there. Even knowing, it was easy to miss the turning into the *domain*. Only a small gap in the tall, impenetrable hedge, which hid the house entirely, signified its entrance to those who were aware of it and turning in through it was sharp and difficult.

The original floor tiles of the house, deep terracotta and stained with age, were mostly intact throughout the ground floor. Outside the kitchen door, roses rampaged over a broken wooden arch. Others clung to the outside wall, splashes of deep red and white. Honeysuckle had colonised one end of it and wild mint in the grass sent up its scent as Fidde and I walked round the outside of the house. 'It takes approximately twelve and a half minutes by car to get from here to you,' he laughed. 'I've timed it.'

He had his arm around my shoulder as we walked round from the back of the house to the courtyard and its *pigeonnier*. 'Do you really like the house?' he asked earnestly, looking at me. We pushed open the door of the *pigeonnier*. Dust caught in a shaft of sunlight danced and sparkled as we climbed the narrow steps to the first floor. It was beautiful, like being in a secret place, full of hope and magic.

He looked at me thoughtfully for a second. He would have Arvid draw up plans for the house quickly and use a local architect to carry them out, he said. With any luck, the workmen could begin soon. He wanted to move in as quickly as possible. It needn't take long to complete the work if the artisans and the architect worked together as a team.

It did. On each of Fidde's visits, he had the same frustrations with his house as I now have at Madame Cholet's. The roofer hadn't finished when he should have done, the plumber didn't come when he said he would and the tiler hadn't started when he should already have finished.

———◆———

'*Coucou! Patriciia!*' The kitchen door opens and Juliana bursts into the kitchen armed with a basket of freshly picked *aillet* and Chloë, accompanied by the pale yellow puddle on the floor. '*Bonjour, ma soeur!*' She kisses me, handing me the basket. '*Aah! Bonjour, Monsieur!*' She tilts her head towards Gilles by way of greeting. He has called by to give me the date of the *chasse* dinner, to invite me along as his guest and to collect more stones for his wall. Chloë looks at all three of us and barks insistently. '*Tais-toi!*' bellows Juliana as she scoops her up.

'*Et alors, quoi de neuf?*' What's new? as she kisses Gilles. '*Tiens*, Patricia, La Tabardy was lit up like Versailles last night. Do you have people there?' It's probably the security light, I say. There's one at the front which comes on when someone approaches. It often does when deer or even dogs pass too close to the house. However, it could hardly be said to resemble the brightness of Versailles and nobody is yet installed as tenant. There's no crime in the area, but Juliana's insistence that she had heard of a house in the area being broken into recently, and that it would be wise to check it out, galvanises us all into action.

We pile into the car and drive over to inspect. I open the front door. We find everything just as it was yesterday when more furniture was delivered. I had simply forgotten to turn the lights off. All the same, we wander round the house to check. Entering the *salon*, Gilles whistles slowly. It is some time since he has last been inside La Tabardy. The *salon* is now furnished. Sofas and carpets, a large dining-room table, chairs and an *armoire* now complement the pale stone walls that were once his *chai*.

He nods in appreciation then looks at the large fireplace that has been built where his cement vats used to be. 'That will never work,' he pronounces dismissively. Why not, I ask. He turns to Juliana, Chloë and me. 'Because there's too much open space between the chimney piece and its base, the chimney piece isn't deep enough and there's not enough drawing power.' I look at the fireplace, which has an expensive, recently installed backplate and fire dogs. 'Mark my words,' he reiterates. 'If you don't believe me . . .' He looks at me again. '. . . We'll try it now.'

We gather up dead branches from the vines next to the house along with some heavier cut-down stumps and some paper left by the deliverymen. Chloë deposits a puddle on the ground. 'Chloë!' Juliana shouts at her and scoops her up into her arms.

'*Elle marque son territoire*' she explains apologetically and heads for the kitchen in search of a cloth while I watch Gilles light the fire.

He's right about the chimney. Smoke curls up from the vine branches, heads towards the chimney flue then sharply changes direction out towards us, the ceiling and the furniture. Gilles steps back. 'You see?' He looks down at the smoking pile in the fireplace. I look up at the smoke fast filling the room and think of the time, effort and money that have been spent on the fireplace, the painting of the ceiling and the furniture fast being impregnated with wood smoke.

The bottling of the white and rosé vats is scheduled for next week. Both wines taste delicious and I'm impatient to have the bottling done. I worry that something untoward might happen beforehand to change their taste, freshness and elegance. Labels have been ordered, as have bottles, capsules and corks. It only remains for the bottling plant to arrive and do its job.

The white and red wines are evolving in barrels. Rows of them sit in perfect symmetry, the sweet smell of their wood and the perfume of wine inside mingling discreetly. The shape of the barrels, the colour of their wood, everything about them is pleasing; gently curved wooden staves moulded into shape with hoops of silver-tinged metal rounds binding them and holding the results of last year's *belle saison*, a marriage of fruit and wood.

My truffle tree over at Les Bûchères still has no weeds around its base. The trees in the woods next to it, however, are bursting with growth, delicate green leaves burgeoning from the tops of the trees. I step in through overhanging branches on its perimeter and to its heart. It is restful, quiet, apart from the crackle of leaves under my feet and the gentle sounds of the forest. Spring sun seeps in through the canopy of leaves above me throwing dappled light on to bark and leaves.

*

Maison Charlois is in the business of wood. The patriarch, Denis Charlois, and his three sons all work in wood. They select it, fell it and transport it. They saw it, split it, dry it and transform it into barrels. They are France's largest stave producers, in existence since 1928 when Denis's father set up his workshop in Murlin, a small village in the heart of the Bertranges forest in the Nièvre region where we now are. His grandfather had also been in the business of wood. They are born into it, bred into it, steeped in it.

Sylvain Charlois steps outside to greet us. In his late twenties, he is tall and slim with long, dark hair tied in a ponytail. I am with my friend Francis Miquel and his director, Charles Cavin. Francis sells me wine barrels. Passionate about them and, most particularly, about what goes in them, he is of medium height and dark complexion. His face is long and interesting with large, expressive eyes and a wide smile. A shock of hair with a white streak running through adds a certain distinction to his appearance. His voice is deep, yet he is quietly spoken with a slow diction which adds weight to whatever he is saying.

Charles Cavin is ebullient. He is driven not just by wine and barrels but also by good food and gossip. Tall, with dark hair combed carefully back, sparkling eyes and a cravat around his neck, he talks almost as loudly as Gilles, laughter bubbling behind every word. Charles greets Sylvain loudly. How is he? What has he been up to since they last met? What news of the wine consignment he arranged? Is Denis well? How are the children? We step from the road into the house and a large room, Charles still talking and laughing.

To our left a table has been set for eight. White napkins bearing the Charlois crest lie beside silver knives, forks and crystal glasses. In the centre of the room and beside a large *armoire* is a glass-topped coffee table with eight champagne *flûtes* on it, surrounded by a sofa and some chairs. Denis Charlois walks into the room with a smile, accompanied by his youngest son, Romane.

Immaculately groomed, well-manicured and with shining

teeth and intelligent eyes, the scent of Denis Charlois cologne hangs discreetly in the air. Dressed in a tailored waistcoat with a starched shirt of dazzling white and a cravat at his neck held in place by a sapphire and diamond tiepin, he has a ponytail, as does Romane, as well as an earring. Small, yet well-built and imposing, he shakes our hands with a slight bow and gestures for us to sit.

Champagne is poured into our glasses by Sylvain. Charles chatters away, to Denis in particular and us in general. Is he well? Has he seen Alphonse recently? What's new? They know each other well: Denis is not just the supplier of wood for the barrel factory but also a major shareholder. Charles recounts anecdotes of winemakers, barrel brokers and people in general as Denis listens, entering into the conversation occasionally, smiling rarely.

I look at Francis, quiet, preoccupied with his own thoughts, and then at Denis Charlois as he listens to Charles. His face and stature are quite different from those of the Gascons and Périgourdins of our region. Although he, like them, is small and stocky, his demeanour is different, his comportment something other than Gascogne. His accent, too, is different and certainly his dress. I haven't seen a single cravat or tiepin on any of my neighbours, ever.

The champagne, allied with aroma of food from beyond the door, increases our appetites. A chef enters the room and with a gesture from Denis we rise and pass to the table as Charles chatters happily to the room about wine, barrels, friends and food.

Foie gras on toast with a sprinkling of sea salt is served with sun-dried tomatoes. The warmth of the toast has slightly melted the foie gras, which tastes rich and luxurious. A bottle of Sancerre made by Alphonse Mellot is fresh and cold and marries perfectly with it. A cool Saumur Champigny is served with the farm chicken that follows. Rich and dark and cooked with *échalottes* that melt in the mouth, it is accompanied by roasted *cèpes* and glistening potatoes, slightly softened by the duck fat they are cooked in, yet with crispy edges.

121

The wines and the food have eased the earlier formality and people chat amiably. Denis observes, listens, laughs occasionally. We discuss barrels in general. Some of the barrels in my *chai* that are not supplied by Francis are not giving the same expression to the wine as I would have hoped. Denis sits up and leans over the table slightly, wiping his mouth with his napkin and fixing me with his eyes. 'But of course,' he states quietly. His diamond earring sparkles as he turns slightly.

He puts down his napkin and leans forward again, picking up his glass of wine. He looks round at all of us, holding up the glass higher to the general assembly. 'If you mix the wine in this glass with twenty-four other wines, you can't possibly know what you might get, can you?' He taps his glass with his fork and the sound of crystal echoes around the table. We all agree. 'It's the same with wood,' he says, turning back to me. 'Like wine, it all depends on its provenance. Those barrels of yours don't give the same expression to your wine because they obviously mix the woods in them.'

He looks around the table then fixes me with his eyes again. 'All our wood comes from the same forest, the Bertranges forest.' A silence as we all listen attentively. 'They are always centenary oaks and they always have fine grain and structure. We know exactly where the wood for the barrels comes from because we buy it standing up in the forest.'

The cheese plate is copious and the *tarte tatin* delicious. As we finish our wine and coffee, Francis asks how Denis's companion is. He smiles. 'Fine, thank you. She doesn't live with me at the moment.' He continues, 'But we still get on well.' He turns to us all, glass in hand again, a faint smile on his face. '*Les femmes*: when they've left me they like me a lot.' His eyes sparkle. 'It's only when I live with them that it doesn't work! *Aux femmes!*' he says laughing and with a bow to me as we finish our meal.

The woodyard that receives and processes the trees that have the age and fine grain that Denis talked of and all come from the same place is right outside Maison Charlois's offices. Sylvain has been deputed to show us round. Lying on the ground outside are five enormous tree trunks. Cut in the forest and delivered here directly by a transporter for a quality control, they are twenty-five metres long and a hundred and eighty years old.

I feel suddenly shaken by the sight of the beautiful oaks that have lived in the Bertranges forest for their long life now lying inert on the ground before me. Some of the wood can be up to three hundred years old, Sylvain is saying; the minimum age of the trunks they buy for barrels is a hundred and thirty.

He points out which sections of the trunks lying on the ground will be reserved for them. The quality controllers have already done their job and we can see, helped by the orange spray paint on them, the knots and grain changes that disqualify certain sections. Other sections have been excluded because of cracks or splits. One of the trunks will be used entirely for barrels, another only twenty per cent, the residue sold on to make railway sleepers, pallets or for general cabinet making.

As we stand next to the newly delivered oaks, huge tractors zoom around the woodyard carrying split trunks. An over-powering perfume of sweet wood and sap pervades the air. The split trunks look raw, their rich interiors open now to the world. Huge piles of them sit in the yard destined for the workshop to make staves for barrels, or to be transported to Spain or further afield. We head towards the woodshed as a transporter arrives with another load of freshly hewn trunks from the forest.

As we enter the workshop, the deafening sound of wood saws pummels our ears. Three teams of six work in unison. One team is standing behind large machines that cut up trunks into stave lengths. Another feeds them into cutting machines, then out at the other end where they have been transformed into staves where yet another team checks them again for quality. Measured and inspected, the now smooth staves are once again marked for faults in the grain or knots in the wood.

We climb a flight of open stairs to a raised platform and look down on the workers and their machines. The sweet scent of wood rises up towards us, powerful and intoxicating. People are everywhere and the sound of saws, of stave hitting stave as they pile up one on to one another, is deafening. Wood moves constantly; through saws, on tables, in piles.

Outside one-metre-high blocks of staves, looking like so many empty pallets piled one on to another, sit in ordered rows. Each layer of each block is separated at its corners by a small cube, creating a gap between the layers and allowing air passages through and around the wood. They will sit outside for two years to dry and season before being utilised for barrels Sylvain is telling me. For the moment, they decorate the yard, each one marked with a coloured and numbered label.

We leave the noise and chaos of the workshop and the yard and head to the forest. Less than five minutes' drive from Maison Charlois and turning left off the main road, we are suddenly in another world. Ancient forestry encircles us, imposing, deep and ancient.

Pierced here and there by shafts of sunlight, as far as the eye can see, are immense oak trees. Tall and proud, they burgeon with fresh, new leaf. Straight roads, their surfaces transformed into mother-of-pearl by the sun's rays, gleam and stretch into infinity through the forest. Birdsong and falling leaves are the only sounds. A feeling of *déjà vu* washes over me, of being part of it, even.

We drive slowly through as Sylvain points out *parcelles* of oaks to the right and left. Although it is not evident to us, the forest is sectioned off into *parcelles*. Sylvain shows us one in the first stages of management, the forestry commission having already graded the oaks in it, guarding those that have straight trunks, marking with a cross those that will be cut out. Tall and straight young oaks stand next to others that are twisted, leaning inwards towards them. The forest floor is littered with leaves, enriching the soil. Tiny oaks spring from the ground, some of which will die or be uprooted, others that will live on for another century.

The Bertranges forest alone has seven thousand hectares of oak trees, says Sylvain. Occasionally, we see an area of what looks like scrubland with young oaks. Mostly the forest is simply forest, kilometre after kilometre of magnificent oak trees. Approaching a crossroads, the four roads seem to lead on forever through them.

A *parcelle* that has reached its final stage of clearance, having been thinned out over a twelve-year period, is before us. We stop the car and look at it. Seven centuries-old giant oaks stand spaced six metres apart. There is no undergrowth, nothing except the oldest, most perfect oaks. They stand huge and tall and straight, black forms reaching up to the sky with mists of new, leaf growth at their summit, reflecting the rising warmth of spring.

We set off towards Burgundy, past Vézelay with its basilica and château perched on the hillside and onwards towards Gevrey-Chambertin. Conversation bubbles, the only topic barrels; the making of them, the wood in them, the use of them, the magical effect of them on wine. We speed on towards the slopes and hillsides of Burgundy scattered with woods of pine and oak, descending sharply down the hillside into Les Côtes de Nuit.

A patchwork of vines spreads across the floor of the valley that opens out in front of us as we descend the hill. Long, narrow rows with the lowest vines imaginable are interspersed with *piquets* so small they make mine look like giants. In Marsannay la Côte vines are planted up and into gardens, even in the heart of the village, abutting the houses and using up every inch of agricultural space. We drive on through narrow streets and out through the other side of the village, vines to the right and left, on through the Routes des Grands Crus, past the village of Couchey with its amazingly tiled, coloured roof tower and on to Fixin.

Small walls divide the tiny vines of Fixin from the heart of the beautiful village. Cherry trees and forsythia from minute court-yards throw out splashes of yellow and dark, rich pink. On to Brochon. Encircling the *grands crus* are beautiful ancient walls. Names I have only heard of are displayed: Morey-St-Denis, Vosne-Romanée and Vougeot.

With barely time to deposit our bags in the hotel room at Gevrey-Chambertin, we regroup for dinner. It has been a long day. Charles is still as irrepressible and full of energy and enthusiasm as he was when he met us this morning at Maison Charlois, in spite of a huge lunch and a visit to the forest. He rubs his hands together and laughs as we meet up in the *salon* of his office opposite the hotel for a glass of Bicard champagne, cool, mineral and fresh.

Supper in a local restaurant is supplemented by Burgundy wines chosen by Charles. He chatters, laughter in his voice, recounting anecdotes about the winemakers of the various wines we drink. A Saumur-Champigny is served as an *apéritif*, followed by a Puligny-Montrachet with the starter. A red Nuit-St-Georges accompanies our main course and a Les Charmes-Chambertin Grand Cru is added for good measure.

I am surprised at how much I'm eating and drinking and talking, given the gargantuan lunch we had at Maison Charlois and the long day. A group of ten or so men seated at the far end of the restaurant are laughing loudly. One carafe of wine after another is delivered to their table. Winemakers and chefs, Charles informs us, waving at them and shouting a greeting. They wave back and send over one of the carafes. What does Charles think of it? We all taste. Old Burgundy, shouts Charles across to them and they discuss its merits from a distance with booming voices.

Dinner over, as we rise to leave the waiter delivers an invita-tion to take a *digestif* with the other remaining customers, now only the winemakers and chefs. Charles laughs and accepts instantly. Chairs are arranged around a huge fireplace in the reception area to accommodate ten of them and five of us, plus the chef and the owner of the restaurant, who has also decided to join the party.

A bottle of champagne is opened, *petit fours* appear. I'm not sure I can drink another drop or eat another mouthful. Francis's face tells me he feels the same. Only Charles is still full of life and laughter and gossip and enthusiasm. '*Qu'est-ce que t'en en penses, Patricia?*' he asks me of the champagne and I force myself to take a mouthful. It is fresh, mineral and biscuity in spite of my jaded palet.

Noise and laughter and more *café* and *digestifs* follow the champagne and *petit fours*. 'Never drink *café* with this,' Charles pronounces, sinking low in a leather armchair as he sups from a huge glass of Armagnac. 'There, madness lies. It gives you a headache and a curtain drops.' My curtain has already done so, the thought of sleep my only desire.

Hidden underneath the house of winemaker Vincent Geantet are deep, vaulted cellars. They sprawl east, south and west; long tunnels, mossy and blackened with mould. It hangs from the ceilings and covers the walls. Rows of barrels down the centre of the tunnel sit on a gravel base, further rows of them along the walls. The pale oak barrels supplied only months before to him by Francis are already changing colour from the mould, which seems to send its spores onwards and over us almost as we speak.

Monsieur Vincent Geantet is a Harley man. Stocky, fresh-faced and in his mid-forties, he has short, spiky, blond hair. He wears cowboy boots. And a gold cross and chain. And rings and a bracelet. A silver chain attached to his belt and draped around his hips from a front trouser pocket to a back pocket holds keys and a wallet. A leather waistcoat and drainpipe cream trousers finish '*le look Harley*'.

He dips the long pipette in his hand into a barrel of white burgundy, a Gevrey-Chambertin from the last harvest, and expels some into each of our glasses with a swagger. I put mine to my nose. Aromas of caramel and flowers dominate and the taste as I swill the wine in my mouth is full of freshness and minerality. We all murmur our appreciation. Vincent Geantet swirls the wine around his mouth, draws some over his tongue then spits it out, nodding his head, a hint of approval on his lips.

We move to other barrels; a Marsanney-Chambertin that has the same minerality and an expression of flowers and fruit, then a Chambolle-Musigny and a Gevrey-Chambertin made from one hundred-year-old vines, dense, with strong tannins, great length and lots of fruit.

A Morey-St-Denis fermented in oak barrels not just from Charles and Denis's barrel factory, but also from another make of barrel, demonstrates the startling difference of tastes and aromas in each type and I understand perfectly Denis Charlois's point about wood. The wine in one of the barrels has good construction with fruit and minerals. Yet the same wine in a different make of oak barrel is aggressive with dryness and green, unripe undertones. Vincent nods at our comments. '*C'est flagrant, n'est-ce pas?*' he says, addressing Charles and Francis.

We taste wine after wine, discussing their structure and balance, fruit and acid content. Confident, yet unpretentious, Vincent talks of his wines with sensitivity, somehow at odds with his cowboy boots and Harley look. A Premier Cru Le Poisserot is mineral and elegant, ageing in a blond toasted barrel and tasting utterly delicious. Another, a Chambertin Grand Cru is round, with aromas of crushed strawberries.

The large numbers of *appellations* in Burgundy are incomprehensible to me. Francis has tried to clarify them. There are general *appellations*, village *appellations*, *climats* and great growths. There are Côtes de Beaune and Côtes de Nuits, Chambertin and

Chambertin-Clos de Beze, Musigny and Chambolle-Musigny, Vougeot and Clos-de-Vougeot, Romanée-Conti and Vosne-Romanée to name but a few.

Some wines smell and taste of chocolate, others of morello cherries. We pass from one *cave* to another, stooping to pass through one-metre-thick vaulted corridors leading to yet more cellars and more tastings. My body temperature is descending, my feet are turning to blocks of ice and my nose drips ceaselessly.

Rows of bottles, caked with dust and mould, line the walls as we are led back to the central corridor where half a large barrel acts as a tasting table. Vincent stands behind it opening bottles now rather than barrels and we taste previous vintages of Gevrey-Chambertin. Ruby-coloured, shimmering and sparkling, they are perfectly balanced with aromas of cherries and pepper and with round tannins, long and elegant.

Not only have I lost all feeling in my feet, my nose is dripping with the cold, damp atmosphere of the cellars, I have also lost all sense of time, hidden deep in the cellars where no sound from the outside world permeates. We emerge slowly from the mossy depths of his cellars, through corridors of bottles and barrels and back to the entrance hall, blinking into the sunlight of the world outside.

Returning home, Francis and I turn up the hill to Gageac. My vines look like giants compared to those of Burgundy. A buzzard is sitting on one of their posts as I return. He surveys the countryside for food, his sharp eyes blinking occasionally. Gilles would regret that he couldn't shoot it. Francis glances at it as we stop outside the house. 'Not much taste to them,' he laughs, nodding in the buzzard's direction as he says goodbye, another hour before he reaches his home near Marmande.

I am happy to be back to my own patchwork of vines and my own grape varieties, though it was fascinating to learn about the pinot noir grape, so different from our merlots, cabernet sauvignons and sémillons. Fascinating, too, to meet winemakers from different regions.

Francis is a bit of an enigma. His interests are not restricted only to wine and barrels. He also loves the *chasse*, cycling, cooking, the guitar and most especially his wife and children. He hunts often, like Gilles, even as far afield as Ireland. Wild quail is one of his favourite dishes and, were I ever to have one to hand, I have the perfect recipe from Francis to cook it along with a sauce of caramelised onions and tomatoes that he serves with it and other wildfowl, a recipe handed down from his grandmother.

His memories of his grandmother and his childhood are as interesting as his recipes. His descriptions of the overpowering smell of hay during harvesting as a child, his grandmother's soups, being seated round the table with her and his grandfather, along with his parents, aunts and uncles. Sunday lunch often lasted all day and into the evening. Children came and went from the table while adults talked, ate and drank.

He remembers the taste of juicy, sweet prunes dried first in the hot sun and then in an oven. And puréed fresh sorrel with confit of duck. Or wild asparagus, green and fresh and full of taste, cooked simply and served with butter and sweet, juicy tomatoes. And country people who ate gargantuan breakfasts to give them the energy needed for the day's manual work.

And snails, one hundred and fifty gathered for each person. Best in the spring, they were purged with bran for a month in a cage and then soaked in vinegar and salt in their shells and stirred until a froth formed. The sound of bubbling water as the *mousse* rose in the bucket and the snails died was unforgettable, he told me. Rinsed, drained and coated with olive oil, they were grilled simply in their shells. 'With good bread and good wine, what else would you need?'

Chapter 7

MID-MAY, WITH TWO DAYS OF REALLY WARM WEATHER, AND THE world outside my bedroom window has gone mad. Ten in the evening and cicadas and frogs sing and croak in their hundreds. Six in the morning and the birds that live in the virginia creeper start yelling at each other. When I drive along the roads during the day, birds on suicide missions fly in front of my bonnet and at night toads boldly sit in the middle of the road, refusing to move. Wild lavender decks the roadsides. With their raised flower heads and two elongated petals looking like so many rows of purple-coloured rabbits' ears, they emit delicate aromas.

Creamy white acacia flowers are in full blossom on the trees in my garden. They float on the air with the breeze, blowing gently on to the swimming pool and blocking up the filter. The pool has just been opened and is awash with it, along with a green gunge at the bottom. I hope desperately that the frogs I hear croaking at night haven't colonised it.

The hedge in the garden is out of control suddenly and the roses and peonies are in full flower. The olive tree that was planted last year, and only a few months ago looked small and meagre,

131

now has leafy branches cascading to the ground. As for the vines, they are growing almost as I look at them. Tendrils wrap themselves around the wires of the *pallisage* and climb upwards, taking with them large leaves and the embryo bunches of grapes.

Juliana brings me *beignets d'acacia*, sweet fritters made by dipping whole sprays of acacia flowers in a light batter, frying them in olive oil and serving them with sugar. I have to approve; for every *beignet* she makes me or Yves or the rest of the village, there are fewer flower heads to float on the air and into my pool. She brings them in a small basket lined with kitchen paper to soak up the excess olive oil. Covered in a lace napkin to keep them warm, they taste delicate and delicious and are thoroughly spoiling.

Benjamin is looking tanned but stressed. The vines are growing so quickly it's already time to lift the wires of the *pallisage* to bring the vine branches into order. Last week he and Alain were thinning out the buds on the *lattes*, steadily working up and down the rows knocking off those considered excessive; time-consuming but important work and essential to reduce the yield and increase the quality. Now they are rushing to finish the task in order not to be behind with the wire lifting. And we are about to bottle the rosé and dry white.

The bottles, cartons, capsules and corks have already been delivered and the wine is ready and waiting. We have changed our bottlers from Monsieur Capponi, who we have used until now. Monsieur Capponi's bottling was always fraught with stress. Flatly refusing to bottle without a filtration of the wine, even though I was prepared to sign a waiver that exonerated him from any responsibility should there be a problem, he would inevitably lose his temper with his workers at some point in the bottling process.

Such was the vehemence of his outbursts, at least one and sometimes more than one of his team would walk off and leave the job. On the last bottling, the sight of him shouting and jumping up and down in rage on the lorry with bottles banking up on the conveyor belt beside him was enough to bring about an overdue decision to change.

The bottlers of the Euralis team calmly walk into the *chai* and inspect the vats. They know already that we don't wish to filter the wine and they know also that we wish to have some of the bottles in cases of six, some with back labels and all with bar codes.

They marry up all available pipes from the *chai* and lay them down the drive and up on to the lorry outside. They link one end up to the bottling plant, the other to a full vat, wine surges through them and in an instant the bottling commences. It is calm and quiet and efficient. The clink of bottles as they pass round the conveyor belt is regular, the hiss of the corking machine is ordered and we marvel at the lack of stress. Two days later and pallets full of shrink-wrapped cartons of wine are standing next to the lorry waiting for a home.

They sit in serried rows on the grass outside the church, glistening in the sun, their clingfilm occasionally capturing rays of sunlight and reflecting them back towards me, flashes of diamonds dazzling my eyes. Relieved and pleased to have the bottling done, I look at the pallets again. We can house them all, but it will take up all the available space we have. As I turn back towards the house the worry that disappeared with the end of the bottling is replaced by another and is back with a vengeance. Where am I going to put the reds and the barrelled white that will be ready for bottling soon?

La Tabardy's chimney problem is a continuing one. I poured water on the fire Gilles had lit, opened all the windows and succeeded in removing most of the odour of wood smoke from the *salon*. I explained the problem to the builder. He stepped into the chimney place, looked up into the aperture leading to the sky outside, stepped back out and measured the length of the chimney front, along with its depth and height from the floor, then shook his head. 'Yes, it's a problem,' he agreed.

Talk of a glass hood in front of the chimney, extractor fans inside the flue and a raised dais at its base is depressing in the extreme. With only a chance that it will resolve the problem, it will be a costly experiment. For the moment, it isn't pressing as the tenants due in a matter of weeks are more likely to need fans to cool them rather than a fire in the chimney. But it is preying on my mind. I am planning to let La Tabardy out in winter as well as summer; indeed, it is the main reason for having the chimney built, along with installing state-of-the-art central heating and triple-glazed windows.

It is undoubtedly true that La Tabardy is a beautiful house. Everything about it is pleasing. Its steeply sloping roof dressed in old tiles, the deep well embedded in a corner and its pale stone walls. The stones for its walls were gathered up from the land around it and many a stonemason in the area would have had the same problems with their backs then as Gilles has now.

The house dates from the early eighteenth century. Peasant farmers lived there, working the land as I do. Perhaps they worked vines here; vineyards certainly existed in the Bergerac area long before they did in Bordeaux. As early as the thirteenth century wines from Bergerac were being exported to England, considered superior to those from St Emilion and Bordeaux. In medieval times they were often used to improve the qualities of lesser wines and in the seventeenth century Holland was importing wines from this region in vast quantities.

Madame Cholet's house is older still than La Tabardy. The architect showed me walls dating from the fifteenth century. I feel glad that I didn't let it fall down of its own accord. Odile and I stand in the large *salon*. She is smoking a cigarette, inhaling deeply and looking up at the replaced ceiling beams in admiration. It has doors and windows and a roof. The builder has laid the cement floor, the plumber has installed the underground central heating and it is transformed.

As we walk back towards Clos d'Yvigne and supper, I glance over towards Madame Cholet's before turning in to the house and our obligatory *blanc cassis*. The beige and terracotta of the dappled roof look harmonious with the stone walls. It no longer looks like a half-ruined barn, its proportions in keeping now that the slope of the roof is back. The mulberry tree sits in front of it, solitary and beautiful.

Odile has just moved into her new house and is busy with renovations too. For the first time in more than thirty years she has neighbours on either side. They are not too intrusive, she says, apart from one who spends hours either singing in the garden or ploughing up the land around his apple trees. 'I don't know why he doesn't just mow it,' she says, laughing. 'At least I don't have moles; the rotivator destroys their tunnels. But his voice! He's always rehearsing – and in the garden!' She lights another cigarette. 'He's got to be in his late sixties. They say he sang at the Bordeaux Opéra,' she continues, giving me a knowing sideways look and laughing. 'It must have been in the choir . . . !'

It's Saturday evening and Gilles is here to pick me up for the Chasse Dinner. He arrives with a large, mustachioed man, Jean-Louis, in a large Audi. Gilles is looking tanned. Work on the wall around his house in Sigoulès is continuing. I've seen rather a lot of him this week as he has made regular trips backwards and forwards from his house to my land to collect the stones for it. Great piles of them are stored in an unused spot on the vineyard, slowly diminishing as his wall is progressing.

'Where are your *couverts*?' he demands as I step into the car. He looks at me in surprise. 'What do you think you're going to eat with?' Our '*couverts*' are our own knives, forks, plate and napkin. 'And what are you going to eat your soup from?' he shouts as he inspects my carrier bag as I get back into the car, armed with everything but a soup bowl.

Pamela has been over to look at the work in progress at Madame Cholet's house with Jean-Louis's wife, Carletta, before meeting up with us at the Mairie. Gilles sees it almost daily but for Pamela it is the first time since she left Gageac to live in Sigoulès. She is astonished at the change; a transformation, she says.

Madame Cholet's is not the only thing to be transformed. It is some time since I last saw Pamela. In place of shoulder-length hair she now has a short-cropped hairstyle. Her pale skin and light-red hair are striking and she looks younger. Her gold earrings sparkle in the sunlight as we stand in the Mairie car park waiting for Jean-Louis to lock his car.

Outside the kitchens of the Salle des Fêtes that is also the Marie, a young girl and two young men are standing outside drinking a beer. Dressed in white chef's uniform with long, white tablecoths wrapped around their waists, they are the outside caterers contracted in to cook the food for tonight. The long tradition of *chasseurs* and their wives preparing and cooking their own dinner has been terminally and brutally ended by EU regulations.

We enter the *salle*. Not many people have arrived yet. The president of the *chasse*, Edward Aublanc, greets us. He is pleased to see us. I know him and his family well. Annie, his wife, is a municipal counsellor at Gageac and her twin daughters occasionally come to me for help with their English homework or simply to practise their spoken English. They have grown considerably in the last year and are now young women rather than children, as is Benoît, their brother, now eighteen.

A series of long trestle tables decked with white paper tablecloths and yellow napkins fill the room, along with chairs. Each place setting has a plastic cup and each table a couple of bottles of unlabelled and already opened red wine. Two large ladies are seated at a table just inside the entrance. On their paper tablecloth, written in black felt-tip pen, are the words 'Famille Lagrange'. Two other tables already have names marked on their tablecloths: Famille Aublanc, Famille Metifet. Gilles congratulates himself on having arrived in time to do the same on the table of his choice.

Half a dozen men are gathered around a makeshift bar at the top of the hall on which stand bottles of whisky, gin and Ricard. They chatter quietly among themselves as they drink their *apéritifs*. Gilles and Jean-Louis approach the bar to do the same, Pamela too, who returns with a whisky. Women and children arrive carrying plastic bags with *couverts* for themselves and their families as more men gather round the makeshift bar and the room fills up. Manu and Jean-Lis appear. Manu, wearing a pink T-shirt, has put on weight since I last saw him at the *chasse*. He now has a live-in girlfiend, on which opinion is divided. She feeds him too much, Pamela says. She lets him *chasse*! Gilles retorts. She loves him? I suggest.

Gilles and Pamela, Jean-Louis, Carletta and I sit down, Jean-Lis and Manu being obliged to sit at an adjoining table. Room at ours has already been taken by people who simply arrived and sat down in the available places. We catch up on news. Jean-Lis has also been over to Madame Cholet's. '*C'est très bien fait*', he adds, grimacing, shaking his head and giving a thumbs-up sign. 'It's dry in the vines over there, though,' he continues. Jean-Louis nods in agreement. Yes, it's a dry year, he says. He can tell by his sunflowers that are showing signs of thirst already.

Vaguely worried about the dry weather myself, not only for the existing vines but for those we are due to plant in a few weeks' time, we all commiserate on the state of the land. Cracks have already begun appearing in the ground, an ominous sign so early in the year. Gilles warns that the sooner my young vines are planted the better; Jean-Lis asks if I'm planting in wide rows or narrow, Manu is behind in the vineyard and can't catch up, he says. The wires need lifting already, such is the vigour of the vines this year.

The contents of a large plastic bottle with what looks like and is orangeade but fortified with quantities of rum and vodka is offered as an *apéritif*. It is poured into our plastic cups by the Aublanc twins and with it the Repas de Chasse begins in earnest. Paper plates of pâté are deposited on each table. 'What?' exclaims Gilles increduously. 'No soup?' He looks at Jean-Louis in surprise, then around at the general assembly in disgust, his eyes searching for anyone who can offer a reason why soup shouldn't be served as it always has been until now. '*Ce n'est pas normal!*' he addresses Pamela, his voice rising by decibels. 'Quietly. Your voice,' she whispers. '*Ce n'est pas bon signe!*' he bellows.

The quartered slabs of pâté on the plates are rich in fat and meat, some plates with paler meat on them than others. 'Venison,' says Gilles, with a nod of his head. I offer the plate to him. 'I don't eat venison,' he announces. 'Never.' He reiterates the point. 'I don't like it!' I taste it. It is rich and meaty, though slightly starchy. Gilles shakes his head and folds his arms, looking at his obselete soup bowl. 'Have some *sanglier*,' says Jean-Louis, passing the darker meat plate over my head to Gilles. Gilles takes some and nods in grudging appreciation. It is juicy, stronger meat than the venison and slightly spicy. It tastes delicious eaten with the fresh, crusty bread that comes with it.

Jean-Louis is a wild boar *chasseur*. Some days when hunting they have an eleven-hour day tracking a single boar, he tells me. When they kill it, they skin it, cut it and share it out immediately. He takes another quarter of pâté. There is nothing nicer, he says, taking another slice, than a whole young *sanglier* of twenty kilos or so cooked the Sunday after it has been killed, preferably on the barbecue with vine cuttings. He and his friends often have one cooked for them by a Moroccan who lives locally and really knows what he's doing.

He helps himself to more *sanglier* pâté as he recounts tales of hunting wild boar. Turning to Manu at the next table, he says, 'I guess you killed this?', holding up his *morceau* of bread smeared with a mound of pâté. Manu looks at him, unblinking, and nods imperceptibly.

Marie-France, the sister of Jean-Lis and Pamela, is seated further down the table with her husband, Prosper, and their niece, whose seven-year-old son is seated next to her. Small and shy, he is dwarfed by his uncle. Prosper is huge and wears a striped black and white sweatshirt that fits tightly round his stomach like swaddling. Unlike Pamela, who is tall and slim, her sister is small in height and heavy in kilos. Unlike either Pamela or Jean-Lis, who both have light-red hair, hers is dyed jet black and frizzled. In her late forties, she has large, watery blue eyes, pale skin and only some of her teeth. She sits quietly, back straight, holding her knife and fork delicately in front of her, eating her pâté in small *morceaux* which she carefully manoeuvres on to her fork. Prosper turns round with difficulty to his nephew Manu at the next table. 'Good,' he pronounces as another quarter of pâté disappears.

A large dish of *civet* of venison is deposited on our table. It has in it carrots, swedes and parsley as well as small lumps of meat. Gilles looks at it with distaste. 'It's the first time I've ever seen a *civet* made like that!' he shouts. We all look at it and Jean-Louis concurs that there aren't normally as many vegetables in a *civet*. '*Non*! It's not that!' Gilles bellows. 'The meat should be melting!' It should be a rich stew with strings of disintegrating meat rather than lumps, he complains.

For a real *civet* the meat, says Gilles, should be macerated for a day or so beforehand, then grilled, before being cooked for at least three hours in red wine with onions and thyme. In any event he is not going to eat what has been placed in front of him as he never eats venison anyway and, even if he did, he couldn't eat that. Things are changing fast and not for the better, he complains. Caterers are never going to be able to cook the dishes in the same way.

He pushes the dish over towards me and the rest of the table and folds his arms again in high dudgeon. Prosper, at the far end of the table, looks at it with anticipation. Jean-Louis serves me then himself with relish. Pamela's sister has already been served. She places small *morceaux* on the end of her fork as she did with the pâté and eats silently, delicately but consistently, concentration on her face. Prosper now has an impressive mound on his plate, helping himself liberally. He dispenses with his knife in favour of a large spoon.

Wine from the opened bottle is poured into my glass by Gilles. He takes a sip from his glass and looks at it in disbelief. 'It's come from the bottom of his vat,' he says, now thoroughly out of sorts. 'It's thick wine, mixed with the pressed stuff. This isn't bottled wine, it's what's left over . . .' He turns to Jean-Lis at the next table. 'It's true, isn't it? And it's yours!' Jean-Lis laughs.

The *civet de sanglier* that follows is undoubtedly an improvement on the venison. Stronger tasting and more tender, it still has cubes of meat rather than Gilles's preferred stewed meat. It is served by one of the *sangliers chasseurs*, a deeply tanned man in his early forties who has been sitting at the far end of our table. His dark hair sits low on his forehead and he wears black jeans slung low on his hips and a white T-shirt. He has a knife in a leather sheath attached to his belt.

Gilles looks at the meat, then at Pamela who raises her eyes and looks at me with a wan smile. She knows what's coming next. Gilles explodes. 'Well, I know what it should be like!' he shouts. 'Why don't they leave the cooking to the *chasseurs*!' The *civet de sanglier* should be stronger and more tender, like a rich stew. There is no doubt that it isn't. Gilles has ordered a bottle of wine rather than drink Jean-Lis's thick wine mixed with leas and offered free as part of the meal. The deeply tanned *chasseur* returns with two bottles to choose from, both from local winemakers. He displays them in front of Gilles. '*Vin de Creyse!*' Gilles mutters, choosing the other and paying the *sanglier chasseur*. He turns to me. 'You've never tasted wine from Château Creyse?' he asks as I shake my head. 'Don't bother! It's bottled vinegar!'

Music erupts suddenly, almost bursting our eardrums and resounding around the hall as a small, emaciated man tunes an electric piano/organ. He is seated at the piano and wears a dark blue shirt, sleeves rolled up to his elbows, and over it a red, hand-knitted, sleeveless jumper. His black hair is worn in a comb-over, neatly parted an inch or so above his left ear, then draped carefully over the bald crown of his head and tucked behind his right ear.

Nine-thirty pm and the general ambiance in the hall is considerably warmer than it was at the beginning of the meal, helped by the *apéritifs*, Jean-Lis's thick wine and the bottled vinegar of Château de Creyse. The pianist has stopped tuning up. An older man is talking into a microphone, the sound of which drowns his voice. '*Passez un moment agréable . . .*' we hear through the screech of feedback. He advances down the aisle between the tables and back again, talking into it and seeming now to be eating the microphone.

He gestures to a small, dapper man attired in a green jacket who bows and smiles in appreciation of whatever the man with the microphone is saying. We are about to have not just music, but song.

The man at the piano thumps the keys as his companion in the green jacket warbles into the microphone. The piano is too loud, the singer can't be heard. Laughter and shouts from the audience while a balance is found. The pianist hits the keys again and everyone claps and shouts '*Olé*!' as the singer launches into an old, familiar song from the Pays Basque region.

The audience sing the refrain with gusto. The women sway and clap. '*Et la nuit . . .*' the singer screeches, straining for the top note. He struggles, moving the microphone away from his mouth with panache until he finds the note. He brings the microphone back and holds on to the note. The audience love the song and

141

love the music. They sing along, clapping. Another song follows as large plates with huge slices of meat ranging in colour from rich, red and bloody to pale and pink and grey are deposited on our tables. At our table, the dark, tanned *chasseur* is opening more bottles of wine as the singer warbles. 'He sang at Bordeaux,' someone says and I know he must be Odile's new neighbour who rehearses in the garden next door. 'God knows what he's singing . . . He sang at the Bordeaux Opéra they say.'

'*Rossignol de mes amours*,' he ululates with soprano-like notes. He reaches our table, turns to Pamela and serenades her on bended knee. She laughs and claps, gazing into his eyes. The microphone whistles. Jean-Louis takes another huge lump of meat. 'I *chassed* this *sanglier*,' he pronounces with pride and certitude. I wonder how he can know.

The singer walks back slowly down the aisle between the tables, singing. With more confidence now, he reaches the high note required to finish and lingers with it, quivering voice and microphone held at a distance for effect. The pianist looks frustrated, awaiting his cue to end with a flourish. He watches the singer intently, hands poised over the keys, eager to hit them. Finally he does so, peremptorily cutting short the singer's finale.

A long platter piled high again with thick slices of both *sanglier* and venison is deposited on each table as the pianist walks back to his table during the short break from musical entertainment. His comb-over has collapsed so that three strands of hair now hang to one side of his left ear. Finding the ends, he repositions them carefully behind his right ear. A plate of meat is passed to him. He picks up his knife and fork with a glance to right and left.

'Yes, we kill them the same day, cut them up and dole them out!' Jean-Louis is saying. Gilles is still sitting with his arms tightly crossed. His arm-crossing takes two forms. One is his usual relaxed posture with arms crossed above waist level, the other, set to red, is high up on his chest, which is where they are now. Prosper is nodding sagely, eating more meat. 'Saves any jealousies,' Jean-Louis continues. Inspecting the plate of meat in front of him, he takes off two more slices. He inspects them, turning the pieces over on his plate with his fork.

Next to the plates of meat on our table is a dish of *pommes dauphinoises*. Gilles takes a large slice of *sanglier*, then sinks his spoon into the dish of *pommes dauphinoises*. Pamela gives him a warning look. 'They're not cooked,' she announces quietly. Gilles bites into a slice. 'I'm disappointed!' shouts Jean-Louis. 'Disappointed?' bellows Gilles. '*Milledieux!* I should think so!' Jean-Louis looks at the last mouthful of meat still on his fork. 'Thought I had *sanglier* but that was definitely venison.'

The short break over, the singer is on his feet again and the pianist is walking over to the electric piano. The Aublanc twins move round each table with a leg of dried ham; one euro to guess its weight and the closest wins it. The dark, tanned man with low-cut hair follows them round, taking down diners' names and their estimates. I guess seven kilos. Gilles says it's much heavier. Pamela thinks its lighter. Jean-Louis doesn't know; he's still tucking into meat and uncooked potatoes.

The pianist in the corner is playing intently again as the singer lifts the microphone to his lips. He looks slowly around the hall and smiles. Turning to the pianist he gives a signal and the opening strains of the next song are played. '*Rien de Rien!*' Jean-Louis shouts, leaping up. 'A great song – I like it!' The audience does too as everyone claps and shouts in anticipation of its rendition. The singer nods his head slowly in appreciation, smiling. '*Non, je ne regrette rien,*' he sings with emotion.

The hall erupts. Everyone is singing, swaying, misty-eyed. Jean-Louis sings the last notes with gusto. It is followed by a French rendition of 'All The Chapel Bells Were Ringing' . . . '*Oh! Elle est belle cette chanson!*' he shouts, nodding and looking at me earnestly to emphasise the point, thumping his fists on to the table. 'All the chapel bells were ringing . . .' warbles the singer accompanied by the audience. The pianist embellishes the tune, a twinkle of the keys here, a twirl there. As the singer's voice rises in search of a high note to finish, he slides along the floor on his knees and arrives at my feet.

Another break for cheese and salad. Tables are awash with plates of meat and half-eaten dishes of *pommes dauphinoises* as people talking, drinking, eating and laughing enjoy their evening at the Repas de Chasse. Children leave their tables to talk to relations or to find their companions. The pianist has returned to his table again, exhausted from the creativity of the last twenty minutes. Cheese and salad are placed in front of him. His wife squeezes his arm. He looks at her and smiles weakly.

Pamela and Carletta laugh and joke. Gilles tries too, but he is out of sorts. He has his arms crossed high on his chest again. The food was not good, he says. The caterers are abominable and it shouldn't be allowed. Why change a tradition that has been in place for as long as he can remember? Why settle for something less good? Why listen to the *fonctionnaires* who have insisted on this change?

The Aublanc twins offer one-euro tombola tickets around the hall for a side of *sanglier* or deer. They pass between tables with tickets. I already have a side of each in my freezer, their father having offered them as thanks for allowing the *chasseurs* to hunt on my land. We wipe our plates clean with paper napkins that are deposited, along with any leftovers, in the middle of the table in preparation for *tarte tatin*, which arrives and is doled out on to each person's plate. Champagne will be offered too. 'Phff!' mutters Gilles, turning to me 'Don't touch that – it's not even champagne . . . made to give you headaches!' The pianist rises for the last time to accompany the singer who croons an old French song.

Pamela throws a *morceau* of bread at the dark, tanned man sitting at the other end of the table, then at Prosper, her brother-in-law. The dark, tanned man smiles. Prosper's wife throws some back, swaying to the music now, along with Pamela and Carletta. The crooner warbles as Pamela throws crumbs at Manu, who turns round and smiles. An old toothless man approaches the table to give Pamela a kiss as the singer sings 'south of Granada . . . ay ay ay ay . . .'

Prosper's wife is talking animatedly now to her husband and Jean-Lis; Manu and a neighbour are shouting at each other so as to be heard as the singer now starts to yodle. 'Mexicoooooo . . .' he soars, hanging on to notes as the now distinctly unhappy pianist, fronds of black hair hanging in front of his eyes, is left in the lurch yet again.

From deep within the bowels of the small electronic piano, the pianist brings forth the strains of an orchestra. The hall erupts with applause. '. . . Mon amour . . .' carols the singer, the refrain resounding around the room as everyone sings with gusto. Laughter and noise are now constant, along with *morceaux* of bread hurled from our table to the next. The dark, tanned man is hugging Pamela and Carletta as they sing together. He is crouching between them, an arm round each of their shoulders. Their cheeks touch, three faces in a row, their mouths moving, singing the words to the song with passion, swaying together with the music.

We have not won the leg of *jambon*. It weighed six kilos ten and was won by the large lady from Famille Lagrange. The *civet* of *sanglier* goes to them too. Shouts of disbelief from the adjoining table, along with laughter and noise and music. I slip away as the *digestifs* arrive.

Outside an ink-black sky with bright stars and a sliver of a new moon looks big and all encompassing. Cicadas rasp as I walk up the road. The grass between the vines has been mown earlier in the day and the smell of hay mixed with wild lavender fills my nostrils. I turn into the drive and head for bed, replete with wild boar, venison and the insistent notes of the chapel bells ringing for little Jimmy Brown.

<hr />

'*Pour le Suédois?*' asked Gilles as we carried chairs from the church over to the kitchen, where a second table erected from an old door and trestles would create the necessary extra eating space for twenty people. Fidde and his children, along with his cousin Svante, Pia and Ekan, their sons and various friends were invited for an Indian curry dinner. Gilles had called over for the loan of some tools and got roped into transporting chairs. '*Ce Suédois,*' remarked Gilles with a shrewd smile. '*Il vien assez souvent.*'

'He was looking for you yesterday,' he continued, as we stood by the door of the church. 'In the vines. I told him you were at the tasting in Bergerac.' Juliana's voice echoed up the road. 'Patriciaa!' she shouted and '*Bonjour*, Gilles!' as she reached us. 'Patricia!' she repeated. '*Ton cheri était ici.*' She smiled, swung her hips and ran her hand over her forehead and hair as she stood in front of us. '*Toute à l'heure,*' she added, with a shake of her head. 'You just missed him. I asked whether I would do, but he didn't seem so keen', and she roared with laughter.

'*Hej!*' said one and '*Hej Hej!*' smiled others in greeting as they piled in through the door, and the house was full. A babble of Swedish, English and Spanish filled the air. Gustaf had brought along his girlfriend from Madrid who spoke no Swedish but some English. Small, with dark hair and smouldering eyes, she seemed dwarfed by Gustaf's height and intimidated by hordes of Swedes. She stood next to him shyly, smiling, uncertain whether to say *hej* or hello or even *holà*.

Fidde stood beside me. '*Hej*, Patricia!' he said with a smile, putting his arm around my shoulder. '*Holà!*' I replied. He laughed. 'I called to see you earlier,' he continued. 'I missed you. I couldn't wait as I had to get back to the architect.' People swarmed into the *salon*. Bottles were opened and *apéritifs* drunk as everyone chattered together. 'Let's eat!' I bellowed and everyone converged en masse from the *salon* to the kitchen, seating themselves around the tables. Bowls of chutneys and fruits, with poppadoms and nan bread, rice and large dishes of curry, along with wine, water and beer were laid out on them. Sound filled the room as people helped themselves to food and drink and continued their conversations.

Fidde was disappointed at the slow rate of progress at his house, he said, as we sat together at the table. Gustaf, Ebba and he had spent most of the day over there. Work was behind schedule again. 'Why don't they keep their promises?' he asked, looking at me earnestly. 'I can't understand it!' he laughed. I laughed too. Pia had the same problems when building her tower and I guessed it was a universal one.

His pleasure at having his children with him had eased any tensions with the builders and he looked relaxed and happy. 'You know, Patricia, I guess you just have to be patient in life,' he said, looking at me with an astute smile and eating a mouthful of curry. He held up his glass. '*Skol*,' he said quietly.

The following day I went with him to see the house. Progress was very slow. In fact I couldn't see any change since my last visit there, I told him. 'Come, Patricia!' he said, taking my hand firmly and striding purposefully from the kitchen to the *salon*. There, the fireplace had been restored from its former delapidated state where some of the stonework had fallen in. 'What do you mean nothing's changed?'

It looked beautiful, immense and ancient. We stood in front of it. He stepped into its hearth and looked up into the chimney. He loved fireplaces and, most particularly, fires in them. He liked the comfort of them, the pleasure of them. In Sweden in winter, he said, most evenings were spent in front of the fire. 'There's nothing else to do there in the evenings!' he laughed.

In the hallway a wood-burning stove was being built into the wall. Fidde planned to install a complicated heating system from it through pipes embedded in the walls and hidden under the floor. The plumber was very nice, he said. He liked him a lot and they had a good rapport but he was being deliberately obtuse on the question of the stove. 'He doesn't understand!' he said. 'Why can't he understand, Patricia?' It was probably quite hard to, I said. Fidde had tried to explain it to me more than once. He laughed his deep, resonant laugh. Yes, he replied, it was a little complicated, but it was not beyond the wit of man and an intelligent plumber like his should have no problem with it.

As we walked from one room to another he described what he had planned for them, how they would be transformed. His enthusiasm for the house poured from him, energised him. 'What do you think?' he asked me of his ideas for the first floor. 'This will be the bathroom,' he said of the large shell of a room. 'Here is the living room,' he pointed to an expanse of floor. 'And this is a bedroom . . .' He looked around for a moment, visualising the finished area, then stared at me in thoughtful silence. 'Come!' he said suddenly, smiling and taking my hand. 'Let's go down and I'll show you the wine cellar.'

We scrambled down the unsteady stepladder and through the *salon*, past the kitchen towards the large barn, half as large again as the house. He had plans for that too, he said, but his first and main priority was to move in. 'Here!' he said, pointing to a small, cordonned-off area between the barn and the kitchen. It would be insulated, he said, and have a sophisticated air-conditioning system to maintain a perfect temperature for his wines. He looked around. 'What do you think? Now that I have all those bottles from you, I have to keep them under the right conditions!' He looked at me again, humour and playfulness in his eyes, and we both laughed. He had an extraordinary selection of great wines in Fribourg waiting to be housed there.

Chapter 8

JUNE, AND THE ROSES THIS YEAR ARE SPECTACULAR. THEY ARE OUT
in force, great splashes of colour. The climbing roses are falling
off the wall such is the weight of their blossoms amd the vigour
of their branches. Along the hedgerow elderflower, dog roses and
marguerites jostle for space with marsh orchids and buttercups.
The irises in front of the wall stand tall against it, pale lilac pokers,
their forms and colour interspersed with delicate yellow and white
varieties. Over at La Tabardy irises I didn't know I had until they
burst into blossom create a border of dark purple; Pamela must
have planted them.

In the vines we are at full tilt. Intoxicated by the warmth of
the sun, their branches and leaves have run rampant, growing at
a ridiculous speed. With the *vendange vert*, where we cut off embryo
grapes to reduce the yield and concentrate the fruit not completely finished, the *épamprage* – cutting off the shoots at the base
of the vines – is yet to be done and the wires yet to be lifted. There
is no time to spare. Alain and Benjamin have Emilie, a young girl
from a nearby village, and Benjamin's girlfriend, Cécile, working
with them for a week in the vines to try to catch up.

Emilie is wearing a cap low over her eyes, blonde hair tied back in a ponytail, working opposite Alain. Cécile wears multicoloured baggy trousers to protect her legs from the sun. They look beautiful, patches of colour against the intensity of green vines, working steadily along the rows in teams of two. Occasionally I hear the sound of Alain's laughter, or Benjamin's voice carried on the air.

Michel Founaud has delivered the first new potatoes of the season. They are sweet and buttery. His vegetable garden has been extended and he now has two, one across the road where he has always had one and where his vines grow and the other next to the pig and rabbit hutches behind his house. In them are planted not just potatoes, but an array of tomatoes, green beans, courgettes, carrots, beetroot, cucumber, red and green peppers and radishes. The rabbit hutches are now empty. Since their daughter, Marie-Céline, kept them as pets, Monique and she banned Michel from killing and eating them. I remember Marie-Céline's rabbits. They were huge, loping around the house and garden at will. Now Marie-Céline has left home and lives in Toulouse; the rabbits are long gone but the ban remains in force.

Arthur, a small, ugly black pig, also exempt from slaughter, grunts and runs up to us as we head towards the potato patch. Some English friends are invited to dinner along with me. They have a holiday home in Gageac and Michel mows their lawn for them. It is their first visit to Michel's and he is giving them a tour of his gardens. We wander from the potato patch behind the house to the garden across the road. Vegetables bare of weeds grow in perfectly straight rows. Michel picks green broad beans for the soup and potatoes for the main course as I look at his vines and the heavy crop of embryo bunches on them. They are well worked and recently sprayed with the tell-tale blue and gun-grey of copper sulphate.

His barbecue is lit in preparation for dinner and the fresh fish he caught this morning have already been cleaned and gutted, ready to be served as appetisers with our *apéritifs*. We sit in the side terrace that runs the length of their house, glassed in by Michel so as to create a closed terrace room rather than what used to be a makeshift lean-to. The table, almost the length of the terrace and covered in a red and white checked oilcloth, is stacked with Michel's *bocaux* of *sanglier pâté* along with boxes of vegetables, cartons of wine, bouquets of dried flowers, seeds ready for planting and dog, cat and pig food. Red and white checked curtains with red satin ribbons made by Monique dress the windows.

The green beans are already in the pot for soup as Michel drops his freshly caught fish into a plastic bag containing flour, salt and pepper. He closes the bag, holds it at its top and shakes it, coating the fish in the mixture. Placing them one by one into the hot oil, batches of them appear on the table to accompany our drinks, hot, crispy and delicious.

Monique tells us he was up at dawn to catch them. '*Tu connais Michel*, Patricia,' she nods with a smile and a wink, explaining to her English guests that she long ago learnt to accept the fact that he's mostly not there when she awakes each morning. '*Ah oui. C'est la saison,*' she continues. Either he's not there because the fish are jumping and he's fishing. Or the hares are leaping and he's hunting. Or the wild boar are running and he's in the woods tracking them. Or the mushrooms are sprouting and he's picking them. He laughs, tipping more fish into the hot oil, then chuckles shyly to himself, standing in front of the hob. With his brown face and ruddy cheeks he looks weather-beaten and healthy. His pleasures are simple and rich. Like Gilles, he is a man of the soil, a man of the seasons, the rhythm of his life governed by them.

Monique now has a dishwasher and a new kitchen, she tells us. The problem is that the dishwasher isn't plumbed in and the kitchen isn't fitted. As Michel will be doing the work and it's now summer, there will be no chance of having them installed for the moment. She will have to wait until winter. She looks at Michel, then adds, 'Even then it's not sure . . .' I say nothing. I was here when the kitchen cabinets were delivered at least six years ago. 'Now that he's retired . . .' she looks at him hopefully, then back at us.

The *soup aux fèves*, broad bean soup, is simple and delicious. The *fèves* are black in colour yet tender, cooked in their skins. Monique drops freshly picked and quartered potatoes into a deep fryer for the main course. I watch, thinking it a shame to fry them. Until I taste them; they are sweet and rich and delicious. We eat them with *brochettes* of chicken. The cheeses have come from Monique's recent trip to see Marie-Céline in Toulouse. The Cantal with a marked crust is mature and succulent. They are wrapped in the paper of Xavier's, a famous cheese shop there. Monsieur Blanchard from Bergerac knows him well.

Supper over, the dogs bound in. They rush around, happy to be with us. Michel dips his hand into a large bag of dog food and feeds them titbits. They sit obediently as he hands them some then stand excitedly waiting for more. The thumping of their tails against the cut-down barrel in the fireplace echoes around the chimneyplace. Disturbed by the noise, a mouse appears from behind the barrel, runs up the side of the wall, along the ceiling beam, then back home again.

We say goodnight under a new moon gleaming in the night sky and drive back up the hill to Gageac. The château looks serene and beautiful as we pass by, its towers reaching up towards a sky littered with stars.

Juliana didn't open her shutters with her usual 'coucou' or her booming voice or her laughter. Nor did she when she opened my kitchen door. Large tears fall down her cheeks as she announces that Chloë has been put down. It had to be done, she says quietly, wiping the tears that drip now from her chin. It was unfair to keep her alive any more. She had stopped eating and was dying. 'Yves is inconsolable,' she says. I put my arms around her and she sobs quietly. 'I'll buy you another,' I say. 'Oh no!' she replies. 'Never. It's too painful.'

Blazing June is definitely here. The cherry trees are dripping with fruit. Banks of poppies with flowering privet and honeysuckle are in abundance as are shorts, T-shirts and sandals. We have leapt into summer with temperatures suddenly in the thirties. The bats are back too. They swarm around the town light and my rooftop at dusk, the sound of their song insistent and urgent. Cicadas, hidden in hedgerows among the wild flowers and grass, chirrup loudly. Owls screech to each other in the early evening, mothers teaching their young to fly and hunt.

Eida's mane is hanging down over her eyes again. It happens every June. She lies in the field, surrounded by wild flowers, occasionally shaking her mane to scatter the flies that disturb her. She canters rather than gallops over for breakfast now, conserving energy against the heat. Michel has cut out a large window for me in her hedge opposite the house. Since he retired as *cantonnier* in Gageac, the hedge has grown higher and higher, making it more difficult to reach over and feed her.

The vines are flowering, a prelude to fruit set. Tiny white petals create star-shaped flowers giving a creamy down to the embryo bunches. They have a perfume too, discreet and delicate. Hermaphrodites, their pollination is vital for a harvest. They need exactly the calm, warm weather we have at the moment. I smell their delicate perfume as I pass through the vines towards Madame Cholet's, La Tabardy and my *parcelle* of vines at Les Ruisseaux. Alain waves in the distance from one of the tractors where he is mowing the grass between the vines.

The ground is cracked and dry. The open field between two of my *parcelles* of vines now has large rounds of hay sitting in it rather than the swathes of long grass of last week. Dried by the sun, they are ready to be rolled on to trailers and stored for winter. The season moves on.

Gilles's warning to hurry and get my new vines in the ground was not lost on me. The huge tractor hired to mulch the chosen *parcelle* of land for the last time before planting is here and working the land that lies between Madame Cholet's and La Tabardy. Where it has already worked the land, what were huge mounds of dry earth and stones with weeds and immense clumps of grass have been transformed into finely tilled soil, level and ordered. The tractor lumbers up and down the *parcelle*, its wheels bouncing over the unworked mounds, dust and stones flying in the air.

I press on towards Les Ruisseaux to check on my vines. The wires there have been lifted and the *épamprage* is done. The view from there strikes me each time I see it. Lush, contoured rows of vines stretch out towards an orchard of fruit trees deep in the river valley. The spire of the church in Bergerac rises gently out of a summer haze in the distance. Surrounding villages dotted on the landscape are interspersed with vines and fruit orchards. Frogs croak periodically in Gilles's pond.

Walking back through the vines I see Yves in the distance, head down, trudging along the road towards the Mairie. He no longer smiles. '*Salut*, Yves!' I shout. He looks up and waves half-heartedly. Since Chloë's death he has lost his bounce. He smiles weakly at me. '*Salut*, Patricia,' he says in a voice that is entirely in keeping with his gloomy disposition.

The Bassin d'Arcachon is the flat, sandy coast that lies between the estuary of the Gironde and the Pyrénées, an hour's drive from Bordeaux. It is a huge, brackish pond linked to the Atlantic Ocean by a narrow bottleneck. The playing ground for Parisians and Bordelais who come in droves for the summer, it has a casino, a golf course, the largest dune in Europe and a long sandy beach. It also has oysters at La Teste de Buche, fished there since the Romans.

La Teste de Buche has salt meadows, *cabanes*, warm water and oyster beds. It also has Gilou. Gilou is an *ostréiculteur*. In his fifties, he is short, stocky and a former jockey. He shakes my hand and smiles widely when I arrive at his *cabanes* with Georges, a friend who lives in Arcachon. His hands are large and thick with the texture of sandpaper. Wearing a bright blue T-shirt and shorts with 'Hot Station' written on the back of them, like Gilles and most of the rural community here he wears black, stained espadrilles and a cotton hat.

Frayed and yellowed, his hat is small and similar to the one Gilles wears in summer. His face is framed by thick-lensed spectacles. He is what Georges calls '*un vrai authentique*'. With a tanned and weather-beaten face, a mouth white and cracked with sun, salt and laughter, his accent is similar to that of the south-west, but more accentuated, lilting and melodious.

Zaza, a pointer puppy, stands next to him, wagging furiously. Unlike Ulma, whose coat is a grey/silver pearl, hers is dark cinnamon and she has pale, golden eyes. We are in one of Gilou's two *cabanes*, a small wooden cabin in which he gives tastings of his oysters to customers and where he works. Made of wooden slats and painted black with a terracotta roof, it has a yellow-painted frontage piece over the door with '*La Cabane de Gilou 157*' written on it. Two draped fishing nets connect the open space between his *cabanes*.

The working yard behind them houses a small cement pool and a huge oyster-cleaning vat. Wooden cartons and whitewashed terracotta roof tiles sit in piles around the vat. They are essential to his work, Gilou tells me. During the breeding season, the terracotta roof tiles are whitewashed with lime and sand and placed on the seabed in the warm waters of La Teste for the floating, microscopic oyster larvae to attach themselves to. The larvae search out warmth, which is why they are in the *bassin*.

The coating on the tiles not only retains heat but captures the floating seed oysters, providing a sticking point for the larvae. Once fixed, the seed oysters attach themselves to each other where they grow together in groups, submerged by the sea twice a day and developing for up to eighteen months when the tiles with their harvest are lifted from the seabed and brought back to shore by Gilou to be stripped.

A red plastic lobster hangs on the wall inside Gilou's *cabane*, along with two terracotta roof tiles similar to the whitewashed ones in the yard outside except these are hand-painted with fishing scenes in blue, white and red. A large black and white poster on the wall next to them, dating from the 1930s, shows women stripping oysters from the tiles. Wearing large aprons, they have mounds of mollusc-covered tiles in front of them. It was hard work scraping the tiles, said Gilou, the sharp oyster shells cutting into their hands. Nowadays they are removed by water pressure.

Once sorted, the molluscs are locked into plastic mesh sacks called '*les ambulances*' and taken back to the beds. Today Gilou, Georges and I are going to take a new consignment out to the beds and bring some back. Gilou's boat is moored only yards away in front of his *cabanes*. We descend via a wooden pier that leads to a wooden jetty on wheels, partly rotten. It shifts slightly and shudders as we step off it and on to the boat.

His boat is one of many moored there. A long, low barge, its wooden deck once painted a deep red has now faded to a pale rose. The cabin and capstans are painted bright sea-blue. On the deck is a box of belongings, a long iron pole and two pallets on which are stacked high Gilou's meshed plastic sacks of small oysters. The '*ambulances*' are the shape and size of flour bags, slim and holding ten kilos of oysters each. 'Yes, Mother Nature is generous,' he says as I look at the oysters through the mesh of the sacks. 'She gives me the raw materials free.'

Zaza leaps on to the deck and is lifted up to the top of the cabin where a red blanket has been thrown. She rests her head on her paws and looks at Gilou who stands behind the cabin in front of her, one hand on the rudder as Georges unties the mooring rope. The motor splutters, coughs into action and we set off. Small boats of all shapes and colours bob gently on the calm waters of La Teste, the halyards on their masts clinking in the light breeze. A long row of *cabanes* like Gilou's, some red or black, some bleached by the sun, adorn the shoreline as we chug slowly by. They have been there in one form or another for almost a century.

We slowly pass other boats. A couple standing aboard their modern, luxurious cruiser, suitably dressed in nautical pale blue and white, wave as we chug slowly onwards past mudflats and sand marshes. Buoys bob in the water. On the shoreline to the left, a line of modern apartment blocks now replaces the row of *cabanes*, their terracotta-coloured walls and blue verandas in stark contrast to the simple, beautiful wooden huts. 'Yes,' says Gilou, nodding towards them. 'There used to be only us, and now look. Six *briques* for an *appart* there!' I was never good on *briques* in francs and now we're in euros it's even worse. Georges translates it as four and a half million francs.

In the distance long black poles jut out of the water randomly, leaning at odd angles for no apparent reason. The water sparkles as we pass through the small port and leave behind Arcachon. '*C'est la belle saison, n'est-ce pas?*' smiles Gilou. He has both forearms on the cabin top, one hand stroking Zaza who is calmly dozing. It's 9.30 am and the sun is already high. He removes his hat now and then to run his hand through thick grey hair. Occasionally he takes off his spectacles, their lenses smudged with thumbprints, and rubs his eyes. His voice has the warmth of the sun in it, lilting and spattered with local *patois*. He used to be a jockey, he tells me, until he became too heavy. Around the same time his *ostréiculteur* father-in-law died and that's how he came to take over the business, now more than twenty years ago.

He prefers to remain a small business. He used to supply oysters throughout France and had five drivers, with lorries to deliver them. He stopped all that because of employment costs. '*Les frais, les frais!*' he grumbles, taking off his hat and folding it in his hands. 'It's a vicious circle. And *les fonctionnaires* . . . !' We look at each other and I anticipate the argument, recognise the sentiments and the inevitable airing of grievances I know is about to follow.

Zaza wakes up and looks at him. Georges sits up. He had the same problem with his estate agency business, he tells us, his voice booming, looking from Gilou to me with passion. The enterprise grew and grew, along with the costs. Estate agent *fonctionnaires* are obviously the same as oyster *fonctionnaires*. I feel I must add the customs, excise and general viticultural *fonctionnaires* to the conversation, as it seems unfair to leave them out. Yes, bureaucracy is getting worse in France, I say. Take the customs and excise! I continue. Or the *appellation contrôlée* boards! Gilou laughs.

Gilou gave up on big business and bought a small shop in Arcachon where his wife now sells their oysters. It has eliminated all employment costs and gives them '*de quoi vivre*'. 'We keep the oysters at a reasonable price and have a good and regular custom,' he says with obvious delight. And yet, returning to the hub of the matter, he still has the *fonctionnaires* to contend with. He has constant controls at his *cabane* where he gives tastings of his oysters, and constant controls on the hygiene of his water, the purification of his oysters and his oyster rearing generally. 'But it's our choice to continue . . .' He smiles now, a wide smile. 'When we get fed up, we'll stop,' he says. I watch him stroking Zaza, looking out to sea contentedly, and feel it won't be for some time.

He doesn't own his oyster *parc*, but has a concession, he tells me. His current concession will last until 2014, at which time he will simply renew it for another ten years. It is a *parcelle* of just over half an hectare. He smiles, taking off his hat and crossing his feet. The sun sends prisms of sparkling light on the water as we gently float through. 'Yes, I'm just like a *viticulteur*, except my *vendange* is in oysters and my *parcelles* are liquid.' A silence, then '. . . in Bretagne or Normandy, of course, they work much bigger lots! *Ce sont les industrielles, les Bretagnes et Normandes!*' he announces. He looks at me and I have that Gilles feeling again. We pass more and more black posts haphazardly sticking out of the sea. They remind me of the brushstrokes of Japanese paintings, scores of black silhouettes with sun, blue sky and sparkling sea as a back-drop. Cap Ferret can be seen in the far distance, a small group of buildings on the horizon with a sun haze shimmering over them and nothing but an expanse of sea between them and us.

Gilou reduces the revs of his motor and turns the boat gently to the right through a gate of black posts. We sail into an enclosed area, a private *domaine*, a sparkling sea courtyard encircled by what I now see are tall, elegant and glistening black wooden columns. We are in Gilou's *parc* and the black posts delineate his *parcelle*. He cuts the motor and throws some of the white and chalky coloured *ambulances* of oysters out of the boat and into the water.

They sink slowly. One after the other he throws, to right and left as Georges ties the boat to two weathered posts. The water is flat and still and there is a calmness, a quietness, around us, save for the lapping of water on the sides of the boat from the wash of a distant motorboat. It causes the boat to sway. Georges grabs one of the posts and attaches a rope from the boat to it, then he too heaves off *ambulances* in the water until all have been jettisoned into the sea.

Georges sits down on one of the now empty pallets and lights a cigarette. His black and yellow hat with 'Kilimanjaro' written on it and his large sunglasses hide most of his face from the hot sun. A small crab swims by. Zaza jumps down from the cabin top, runs round the deck then flops down again in front of him. Gilou crouches down near his cabin and sits on a small wooden plank. He takes off his hat and rubs his head and eyes, then yawns, elbows on his knees.

The quality of light is wonderful today, he remarks, looking out and rubbing his left leg with his hand. I sit down on the other empty pallet. We are waiting for the tide to drop, he says. I look out over the deck and into the water. It is hot. A small group of minute silver fish dart through the water. They sparkle. '*Les Loubines*,' says Georges.

We wait, the boat swaying now and again with wash from distant pleasure boats. Zaza pads over to Gilou and tucks her head under his arm. She sits in front of him, facing out to us. He caresses her, hat in right hand, his left patting her breast. She looks first at us with pale golden eyes, then further on out to sea, blinking occasionally. 'It's magnificent, isn't it?' says Gilou, smiling and looking out to sea with her.

His gentle, lilting voice coupled with the rays of the sun are soporific. He takes his life calmly, he says, working at his own rhythm, tranquilly. '*Eh, ma Zaza?*' Zaza wags her tail gently. He stands, lifts the motor up out of the water, then returns to his plank of wood. '*Oui, le Bassin est beau*,' he repeats. 'You fall in love with it easily. That's why there are more and more people here now.' A silence. 'After all, you can't really stop people coming.' He stands up, looking down into the water. The water is normally clearer, he remarks. Today it's cloudy but yesterday when he took his *ambulances* out it was as clear as a rock pool. I look into the water and see through its cloudiness the outlines of the *ambulances* he has dropped over the side on to the seabed. In the distance a boat with two men and a dog in it is moored to a post.

In July, Gilou continues, he will put his tiles down on his oyster bed, restocking for the next three-year cycle. He reaches into the box on deck for two trestles and sets up a makeshift table with them and an old top made of compressed cork lying on the deck. He scoops some water from the sea into a bucket and swabs down the table. Georges opens my bottle of cold rosé. The cork pops as the men in the distance throw *ambulances* of oysters to left and right with steady movements. They are silhouetted against the sun, animated marionnettes. Their dog jumps off the boat and into the water where a sand dune slowly emerges as the tide drops. The dog trots on it like a dancing horse, a black form pirouetting on the horizon.

Looking down into the water beside us I see now long rows of mesh *ambulances*. The rows have the same distance between them as my rows of vines, almost as high, sited on raised iron rails positioned there by Gilou earlier in the season. Perfect rows, not of vines but of oysters. They are beautiful. 'As I have lots of space, I spread them out,' Gilou is saying. 'Not like in Normandy and Bretagne where no one respects the rules.'

Mesmerised by their appearance, I watch. With the ebbing tide, row after row of *ambulances* reveal themselves, an island of oyster paths and posts. Gilou is drinking rosé, as is Georges. He points to the two long rows he will gather in today. He will remove the *ambulances* from their rails, take them back to his *cabane* and boil them in a vat for thirty seconds or so, enough time to remove the parasitic baby oysters that have attached themselves to the older ones' backs. Boiling for such a short period doesn't harm the larger oysters, he says, and the younger ones simply fall through the mesh. Then he will pile the *ambulances* back on to his boat and return them to his *parc*.

Arcachon, Gilou tells me, is the biggest centre of oyster larvae in France. Seventy per cent of all the oysters in Europe come from this *bassin*. A pleasure boat hurtles past in the distance. 'Look at him,' Gilou nods gently in the direction of it, drinking his *rosé*. 'It should be forbidden, you know. *Mon pauvre*, he makes waves!' Zaza is waiting to descend into the water. She looks at Gilou. 'It should be forbidden', he repeats softly. 'Look what it does to my *ambulances.*' Rows of oyster *ambulances* ripple and undulate violently from one end to the other as bow waves roll in from the fast-moving boat.

A white heron lands on the distant sand dune where the men are working. Gilou looks out towards the sand dune, then turns to me. He smiles broadly. 'An *aigrette,*' he says. 'In October we have migrating geese here – millions of them,' he adds. 'They land and stay awhile, then suddenly they fly, twenty thousand of them!' He raises his huge hands in the air to demonstrate. 'People come to film them from all over the world.'

He sits on the deck to don his wellingtons, then gets into the water. The water level is higher than both his wellingtons and his knees. The wellingtons are not to keep his feet dry but to protect them from the sharp oyster shells which cut into his feet on the bed of the sea. Zaza jumps up from the deck where she was lying and Gilou lifts her off, carrying her across the water to a row of oyster *ambulances*. She walks up and down proudly, crossing from one to another, then jumps into the water and swims off in search of fish. The white heron joins her in the distance, both of them intent on the same catch.

Gilou lifts some of the mesh packets of oysters he threw haphazardly down on the seabed up and on to one of the raised iron paths, already full of existing packets, about to be detached and taken back to the *cabane*. Once he's attached today's batch they will stay there until next March, he says. Detaching the rubber ties from one of the oyster *ambulances* and lifting it off the rail, he throws it on to the boat.

His boat, he says, is better to work with than most of the others, being a traditional long barge, flat and low. It floats in only a foot of water, much better for his back than the higher models. He climbs back on to the deck and opens the bag of oysters just thrown up. Tipping some of them into his steel bucket he shows me a small, wild oyster born last August and living on the outer shell of the two-year-old one.

It is minute, smaller than a shirt button. Georges has already put *saucisson* and pâté on the table along with a knife as Gilou expertly opens fresh oysters from the bucket.

Silver-tinged with a black frill and a fat, creamy centre, they glisten and sparkle, the sun reflecting on the pearly white interior of their shells and bodies. 'A bit *laiteuse*,' says Gilou. 'It's almost the start of their breeding season.' Georges hands me one with a small knife for scooping it out of its shell and pours some of my white wine into plastic cups. '*Aux huîtres!*' he says and swallows his oyster, smacking his lips. I swallow mine.

It tastes of the sea, salty, juicy and luxurious. 'Yes,' says Gilou smiling as we eat oysters freshly gathered from the seabed with *saucisson*, pâté, bread and crisp white wine. 'It may be hard work here in the *parc*, but I recognise I'm spoilt.' We laugh, three people in a small paradise of sand, sea, sun and oyster beds.

'All the same, the older I get, the less I like the winter work,' he continues after opening another four or five oysters. 'You have to love *la nature*.' Georges and I agree. When Gilou was fourteen, he says, he was already working as a jockey at Casteljaloux, three hours or so from Arcachon. He loved horses and was sorry to give up. Yes, he continues, his nephew, who's twenty-seven, has only just found a job; at his age Gilou had already been working for more than twelve years. He holds up his cup for more wine. 'We should give more credit to manual work,' he says. 'Doesn't the oyster maker deserve respect and money? His hours are not counted. Not like the *fonctionnaires*.'

In the distance, Zaza looks like a ballerina, gracefully making her way over the oyster *ambulances* on her way back to us. '*Tu es content?*' Gilou asks her as she returns. He gives her some pâté. 'No, I wasn't a phenomenon at school,' he continues, returning to his nephew and the subject of work. I wasn't an intellectual, he says, but at least I could write a letter and read when I left at fourteen. 'Now they stay at school until they're thirty and it's not even certain they can write letters and read after all that. They should stay at school until sixteen then work.' Georges mumbles that his daughter is about to enter into years of study and will probably follow in the same steps as Gilou's nephew. 'What about manual workers? There are none left — no more masons, no more plumbers. Where are they now?' says Gilou with feeling.

His voice is musical and gentle. He doesn't shout as Gilles does yet his views and opinions fix themselves firmly in my head in the same fashion. No, he continues, his nephew is now a surgeon and earns only twelve thousand a month after all his studies. I listen, looking out into the sun and on to the sea, dulled by the wine and the oysters. A fish jumps out of the water. Zaza has her paws on the table now, like Ulma. She watches Gilou's *saucisson* and bread, following it from his hand to his mouth with her eyes. She jumps down and complains.

The oyster *ambulances* look extraordinary. We are encompassed by rows of them, ordered and beautiful. They are already dry from the sun; pale, bleached grey sacks raised from the ground by their iron rails and encircled by long, thin black posts standing proud and gleaming like exotic plants. The posts are encrusted at their base with groups of wild oysters and mussels growing together, generation after generation; some are huge, others minute.

Gilou is at work among the rows. Astride the iron rails and taking the *ambulances* that were thrown into the water on our arrival, he has a bucket of rubber ties, some *crochets* and a rubber mallet in front of him. He taps the iron rails at their edges to dislodge wild oysters attached to both it and the *ambulances* fixed there, detaches each *ambulance* deftly from them and throws it on to the seabed, working along the row replacing detached *ambulances* with the newly arrived ones.

Pushing one end of a rubber tie into one of the holes at the corner of the mesh *ambulance* and around the rail, he secures them to each other with a *crochet*. Sometimes the *ambulance* already has a rubber tie attached to it from its last stay in the oyster bed; he simply hooks it to the rail with a *crochet* in the same way I attach *crochets* to my wires in the vines to bring my branches into order. The ambulances are attached to each other quickly, creating serried rows of ordered sacks.

Each of us works a row. I look up from my row and see Zaza parading up and down the pale rose deck of the boat, the table still mounted there but cleared of oysters and bread. The black sides of the boat and the deck are only just higher than the iron tables we are working, its hull completely grounded, embedded in the glistening seabed. A crab runs over the wet sand, then buries itself in it – in three seconds it's gone. Small empty oyster shells lie on the seabed. In the distance, two herons, their legs long and thin, peck at the ground. They stab at the sand in staccato movements in search of food. A prawn rushes by.

Gilou and I are working on adjacent rows, Georges at the other end of mine. Yes, oysters must pass through the hands of man, says Gilou as he detaches and reattaches the sacks, tapping off wild oysters as he does so. I ask him about the Brittany and Normandy oysters. 'Their oysters come from here,' he says calmly. '*Ce sont les industrielles.*' They produce the maximum oysters they can from their beds instead of respecting the rules. They ruin the prices by selling too cheaply, they mechanise wherever they can and they don't respect the *métier* of *ostréiculteurs*. He is silent a moment, then smiles, changing the subject. In the same way you work the land, he says, I work the sea.

Georges and I unhook rubber and *crochet* from the *ambulances* and throw the sacks over and on to an adjacent row, ready and more accessible for gathering up to take back to the *cabane*. Gilou continues to attach today's delivery. The rubber ties are made by him, he says. He laughs. 'As soon as we find a source of inner tubes, we jump on it.' The inner tubes surrounding my vat lids in the *chai* are exactly what he needs and I tell him I'll send on my obsolete ones to him from now on.

The tide is beginning to rise, with an accompanying hot wind. Gilou is working faster. I am too. Darting, minute fish flash by. The white heron takes flight between the rails of oyster *ambulances*. Only minutes ago the boat was firmly embedded in the wet sand, now it has water lapping around its edges. Yes, it comes in quickly says Gilou, gathering up his bucket and rubber ties and moving off purposefully.

Rivulets of water run between the rows of rails. Gilou is gone to a distant row near the perimeters of his *parc*. He strides along, working quickly now, tying in, picking up *ambulances* from the seabed and laying them on the tables. Hunched over the rails, only a hat, blue T-shirt and bronzed arms are visible. Within minutes the rivulets of water are a stream. Ripples of baby waves sweep under the rails.

Georges has dismantled the makeshift table on the boat and is arranging the empty pallets on the deck ready to receive the returning *ambulances*. He puts empty bottles into boxes, and clears the deck. '*Ma pauvre fifi!*' he says to Zaza who has returned from her forays at the far end of the *domaine* and is asleep on deck. He removes her from her chosen spot and places empty pallets in her place. Another heron standing on one leg nearby stabs at the seabed. She too knows time is running out. Gilou returns and she flies off, low and graceful, along the rows of oysters.

Gilou is waist-deep in water now, me too. Georges points to my arms and I see fine rivulets of blood, minute, sharp cuts from the oyster shells leaving their mark as I work, the warm waters of La Teste anaesthetising any pain. Gilou passes *ambulances* to Georges on the boat, as he does so tapping each one deftly with the wooden mallet to remove the baby parasites from the larger oysters. This time he taps the packet all over rather than at the ends. The water is rising more quickly. With each *ambulance* piled higher still on the pallet, Georges lets out a grunt. A small crab falls from one of them, scuttles along the deck and plops back into the sea.

. The oyster rails are almost immersed in water as Gilou works the rows. Tap, tap and the rustling of shells, waves, shingles. The ordered rows around us look beautiful, some of the *ambulances* pale ivory and sand-grey, others darker and glistening as water washes over them. Gilou and Georges unhook the ropes from the mooring posts and Georges plunges the long iron pole lying on the deck into the water. He heaves on it to push the boat along a little further. '*Gondolée*,' he sings as we move slowly down the row. Attaching the rope to the next post, he lifts the iron rod back out of the water. Gilou piles more *ambulances* on to the deck, Georges heaves them on to the pallets. Gilou wears thick blue rubber gloves now to protect his hands and arms from the cuts of oyster shells.

The boat sways backwards with the tide as they heave and pile *ambulances* on to the boat. They clink and rustle. Georges groans more loudly with the effort as he piles them higher and higher. Gilou heaves the boat towards him with force and Georges passes back to him the long iron rod that sits on the deck. He rams it though an iron fasting loop on the edge of the deck and into the seabed to stabilise the boat, the wooden pole no longer sufficient against the current of the incoming sea.

Time is running out. The mesh of silver-white and pale grey on the dried sacks has been transformed into glistening and shining black gossamer as the waves hit them. In the near distance, the *ambulances* are already underwater again, the sea having reclaimed them.

Three large pallets of oyster *ambulances*, each over a metre high, are now safely on the boat as Gilou scrambles back on deck. The sacks of oysters in the sea are disappearing from sight as we look at them. Gilou heaves on the iron rod and lifts it back out of the sea. The rim of his hat is curled up above his left ear, his thick spectacles spotted with water and stained with thumbprints. He lifts Zaza on to the roof of the cabin, throws off his wellingtons and blue gloves and slips espadrilles back on to his wet feet.

He lowers the motor back into the water and starts it, taking up his position behind the cabin as if he had never left, forearms placed on it. We pass the posts encrusted at their bases with wild oysters and mussels. They glisten too, the sun reflecting on the last of the black shells visible before they are submerged. Paths of shimmering *ambulances* dip in and out of the water as we pass by. Gilou gives a bowl of water to Zaza. She drinks it lying down, then licks her paw, tired and happy. The wind rises as we head back towards Arcachon and La Teste. A motorboat zooms past, breaking the calm and silence of the day. 'Yes, *le calme est fini*,' says Gilou looking out towards it as it bounces over the waves.

Georges takes a long drag on his newly lit cigarette as he watches the boat disappear into the distance towards the open sea. He has always had a boat, for fishing, he says, much larger than those 'scooters of the sea,' nodding in the direction of the motorboat. He looks out towards it and the wider sea. It's late for it to be going out, he remarks slowly, as it disappears. The sea is dangerous with tidal creeks and huge waves, bringing with them tons of sand. The Bassin d' Arcachon is deceptively beautiful. But the bed of the sea is constantly shifting. The Atlantic waves at high tide are so strong they can displace tons of sand from the dunes in seconds.

Years ago Georges went fishing with his brother-in-law and was late returning. His brother-in-law turned to look behind him and shouted suddenly, 'Open up the throttle!' The wave coming up behind them was higher than the boat. Gilou nods his head in agreement. They sped back, Georges said, just beating the wave.

'The waves can split the boat into matchsticks,' Gilou explains, looking at me. 'You must respect the sea. Respect nature.'

'Yes,' he continues as we head slowly back to La Teste, 'you must be humble in the face of it. These Parisians who spend eleven and a half months in their offices then come down here with their big boats to play . . .' He shakes his head. 'I had a brother-in-law like that,' he says, looking out towards the harbour. 'Always knew best. He soon changed his mind when the water came. When you don't know what you're doing, you should be careful.'

Zaza is asleep on top of the cabin. Georges is next to her, arm on the cabin top like Gilou – me too. The posts in the distance are disappearing with the incoming tide. '*Ah, mon pauvre chien,*' sighs Gilou with a smile, stroking Zaza. '*La vie est dur, n'est-ce pas?*' He laughs, his lips white with sun and salt. It's her chosen place on top of the cabin, he tells us. Mostly he only has her to talk to out in the *parc*.

'And she sometimes talks back,' he laughs. Georges laughs and lights another cigarette. His own dog, he said, used to put her head on his lap and gaze at him often. 'Never had a woman look at me like that in my life,' he laughs. 'And mine didn't talk back either!' We all laugh, windswept, sunburnt, tired and happy. Two motorboats cruise by creating waves. The boat rocks as we sail back through the *bornes* marking the confines of the *bassin*, past white, modern motorboats with their coloured buoys and clinking halyards.

Two swans sail serenely past as we approach the beautiful *cabanes* of La Teste with their black wood frames and terracotta roof tops. Another oyster boat is moored nearby, its owner and Labrador dog on the deck. A duck drifts between the two boats and quacks. '*Le pauvre!*' laughs Georges. 'Surrounded by *chiens de chasse!*' Gilou cuts the motor to low and I hold the rudder while he and Georges moor the boat.

We descend from the boat, heavily weighed down with its

harvest of oysters. Gilou carries one of them with him to the working area behind his *cabanes*. He tips some oysters from it into a machine. Its barrel pierced with holes rolls round in the same fashion as my grape de-stalker as Gilou pours not grapes but oysters into it. High-pressure water gushes through as the barrel turns, cleaning the oyster shells and spurting them out at the other end.

When tipped in they were stones and sand-coloured, dull and dry like sculptor's clay. Now they are pale cream, green-tinged and glistening. '*Regarde comme elles sont jolis*', he says, shaking the steel basket in which they sit and selecting some carefully. He puts them one by one into a large carrier bag then adds the rest of the basket, handing the bag to me.

We wave goodbye to him from the car as he walks down to the boat and his sacks of oysters. I look back towards him and his beautiful boat with its pale rose-coloured deck and blue cabin. He waves back, Zaza next to him.

'*Je ne sais pas*', says Juliana. She is in my kitchen and I have repeated my offer of a new puppy for her and Yves. It's the least I can do for them after all Juliana has done for me over the years. Yves is so depressed that everyone is worried about him, particularly Juliana. He no longer bothers to take any exercise, she says, which he needs to for his heart problem. He doesn't take any interest in the garden either, something he loved doing.

Furthermore, Gageac is silent without Juliana's laughter. Her face is no longer lit up, her smiles are rare and even her shutters make less noise, with no greeting from the upstairs windows. The insistent barking of Chloë that everyone found trying is now sorely missed. 'But I can't let you,' she says hesitantly. Yes you can, I reply. Won't you let me? She looks at me, laughs loudly suddenly and nods her head.

Chapter 9

IN THE OLD *QUARTIER* OF BERGERAC WITH ITS WINDING BACK
streets and alleys of timbered houses and small, unexpected
courtyards, the streets buzz with activity. It's a *quartier* I know well
as most of my professional life takes place there. The laboratory
where my wines are analysed, the tasting rooms where the *appellation côntrolée* tastings are held, the Federation of the Wines of
Bergerac and the Institut des Appellations d'Origine offices are all
to be found there, housed in the beautiful buildings of an ancient
convent and in the thirteenth and fourteenth-century houses
surrounding the small square where the statue of Cyrano de
Bergerac stands.

Only a stone's throw from the convent and the statue, the
tables at l'Imparfait restaurant in the rue des Fontaines spill out
on to the pavement. Large yellow parasols perched above them
jostle with each other for space, their deep ochre colour com-
plementing the silver-green leaves of the olive trees which stand
in terracotta pots at the entrance to the restaurant. The table
settings reflect the ochre and orange of the parasols, the tables
themselves stretching from one end of the alley to the other, two

deep and leaving just enough space to pass through. The restaurant building, like those of the laboratory and the Wine Federation, dates from the thirteenth and fourteenth centuries and is a mass of thick stone walls, winding staircases and myriad small rooms hidden under its roof.

Life in the restaurant begins at 9 am. Jean and Annie Rolland who run it are my friends and have been for many years. Jean is large, expansive and welcoming, Annie discreet, smiling and gentle. Their restaurant is always full; their welcome always warm. They buy copious amounts of both my red and white wine to serve with their food. Their season has begun too, the warm weather increasing their trade.

Inside the restaurant, tables are positioned around a large fish tank holding live lobsters. A carved figurehead from the prow of a nineteenth-century ship dominates the room on the wall opposite. A voluptuous woman with blonde hair curling round her face and neck and with full red lips slightly open, she smiles into the *salon*. Her left breast is bare and in her outstretched hand a lobster is being offered to the room. Jean says that she herself signifies the sea, her breast proffered to nourish the fishermen. 'I added the lobster myself,' he laughs, a conspiratorial laugh that begins deep in his stomach and bubbles up and out from him as he speaks.

At the far end of the *salon* a brown, swinging door with a round window in it leads to the kitchens and the working heart of the restaurant. Directly behind the door a stainless steel counter with three infra red lights hanging above is the reception point for the dishes prepared to order for customers. Philippe, the chef, and his sous-chef, Jean-Pierre, occupy the main kitchen. A large cooking range with a number of hobs and ovens provides ample space for Philippe, the meat chef, and Jean-Pierre, the fish specialist, to create their dishes. An open hatch in the room divides their working spaces neatly into two.

To the right of the main kitchen is a room housing cutlery, crockery, dishwashers and a large and deep stainless-steel sink. Further on still and looking out on to the tables in the alley is a light, open room with mixers, ice-cream makers and ovens where the *pâtisserie* chef creates his desserts.

A side entrance leading off from the main kitchen has a steep step down to one of the small alleys beside the restaurant. Like the swinging kitchen door, it too has a round window in it. To the right and one step down from it is a small, dark back kitchen with oven, hobs and fridges. To the left, another room contains large, walk-in, meat and vegetable fridges and a winding stone staircase in one corner which leads up to a labyrinth of dark storage rooms.

Philippe, in his early forties with curly dark hair peppered with silver, and Jean-Pierre, heavier in stature with short, spiky hair and a smiling countenance, are already at work, assembling their ideas and preparing their menus. In the small back kitchen two assistants, Maya and Olivier, work on the starters. In the crockery room a thin youth, Patrick, is the dishwasher and spends his time with his hands and arms elbow-deep in the stainless-steel sink. In the *pâtisserie* room resides Sébastien, who mixes sorbets, makes ice creams and small, delicate cakes and hums to himself, industrious and efficient. Two, sometimes three, servers complement the team.

Sabrina, one of the young servers, carries a tray of three espresso coffees and places it on the cash counter. From the half-timbered house opposite a man in open shirt and a suit crosses the alley. Looking *mondain* and un-Bergerac like, he shakes hands with Jean, hurls his keys on the table and throws a sugar lump into one of the espressos. He leans one elbow on the counter.

Jean is leaning on the counter too with one hand on his hip. Dressed in a black long-sleeved T-shirt rolled up to the elbow and black trousers, both he and his neighbour look Parisian. In fact, we could easily be in any one of the small *quartiers* of Paris rather than in Bergerac. A mother passes with two small children and shouts a greeting. Jean's neighbour lights a cigarette; he is off to buy his morning paper. The coffee he takes with Jean is part of his morning ritual, like the first cigarette of the day and the paper run.

Already at the side entrance of the kitchen the door is open, a vegetable van delivering today's produce. Bright morning sun sends a path of light into the kitchen. Maya and Patrick carry wooden cartons of vegetables into the cold room. Fresh green asparagus and small new carrots with delicate green fronds jiggle in the basket as Patrick mounts the steep step up from the road to the kitchen. On the ground outside, waiting for his return trip, are baskets of spinach. Maya has a box of fresh, white mushrooms, lemons still with their stalks and green leaves attached and black, shining aubergines.

In a small fridge next to the cold room, fresh foie gras enveloped in roughly broken peppercorns and wrapped in clean tea towels sit in rows looking like so many cloth sausages. They will stay there for four days before being served in thin rounds with a marmalade of fresh oranges and cumin. In the meat fridge next to it, pink veal fillets, round, lustrous kidneys still half-wrapped in creamy white fat and dark red cuts of meat, succulent looking and fresh, are arranged in separate plastic containers.

Outside the restaurant on a table next to the olive tree, Jean has deposited packages of roses of all colours, brought with him this morning. Sabrina will separate them into jugs. For the moment, she is in the crockery room wearing white cotton gloves and cleaning silver forks and spoons. Alain, the main waiter and an old hand, points to the tips of the forks she has already cleaned and suggests gently that she cleans them again.

Small with dark, gleaming hair, large eyes and fulsome breasts, she looks up at Alain and nods, eager to please. Beside her, coloured wicker breadbaskets, neat piles of clean tea towels and scores of large serving plates await the working day. Patrick is podding peas. Thin, with long arms and bony elbows, his hands are pink. His nose, too, is pink at its tip. Young and shy, he works quietly, occasionally casting a nervous eye towards Sabrina.

Alain has worked at the restaurant for fourteen years and is as much a part of it as Jean and Annie. Fair-haired, and in his early fifties, he lives with his mother and owns a large farm with cows and wheat fields. He spent some years serving on cruise ships that worked the islands around Florida before returning home to his farm and his life here. As a result his English is excellent. He is a Bergeracois, like his parents and grandparents before him. When he is not working in the restaurant, he is working at home. 'Ooui!' Jean laughs. 'He's richer than all of us put together with his farm and his cows.'

In the small, dark back kitchen where the starters are prepared, pots of fresh herbs are laid out in a row along a tabletop. Next to them small cherry tomatoes, still with their stalks attached, sit in containers along with fresh fronds of aniseed, frisée and lettuce leaves. They are the garnishes for the starters on today's menu. On the stove nearby, a *velouté* of asparagus is just beginning to bubble. Maya, a young, thin Spanish girl with dark eyes and short black hair, turns down the heat. She previously did Patrick's job, working for three years at the sink washing dishes or peeling vegetables, learning her trade from the bottom. Now a kitchen assistant, she is dressed in blue checked trousers and a starched white chef's shirt. Around her waist and tucked under the belt of her apron is one of the clean tea towels from the pile next to Sabrina.

The baker delivers large rounds of fresh bread in a huge basket balanced on his shoulder and carries them through the *salon* to the crockery room. With him the morning begins in earnest. The fishmonger arrives at the side door of the kitchen. Monkfish with creamy white and rose-tinted skin, fresh flat sole and large, firm-textured turbot are handed over. 'Where are the lobsters?' asks Jean-Pierre. There are no lobsters left in the fish tank and one is needed this morning for the sauce that will accompany the langoustine starter. The fishmonger promises to return with them within the hour. In their reproduction cycle, the texture of their meat is firmer at the moment, sweeter and more succulent. '*C'est la belle saison*,' says Jean-Pierre.

The main *salon* is almost ready for today's customers. Fans are switched on and Sabrina has placed jugs generously filled with roses on the tables that also now have her freshly polished silver and large white plates. And the Breton lobsters have arrived, eight of them. They come from Jersey and Guernsey, says Jean. Which are, he pronounces with a flourish, naturally, French in origin. '*Les Anglais* have pinched our isles because of the lobsters!' he shouts, laughing and picking one up by the back of its head.

He strides with it to the fish tank, its long, thin and dark blue legs oscillating and its antennae waving. Its claws are firmly wrapped shut with sticky tape. He holds its head just beneath the surface of the water for a moment before plunging it into the tank. What do you suppose they think, I ask, as he puts one after the other into the tank. He splutters, laughter erupting from deep within his stomach. He looks at me with knowing eyes and a large smile. 'Probably that they'll soon be put in the pot!'

Jean grabs a handful of coarse salt, strides through the restaurant and scatters it outside on the ground in front of the restaurant and next to the tables with a flourish. 'To encourage the customers!' he laughs. The owner of the first restaurant he worked in in Paris did the same every day. 'I've done it ever since. Doesn't work a hundred per cent, but almost,' he laughs.

Alain has changed and is now wearing a black apron over black trousers and a white shirt. Sabrina is similarly attired except she wears a short black skirt. The buttons of her white blouse are straining. She has plaited red and blue ribbons into the fringe of her shining hair. '*Oh, que tu es belle*,' Annie laughs. Sabrina smiles, delighted at some recognition of the effort she has made.

Four minutes to twelve and the first customers wander in: an English family of three children with their parents. A French couple follow and Alain is instantly in professional serving mode. 'Make sure to take care of the customer,' Alain instructs Sabrina. 'As soon as they arrive give them bread and olive oil. Then ask them if they want an *apéritif*.' He heads to the French table with bread and olive oil as Annie welcomes the English family and puts on some music.

The English family look around. Seated next to the lobster tank, the children gaze at it and the voluptuous blonde figure-head opposite. They gape at Alain too, mesmerised by him. One of them lifts the covers on the salt and pepper pots on the table.

'*C'est parti*,' announces Philippe as the first orders are pinned on the wall next to the pile of plates. Dishes out, fridges open. '*Queues de langoustines et Pissaladière!*' he bellows towards the back kitchen. '*Oui!*' shouts Maya from its depths. '*Lotte pour toi*,' he announces to Jean-Pierre who is already removing the outer skin from the monkfish.

He makes a small cut on the skin and pulls it off in one action, then cuts down the backbone and removes two white and glistening fillets in a second. Laying them flat, he removes any residual skin and taps them into shape, like Sébastien at the bakery with his baguettes. Placing them on a dry cloth for a moment, a pan is already sizzling on the hob to receive them.

Philippe is preparing a heart of fillet of beef with hot foie gras. '*Tampina de légumes!*' he shouts to Maya. '*Oui!*' she calls back, appearing from the depths of the dark back kitchen with two white porcelain cups of *velouté* of asparagus. She speeds to the reception point, placing them carefully on curved, wavy bases and wiping a drip away with the clean tea towel hanging at her waist as Alain sweeps in through the swinging door and carries them out to the restaurant, the soup a prelude to the French couple's meal. The door swings shut.

Maya is back again, rushing towards Philippe and Jean-Pierre with the starters. Three crayfish tails sit in a delicate pyramid at the centre of a plate, a butter sauce of orange and ginger beneath them and deep fried *beignets* of dandelion beside them. Surrounding them are fronds of delicate *aneth*. The other plate holds a succulent looking round of pressed aubergine with minia- ture tomatoes. 'OK,' shouts Philippe and she turns to him with the plate. He places hot foie gras from his pan on to the aubergine and rearranges the dish. Maya places both plates under the infra- red lights and disappears back into her kitchen as Alain sweeps back in through the doors. 'Oysters!' shouts Philippe to Olivier. '*Oui!*' he replies from the back room.

In the *salon* and outside the tables are filling up. It's only twenty past twelve and almost every table is full, both inside and out. '*Ça marche, le sel!*' says Jean with a smile. '*Allo!*' he calls sharply now and again to Sabrina or Alain to attract their attention. 'Clear those *apéritif* glasses, *s'il te plaît*' or 'You've forgotten to serve the soup' or 'Their wine glasses need filling'. He speaks quietly but insistently as he sweeps by.

Occasionally he simply calls '*Allo!*' and indicates with his eyes that a table needs clearing as he passes on his way to and from the kitchen with orders or dirty plates. Sabrina's apron straps have fallen and one of the buttons on her shirt has given up the ghost and left it altogether. She bustles in and out, not quite in the swing of things but with a willingness to please.

In the kitchen, ever-increasing orders are stuck on the wall above the pile of fast-diminishing clean plates. Piles of used ones surround Patrick in the crockery room, along with dirty casserole dishes and frying pans. His hands are plunged into the deep sink, working rapidly and silently, no time to talk, no time to waste. Three large pots of warm water hold soaking knives, forks and spoons that await the hot, soapy suds of the sink. The dishwashing machine whirrs as more dirty plates, piled dangerously high, amass beside him.

The pressure, along with the heat, is extreme: '*Marmite de poisson!*' shouts Jean-Pierre. '*Oui!!*' shouts Maya from the dark dungeon behind. '*Purée de châtaignes!*' shouts Philippe. '*Oui!!!*' screams Maya. Her helper, Olivier, rushes through with a plate of crayfish tails and another of foie gras, the latter deposited on his plate by Philippe as he passes.

Jean coasts through the door to collect them, spectacles perched on top of his head now, sleeves rolled up and wiping his brow with a napkin. '*Erreur!*' he says sharply. 'Not crayfish tails – two foie gras.' Olivier looks at Philippe and Philippe looks at Jean then the order slip. 'Foie gras!' he yells into the back kitchen, opening the fridge and removing a foie to start cooking. '*Merde!!*' screams Maya.

Outside in the *salon* and on the terrace, clink of glasses and laughter is loud. Alain is uncorking bottles, cold whites and reds. Sabrina is working hard. In her hands, two of the carefully pre-pared pyramids of crayfish totter dangerously as she leaves the reception counter, the orange butter sauce sliding gently across the plate as she turns towards the *salon*. '*Allo!*' says Jean, entering through the doors and turning her smartly back to the reception point with them.

'*Ma petite belle*,' he says with laboured patience. Her hair has fallen down in front of her face and her breasts are bobbing out of her shirt. Jean takes the plates from her and replaces them on the reception point. Philippe and Jean-Pierre arrive with two clean plates and more sauce and the contents of the now demolished dishes are transferred to the replacement plates and their former glory.

Placing clean napkins in each of his hands, Jean looks at her knowingly. He slowly pulls the hot plates towards him until their edges leave the counter. Releasing his hands from the plates, he holds them up like a magician, clean napkins still in them. He looks at her again, then bends his knees in an exaggerated fashion, takes the plates and scoops them up carefully.

Holding them at the same level as the counter for a few seconds, he raises them gently in the air by a foot or so then puts them back down on the counter carefully as she looks at him and them with large eyes. He places the clean napkins in her hands with a flourish and says, 'Now, *ma belle*, lift them up properly', and she does. He smiles at her. 'Bravo. Keep them at that level!' he says as she wanders into the *salon*, carefully regarding the contents of the plate and smiling broadly.

Puddings leave the pastry room at a pace as the main kitchen calms down, most of the customers now served. Jean is waiting for the last of the main dishes at the reception point, hand on hip, napkin in hand. Everyone is feeling jaded. He drinks a large glass of water. Annie is at the cash counter, head down, preparing bills, Patrick still steadily washing up. Each time Sabrina bends over him to deliver more dirty plates his back straightens and his eyes try unsuccessfully to evade the sight of her open shirt. '*Eh oui, mon pauvre!*' laughs Jean. '*Ça fait rêver, n'est-ce pas?*' The kitchen erupts with laughter, the pressure suddenly gone.

Jean-Pierre cleans the hob of his hot oven with sandpaper and order is restored. Patrick gathers up frying pans and casseroles from the kitchen. It is the first time he has left his post since midday.

Tables are cleared and relaid. '*Allo!*' Jean calls gently to Sabrina. '*Café pour table neuf*' and she rushes off for the coffees and *petit fours*. Each time she prepares a tray of *cafés* with *petits fours* cakes, she slips one of them into her mouth.

In the kitchen, Maya has recovered her calm. All dirty tea

towels and dishes have vanished, whisked away into a laundry basket. Patrick is silent at the sink, finishing off the last of the dishes, surrounded by pan scrubbers and washing-up liquid. The cutlery pots are empty now too, as are the dishwashers.

'He's a bit slow, *n'est-ce pas*?' Jean-Pierre says, patting Patrick on the shoulder. Patrick smiles shyly. The tops are shining and the plates are clean, dry and back in their place next to the reception counter. Jean-Pierre wipes his face with a huge piece of kitchen paper. He does so slowly, happy to have the time to do so, pleased to have the lunch period over. 'This evening will be easier,' he says, taking off his apron.

Le personnel have on fresh *tabliers*, check trousers and clean shirts, their three-hour break over. Downstairs in the kitchen, Jean-Pierre has already cleaned the turbots for this evening. They glisten, white greaseproof paper covering them for the moment. Philippe is singing along to some blues on the CD player as he cuts up fillet of beef into rounds. Jean-Pierre is drinking a bottle of water, rehydrating himself in preparation for an evening in front of the hob. It's 6.50 pm and the restaurant is ready for action again.

Jean stands by the cash counter waiting for customers. His first *patron* in Paris with whom he worked his apprenticeship was Gilbert Spiegelle. 'All Paris came to eat there,' he says. '*Les artistes, les politiciens*, Pompidou, Wittgenstein.' When he retired, he continues, he sold his cellar of four thousand bottles of Mouton-Rothschild to Christie's. '*Pas mal*,' laughs Annie, who is listening. 'Yes, it was the first real *restaurant à la mode*,' he says. 'Next to the river, the other side of the Pont Neuf. Bistroquet it was called.' The ambiance in the restaurant was incredible, he recalls. It was open from 7 pm to 3 in the morning.

'He taught me the importance of ambiance,' he continues. 'He taught me the *morale* of our *métier*. You can't cheat it. What you get is what you get. Real cuisine is preparation. Real cuisine is tradition. It must be good. If you eat badly, even if it doesn't cost a lot, it's expensive!' He laughs as the first customers arrive and he strides out to welcome them.

The atmosphere is very different from that of lunchtime. The music playing in the restaurant is blues or jazz, Jean's favourite, and in the kitchen the ambiance is notably relaxed. Jean-Pierre is preparing '*les petits turbots*' for the first customers of the evening. They will be roasted and served with a lobster butter sauce. He and Philippe joke together; even Patrick is in the kitchen rather than at the sink.

A head appears at the open side entrance door. A small man is smiling and waving. Weather-beaten, with an olive-brown face and a straw hat, his teeth are missing and he sways, slightly worse for alcohol having just left the café opposite. He looks minute, cut off by the height of the steep stone step. '*Salut le Matelot!*' shouts Philippe as he cuts up meat. Jean-Pierre waves at him with the knife he holds. The *Matelot* who drives the barges on the river makes a half-hearted effort to mount the step, then thinks better of it and wanders off.

'*Allo!*' and the restaurant is in business again. Champagne corks pop as Alain opens bottles for the *apéritifs* and Annie and Sabrina deposit *rillettes* of duck on tables to accompany them. Orders are taken and delivered to the tables with speed. Plates of oysters from La Teste opened by Olivier in the small back kitchen arrive, crayfish tails and foie gras made by Jean-Pierre and Philippe and *veloutés* of *asperges* prepared by Maya. The fridge door beneath the figurehead opens and closes constantly as bottles of cool white wine or water are removed and served, along with red wines.

Jean-Pierre and Philippe work speedily and with concentration in the intense heat of the kitchen. Another face appears at the window of the side door. It's the man from across the road who came for his morning coffee. He laughs and gesticulates like a clown, then disappears as quickly as he appeared. 'He's fallen off the step again,' remarks Jean-Pierre. 'Just come out of the café,' replies Phillipe, smiling.

Laughter, the clink of cutlery and glass and the restaurant, both inside and out, is full to the gunwales. It is a hot evening with not a spare table or seat available. Ella Fitzgerald's 'Summertime' drifts into the kitchen as Jean-Pierre flash-fries creamy, glistening scallops. Philippe cooks two thin slices of foie gras. They are served together, placed delicately on two plates, already garnished by Maya with a *mirepoix* of seasonal vegetables. Philippe adds the finishing touch of *lamelles* of summer truffles with care.

'Fresh ingredients and a marriage of tastes,' says Jean as he gathers up the plates, turns tail and sweeps through the swing door into the restaurant, placing them on the table in front of his customers with a flourish. The unmistakable aroma of summer truffles hangs in the air behind him.

Annie is back at the cash desk, head down, adding up bills. Most of the customers inside have left and in the kitchen the cleaning up is over. Patrick is at the sink but almost finished and Jean-Pierre has taken off his *tablier* and wiped his face. Sabrina has delivered the last of the coffees to the tables outside.

Jean, Annie and I sit under one of the yellow parasols, a welcome breeze cooling the sultry evening. Desultory conversation drifts over from the last few customers still sitting at the tables outside. We sip cold, refreshing champagne and take in the warm evening air. Jean is in expansive mood. His legs are stretched out in front of him, one arm resting on the table, the other holding up his glass. He takes a long sip. Did we keep the customers happy? Was the ambiance good? Music floats on the air, Ella Fitzgerald singing 'I Love Paris'.

Laughter drifts over from the remaining customers. I say I think the ambiance was excellent. Gilbert Spiegelle would have been pleased, I tell Jean. He laughs loudly and looks at me. 'Ah. It's like your wine,' he replies. 'You must be proud of your talent.' He takes another sip from his glass. 'It gives you freedom. The better you know your *métier*, the freer you are. The more you are respected — Gilbert taught me that. Here at the restaurant, you need real products, made by real cooks, with seasonal tastes. And as a customer, you need to feel pleasure in the meal.' He looks at me. 'Why do people come to a restaurant?' He answers for me. 'To *faire la fête*, of course. It has to be good. The food must be good and fresh and creative and the ambiance must be conducive to the meal. *Santé!*' he shouts and we lift our glasses as Ella's voice fills the night air.

Fidde told me that real freedom comes when you know yourself. We were driving back from dinner at l'Imparfait on a summer's evening with the honeyed scent of hay in the air and a white, luminous moon. It hung in a sky, black and littered with stars. 'For instance, why do you work all the time?' he asked me. 'Do you know? And why do you go out so much in the evenings? Why are you so hard on yourself, Patricia?' He gave me a searching glance that looked deeply into me.

Time seemed to slow down in the dark interior of the car. Stunned by the questions, I said nothing. I didn't have an answer. As if someone had opened a trap door, I had a sense of falling, of weightlessness. Fidde had stripped away all the layers of protection I had given myself. I was a million miles away from vines, *chais*, tractors and even from Fidde. A great wave of loneliness swept over me.

I saw a mirror image of myself. I saw the echo of

early dreams and hopes with James, I saw the shadows of aching voids when I had missed the children, I saw the solitude of a slow and painful mourning of the loss of love. I felt the fleeting touch of Fidde's hand on my knee. 'It's good to face it,' he said as we drove home.

I looked out at vines flashing by in the night, at fields of mown hay, at houses with people living their lives in them, swallowed up in the darkness of the car and wishing that the whispered conversations in my head would go away.

As he left, he stared at my face for a long time in silence then kissed me gently goodnight. Light from the moon shone in through the French windows and settled on the tiled floor of the kitchen. I looked down at it. The house was silent, like me. The whispered conversations in my head had gone. There was nothing in it now, not even anger or bitterness. Just a terrible sadness.

Fidde was right. I did fill up my days in order not to think of other things, in order not to look at myself. I only ever looked at bits of me. I didn't want to see my own pain and I didn't want others to, didn't want them to think badly of James, didn't want to face reality. As a form of self-preservation, I allowed no one to see the real me, not even me.

Chapter 10

MOST OF THE SOUTH-WEST OF FRANCE IS ON A MISSION TO FIND A
Yorkshire terrier puppy for Yves. Odile has asked her vet who has
no leads for the moment. She reads the adverts in the *Petit Foyen*,
the local newspaper for Ste-Foy-la-Grande, in the hope of finding
litters for sale. Bruno and Claudie scour their local paper, the *Petit
Bergeracois*, for advertisements too. Every so often, Claudie faxes
over a telephone number for me to ring. Usually they are either
not yet born, or only just born and not ready to leave, or have
no pedigree. Jacques and Marie-Christelle have asked their friend
who breeds them but she has no litters for the moment either
and thinks we must wait. Gilles thinks Yves and Juliana should
simply go to the SPA, the equivalent of our RSPCA, and get any
old dog for nothing.

'*Ecoute!*' says Odile. She is here for supper and we have had the
obligatory trip over to Madame Cholet's before our *blanc cassis*. We
are sitting in the garden under the shade of the acacia tree. The
lauriers-roses are in blossom with clusters of delicate white and rose-
coloured flowers. The hydrangeas too are in bloom, their huge
blowsy flowers bursting out over their leaves.

'*Oh, que c'est bon, un petit blanc cassis!*' she laughs, taking a sip from

189

her glass and a long drag on her cigarette. 'Gilles is right. After all, why not try the SPA?' She holds her cigarette close to her mouth as she speaks in order to catch the odd curls of tobacco smoke that escaped the last inhalation. 'They don't need a pedigree!' I ask her whether she would be prepared to accept a non-pedigree dog from the SPA herself when Gaiaa, her beloved but ancient Labrador, eventually dies, given that she has always had pedigree Labradors. She looks at me for a moment. '*Oui, tu as raison,*' she agrees, sticking the cigarette firmly back in her mouth and lifting her glass.

On the wide back terrace at La Tabardy, the light on the outside wall above the kitchen door is caked in baked owl pee. On the floor beneath it a pale grey pool has a mound of large droppings in it, proof of its nightly visit. Where the beams of the terrace roof join the wall, newborn starlings, hidden somewhere inside the wall, shout to be fed. The noise is deafening. Their parents dart to and fro under the eaves and into the wall, supply and demand feeding their chicks.

With the aid of a stepladder, and unscrewing the glass covering of the light above the kitchen door, I remove and soak it in hot water then set to in the kitchen for a thorough clean as Juliana arrives. '*Coucou!*' she shouts, then, '*Ah là là! Quell bruit!*' as she looks up at the starlings darting in and out of the terrace walls. A rabbit appears from the side door of the barn next to the house as we stand on the terrace. We watch in astonishment as four more appear from the same place. They look at us sideways, sitting stock-still on the grass, ears to attention.

Madame de la Planche has Yorkshire terrier puppies for sale. She lives the other side of Angoulême, a good two and a half hour's drive from here. Juliana and Yves would prefer a bitch and two are available, one eight weeks, the other almost five months. Odile had seen an advert in the *Petit Foyen* and rung the number. 'She sounds *très sympa*,' she said when she called me afterwards. 'Give her a call. But God, can she talk . . .'

I know nothing about Yorkshire terriers, other than that Chloë was one, they bark a lot and they pee on my kitchen floor. Madame de la Planche knows all there is to know about them. She speaks rapidly, breathless with excitement and enthusiasm for life in general and Yorkies in particular. 'Madame!' she warns. 'Even if you don't take one of mine, *faites attention* when buying one!' She continues, 'Don't think they can be bred by just anyone, Madame. They must be small. They must have the right shaped head, Madame. They . . .' I stop her and explain the situation. I know nothing about Yorkshire terriers, I say, but I want to buy one for my friends.

'*Attention, Madame!* Are you sure they know how to look after Yorkshires? I have bred them all my life and . . .' I try to break in. 'All mine have been tattooed, they have their inoculations. They need to be wormed regularly, Madame!' she continues, ignoring the interruption. 'And . . .' I open my mouth again, '. . . they mustn't be given too much to eat! They have delicate stomachs and . . .' 'Which puppy would you recommend?' I shout, my voice bursting through the avalanche of words. '*Ah, là!*' she opines. '*Tout dépend des clients . . .*'

I had thought it might be nice simply to present Yves and Juliana with the puppy without prior warning, given that they both already knew I was hunting for one. I now think better of it. '*Celui de cinq mois, Madame . . .*' The five-month puppy's weight hasn't increased for a month, she says, and so she can vouch for it as a perfect specimen of a Yorkshire terrier. She's called Venus, she says. La Petite Venus. She is very beautiful, she continues. '*Elle est très joueuse, Madame!*' She's very playful. She follows her everywhere, she hands over her paw to play, La Petite Venus . . . 'I'll ring you back,' I shout.

Does Juliana think it should be La Petite Venus, I ask her, or an even more *petite* eight-week-old specimen? She decides on La Petite Venus, then instantly changes her mind. What would Yves prefer? I feel we ought to be clear on this before I ring back Madame de la Planche. In any event, I have told Madame de la Planche that we will pick up one or the other tomorrow, and that we will meet halfway between Angoulême and Gageac, outside the church at Ribérac at 6 pm. Meeting at Ribérac suits me well as I have a *dégustation* and dinner not far from there. Yves and Juliana will follow me in their own car to pick up La Petite Venus, who has eventually been chosen after great discussion and many moments of indecision.

Yves is beside himself with excitement, says Juliana. They have been to buy La Petite Venus a basket of her own, rather than use Chloë's, and Yves wants to know what time we are leaving. Yves rings me ten minutes later to say he has decided to start off half an hour earlier than me because I drive faster than he does. I can hear urgency and excitement in his voice. He rings me again mid-afternoon to say he's leaving. He will arrive hours before La Petite Venus, Madame de la Planche and me, I tell him. *Peu importe*, he replies. Do I know exactly where the church is and is it the collegiate church or the temple or some other church? No matter, he exclaims when I tell him I have no idea. In fact, I don't know Ribérac at all, having been through it only once or twice and always en route to other places. I suggested the church as a meeting point to Madame de la Planche on the grounds that there was sure to be one there.

As I approach the *centreville* of Ribérac, driving slowly and looking for the church, the waving and gesticulating figure of Juliana beckons me up a small road to the right. I wonder how long she has been waiting for me, given that she and Yves left more than three hours before me. She laughs, waving me up a steep hill to the church.

It is hot, breathless and humid as we await the arrival of La Petite Venus. Her new basket is on the back seat of their car. Yves is sitting in the car with the door open, fanning himself with a map of France. He has managed to find some shade for the car by parking it across the access to two garages. Although they have been here some time, he says, *peu importe* – better to be early than late. Each time a car enters the car park, he leaps out of his car, searching anxiously for signs of a puppy.

Cars arrive in the car park regularly, mostly driven by large firemen in navy uniforms with red stripes across their chests. They stride backwards and forwards in their heavy black boots carrying chairs from the church, which they load into a small van and into each of their cars. They must be having their annual *fête*, surmises Juliana. They glance at us now and again, nodding in greeting.

The church looks Russian with a bell-shaped roof and wide steps, busy today with a constant stream of chairs and firemen. It is the collegiate church, says Yves. Does Madame de la Planche know this? Should we not ring her on her mobile? A car draws up; inside it are three small children, their mother and a large grandmother. The driver gets out of her car and opens the boot. '*Ça y'est!*' says Yves, springing out of the car again. We rush towards her as she leaps back from us in fear and surprise.

Yves returns to his car for some shade as Juliana and I lean against mine. We wait, dulled by the sun and the heat, watching the activity in and around the church in a desultory fashion. It is half past six and we are tired and dehydrated by the heat. I am beginning to worry that I won't have enough time to get to my *dégustation* and dinner when a car sweeps up the steep slope to the church.

It has an Angoulême registration number. Yves scrambles out of his car and stands to attention as Madame de la Planche leaps out of hers before her husband has brought it to a stop. 'Madame!' she rushes over to us. '*Bonjour*! We are sorry to be late!' Juliana gazes at her open-mouthed. Curvaceous and wearing a short black skirt and a low cut black T-shirt, her breasts are elevated to gravity-defying heights by a bra with wide purple and pink lace straps, her painted toenails and open shoes in the same vivid colours.

'*Il fait chaud!*' she exclaims as we all stare at her, transfixed, and she pats her neck and bosom with a handkerchief. '*Chéri! Où est-elle?*' and she swivels in search of her husband and the dog, waves of perfume drifting towards us. The car door opens and her husband steps out. Two small Yorkshire terriers with beribboned topknots and hair falling over their eyes tumble out of the car with him. One rushes around, happy to escape the confines of the car, while the other collapses, hyperventilating on the hot tarmac of the car park. 'La Petite Venus!' exclaims Madame de la Planche with her hands in the air, looking at her husband who immediately scoops La Petite Venus up in the same way as Juliana used to with Chloë.

La Petite Venus is very hot and very wet. Monsieur de la Planche hurriedly wipes her mouth and rearranges her hair. The roads were winding, explains Madame de la Planche, La Petite Venus is hot and not used to the car, she says, and that's why she vomited. 'But normally she's very good in the car!' she continues hurriedly. '*N'est-ce pas, chéri?*' she asks her husband, who nods. '*Elle est très joueuse!*' she continues, rearranging again La Petite Venus's topknot and smoothing out her coat.

'Get the toy, Denis!' she commands with authority as she takes La Petite Venus from her husband and tucks her under her right breast. We gaze at it and her. Her husband removes from the car a beanbag lizard and Madame de la Planche deposits La Petite Venus on the ground next to it, smartly lifting her back legs up as she collapses once more in a heap on the ground.

'It's her mother?' asks Juliana of the other Yorkshire terrier with the red-ribboned topknot, finding her voice at last. '*Non, non!* Her father!' replies Madame. '*Tiens*, look!' and with dramatic gestures she turns towards the car, bends over and takes out a large photograph. '*Son grand-père!*' she announces, displaying the picture to our group. A silky, beribboned Yorkshire terrier, brushed and gleaming with perfectly straight hair cascading to the ground, stares out at us from the photo. It has red and blue ribbons in its hair. 'He's a champion!' she announces with pride. Meanwhile, the soft toy and La Petite Venus sit together motionless on the hot tarmac.

I lift her up gently as Madame chatters noisily. She is light, minute and trembling slightly. Removing the hair from her eyes I look into her face. She is beautiful, a real Petite Venus. She looks back at me with black, intelligent eyes. 'Look at her ears!' exclaims Madame, rushing to me and pulling them smartly up. 'Perfect small ears! You should look for that in a real Yorkshire!' Yves has said nothing since her arrival. I hand her over to him. He looks at her, then puts her to his shoulder. She buries her face in his neck. 'This is supposed to be a happy moment!' splutters Juliana, laughing as a tear falls from Yves's eyes.

'She must have her teeth brushed regularly! Very important. She's very intelligent!' Madame is saying to Juliana and Yves who are now chattering too. Juliana has had many a Yorkshire, she informs Madame; in fact she has only ever had Yorkshires. I drive out of the car park to my *dégustation*, leaving behind the perfect example of a Yorkshire terrier and its admirers.

The children will soon be here for their annual holidays. John, now back from Thailand, lives and works in England again. Chantal works too and as a result they can manage only one real holiday here a year, always in August. Amy and Beth, my grandchildren, have spent every summer of their lives here; in their younger days before work and school, their visits lasted the entire summer.

Now twelve and ten years old, they are full of life and vitality.

I speak to them often on the phone. I have told them of the sad demise of Chloë, tempered rapidly with news of the arrival of La Petite Venus. The memory of their reaction when my setters, Sam and Luke, died, hip dysplasia and old age having taken their toll, is still fresh in my mind. They were mortified. About to debark for their annual holidays, Chantal had thought it better to get the bad news over with beforehand. 'Mum,' she had said on the phone. 'Can you just speak to the girls, please? I've told them.' In the background I heard the sound of muffled sobs. 'Grandma,' said Beth quietly. 'I don't want them to be dead.' Amy sobbed, 'It's not fair, Grandma!'

Now they are on the phone again. 'Grandma! What's she like?' asks Amy excitedly. 'I need to talk to Grandma!' says Beth, taking the phone. 'Why is she called La Petite Venus, Grandma? How big is she? Is she allowed to come to your house?' Amy takes the phone back. 'Does she pee on your floor, Grandma?'

Like Gilles and Gilou, Michel Founaud often wears espadrilles. It's 6.30 am and he is wearing them this morning. We are going fishing on the Dordogne, meeting up at his house. His dogs leap at the fenced gate as I arrive, eager to greet me. They are not coming with us this morning, says Michel, as the bank is steep and only one of them can manage it. Minou's legs are now too arthritic for her to descend and ascend.

We drive to Gardonne, cross the bridge then turn right down a small and bumpy country track. Rabbits are everywhere, bounding over fields or huddled in groups on the lane. They look at us boldly, lope away nonchalantly, bob over meadows then stop momentarily to turn back and gaze at us. Adorned with large hay bales as well as rabbits, the fields belong to Monsieur Martin, a long-time friend of Michel's.

The fresh cream from his cows is without match, says Michel as we bounce along the track. The cowsheds to the right where the matchless cream comes from look medieval. The bumpy track narrows as the grass growing at the side and in the middle of it lengthens. We come to a halt next to an old, abandoned house. Monsieur Martin is restoring it when he has the time, Michel tells me.

Would I carry his buckets down to the riverbank, he asks me as he gathers up his rods and tackle box and we cross the track to the bank. Michel was not exaggerating when he said the bank was steep. Almost a sheer drop, five steps built into the top of the bank of dry soil and scrub and made from small wooden planks shored up by makeshift pegs are the only aid to our descent. 'I must make some more,' he says as we stumble between each one.

The steps end, the descent is steeper still. A knotted blue rope provides scant but welcome aid to our descent. Michel has attached it to tree trunks at the top and bottom and woven it in and around others, slotted through an occasional stump of tree cut in to a V shape. We slip and stumble down to the riverbank.

A mist hangs over the surface of the wide river, pale and delicate, like gossamer. Gentle prisms of light shine on the water. Acacia trees overhang it, the only sound that of birdsong, calm and tranquil. We are in Michel's private fishing domain.

Three small iron stakes embedded into the earth next to the river's edge with small sections of cut-down plastic pipe encircling them serve as holders for his rods. He deposits his fishing tackle box that also doubles as a seat next to them and sets to work.

Fish love fennel, he tells me as he sprinkles some on to the contents of a tin of sweetcorn and throws both into the river. Tablespoonfuls from a large container of what looks like moist curry powder from a large container follow. They create pools and ripples of increasing circles in the river, disturbing its tranquillity. It is, he explains, bait. The sun gleams on the rippling water as the bait disappears and sinks to the riverbed.

'Is it the first time you've been fishing?' he asks me, as he fixes a line and coloured floater to one of his rods. Yes, I say. Is the coloured floater there to attract the fish? '*Non, ma pauvre*. It's to locate the line in the water!' he laughs as he takes out a plastic plant-pot base filled with maggots from his box, two of which he attaches to the end of his line. He casts the line, hands me the rod and tells me to pull the line out as soon as the floater bobs beneath the water, affixing the pot of maggots firmly on to an iron rod next to me as he does so.

I sit beside the large open pot of bait and a squirming mass of yellow and pink maggots. Michel watches me watch them spill over the edge of the container, periodically dropping to the ground and writhing at my feet. They are coloured to attract the fish, he says. He used to produce his own, but Monique complained about the smell. 'You need a dead animal and a dead animal smells,' he explains. 'Now I just buy them and keep them in the fridge.' I look at the maggots and sympathise with Monique.

'Pull!' shouts Michel as my floater bobs under the water and I pull on the line with such force it jerks out of the water and flies high into the air. Attached to the end of the line is a small, silver fish. It pirouettes in the air like a bird as I try not to lose it in the branches of the overhanging acacia, panic at the reality of a live fish on the end of my line and adrenalin at having caught one washing over me simultaneously. '*Attends!*' shouts Michel as the line sways and the fish appears to fly through the air. 'Lower your rod!' and he catches the end of the line and the fish.

Only its tail moves as Michel holds its flashing silver body firmly in one hand. He gently unhooks its mouth, which opens and closes soundlessly as if to speak, from the line. Michel throws it into a bucket of water next to him where it swims around frantically, relieved to be free. An *ablette*, says Michel, a bleak. I am none the wiser. It looks like whitebait, but flatter and fatter. It's what we ate with our *apéritifs* the last time I was at his house for dinner, he tells me.

'*C'est parti*,' he says as he hands me back the rod with replacement maggots on the end. His own two lines have been cast and sit in their holders awaiting a passing fish. They are cast much further out than mine and stay where they are, whereas my line moves downriver rapidly with the current. I remove it periodically from the water and recast further upstream, trying not to catch the line in the trees or in his lines, the rods of which are only a metre away.

It is calm and still. The mist is disappearing from the river as the heat of the sun disperses it. I watch my floater for signs of bobbing on its journey downstream. As it reaches the sun's direct reflection on the water, I see nothing but dazzling light and a wide circular rainbow on the river's surface. Michel explains it's simply the sun's rays dispersed by the river. It's always there at this time of day, he says.

He rolls up a cigarette and lights it as we look out over the river. I stand at a safe distance from the maggots with my rod, Michel now seated next to them. An embroidered *sanglier* peers out from the hat on Michel's head, one of its feet resting on a felled tree trunk. '*C'est moins pénible que la chasse, n'est-ce pas?*' says Michel quietly, laughing. Birdsong is the only sound.

A small wooden fishing boat is moored next to us, waterlogged and bleached by the sun. Michel is going to fix it one of these days, he says. He'll take it into the middle of the river to fish for the bigger fish. Upriver another small boat is moored, belonging to his neighbour who fishes occasionally but is never here before 8 am. A shame for him, Michel says, as by 10 am it's all over and the fish stop biting. '*Ecoute*,' he says suddenly, pointing over to the trees on the other side of the river. 'Can you hear? The wood pigeons are singing.'

We sit by the edge of the river eating some of Michel's homemade *saucisson* with bread rubbed with garlic and coffee served in a small glass. He cuts the finger-thin *saucisson* into small chunks, handing some over the maggot dish to me. He and Monique had a problem with Arthur the pig the other day, he tells me. He escaped while they were both out. 'It's the rutting season,' he explains. Monique was not happy, he said, smiling guiltily. Arthur had run rampant first in the garden, then in the outhouse, upturning baskets of vegetables, boxes of seeds and lime flowers and causing general chaos. He had even made it to the kitchen tearing open bags of flour, before they returned.

My floater is bobbing beneath the surface as we speak and I pull, the line emerging sharply and flying into the air with another wriggling fish on the end of it. It's a gudgeon, says Michel. '*C'est bon, le goujon*,' he smiles. They are delicious to eat, full of taste. He points out its flashing green back and slim body before throwing it into the tub with the bleak.

Yes, says Michel when I ask him whether he managed to recapture Arthur. But it was difficult. Normally, he's gentle and malleable but the other day he was possessed. Another bob of the floater almost immediately and another fish is dancing on the end of my line. '*Dis-donc!*' says Michel, laughing. '*C'est le concours de pêche ici!*' as he removes another fish, a small carp. '*On a toutes les nations*,' he laughs gently as he throws it in with the others.

Both Michel's lines are straining. He leaps up and starts to reel one of them in. It tenses as he pulls it through the water. '*C'est un gros Gardonne!*' he exclaims as the form of a fish appears through the water. '*Non, c'est une brême.*' A large, flat bream, pale green and golden in colour, is drawn in. The other line has a carp on the end of it. 'Look,' he says as he pulls it in gently towards the shore.

The fish twists and turns, effectively catching the line on its fin. 'It's their defence,' he says. 'The more you pull, the more likely he is to be able to cut the line.' The fish, however, is not as adept at cutting the line with his fin as Michel is at drawing him in. Pulled out of the water, it has golden green scales and a sharp fin on its back. The bream caught earlier is on the ground next to us, beached and flapping occasionally. Michel picks it up and throws them both over to the small boat. They swirl around in the well of water in its base.

His lines are thrown back into the river as I pull out mine with a jerk, the floater having sunk again. The small fish on the end leaps into the air with the line that promptly wraps itself around one of Michel's in an instant. 'Oh, my God!' I shout, 'I'm so sorry!' '*Ça arrive*,' says Michel, laughing. 'But we're gonna be out of action for a while.' The fish is another bleak and has joined the fishes of all nations in the white bucket.

Patiently untangling my line from his, '*Ecoute!*' he says as we hear the distant shrill song of a bird. 'It's the song of the *faucon*.' I know them well as I see them often in the sky over Gageac. Small falcons, they hover and waver in mid-air above their prey. Gilles calls them '*les petits morpions*' as they *chasse* and kill the pigeons that he might otherwise hunt. They're not even worth eating, he once told me with disgust, as their flesh is too firm and dry.

Michel has given up on the hopeless task of untangling my line and has simply cut it. 'We'll start again,' he says. As he threads new line through the rod the sound of flapping wings makes us look up with a start. A swan is taking flight. Its wingspan is huge and we watch transfixed as it flaps across the water, the slow beating of its wings and the sound of wind under them echoing along the river, its wing tips touching the water fleetingly with each beat of its wings. The swan rises slowly and takes flight low over the river towards the bend, pools of ever-decreasing circles from the touch of its wing tips in the water witness to its passage.

We are back in business again and I have caught two more small fish. The floater bobs again beneath the surface and I pull, more gently than on my first attempts, in order not to wrap the line around one of Michel's. 'Pull!' says Michel as I heave on the line. 'It's heavy,' I say as I heave it in. '*Mon Dieu*,' says Michel, laughing quietly as my line drags in a large carp. '*Dis-donc, tu es douée!*'

Removing the line from its back and throwing it over to the small wooden boat with the others, he laughs and replaces more maggots on the end of my line.

Fewer small fish are taking my bait. Michel says that's because the bigger ones are heading downstream now and frightening the smaller ones away. Occasionally fish jump out of the water with a splash. Why do they do that, I ask. 'It amuses them!' laughs Michel. He has pulled in another bream and his line is tugging again. The carp on the end of it escapes, pulled in too quickly.

It's nine o'clock and we decide to call it a day. The river level is falling with the outgoing tide and Michel's neighbour has arrived further upstream. He waves from a distance as we gather up our belongings and head back up the bank.

If the blue rope was helpful in descending the steep bank on our arrival it is essential as we scramble back up. With gratitude I grasp and find each knot in it to heave myself up the bank. Michel is carrying the small fish in a bucket along with his tackle box. Ahead of me, stumbling and heaving, he sends soil and dust down the bank. I struggle to grab each knot with my left hand, my right carrying fish bait and rods, spluttering with the dust kicked up by Michel's passage back up the slope. We reach the top, breathless. 'At least it puts anybody else off,' he says, gasping for breath.

We sit on the ledge of Michel's van, recovering from the effort of the ascent. '*Qu'ils sont jolis, les petits goujons*,' he remarks gently as we look down into the fish bucket on the ground. The fish swim round and round the bucket. He lifts the *goujons* out of the water and we peer at their minute green and silver bodies, smaller still in his hands. He throws the fish back in the bucket, stands up and stretches, yawning. Yes, he says, it was relaxing and beautiful down by the river.

'*Zut!*' he exclaims, searching in vain for another bucket in the back of the van. '*Eh, beh!*' he says, removing the small fish from the bucket and temporarily housing them in the curry powder bait. He will need the bucket for some fresh water. He descends the bank again for the larger fish, more water and his fishing net. I look at the small fish left behind, arcs of silver and fluorescent green among the dark yellow mixture of the bait. They flounder, opening and closing their mouths, some of them taking small grains of the bait.

Michel reappears, breathless. He has fresh water in the bucket and the larger catch of fish in his net. They flap occasionally. He carefully lifts the small fish out of the curry powder bait and back into the fresh water. '*Oui, mes petits, vous êtes jolis*,' he says softly, then tips the large fish on top of them, closes the lid, puts them in the back of the van and we drive back down the bumpy lane to the sound of slopping water and an occasional flap as the fish flounder in the bucket. He will store the big fish in my pond over at Les Ruisseaux, he tells me. Then, when he needs some, he knows where to find them. As for the small fish . . . He looks at me. '*C'est la bonne friture pour ce soir!*' He roars with laughter.

<hr>

'Are you really making me Peking duck?' asked Fidde on the phone from Paris where he and Ekan were visiting the factory. Peking duck was his favourite and I had promised to make it for all four of us; a potentially rash promise as I'd never cooked if before. I started coating the duck with honey two days before and the morning of the dinner I made the pancakes to accompany it, buying a Chinese covered palm basket to store them in. Authentic aromas of cooked Peking duck permeated the kitchen as I cut it into thin pieces just before they arrived. '*Hej*, Patricia!' said Fidde, kissing me and smiling as he stepped into the kitchen with Pia and Ekan.

We ate as we caught up on our news. He and Ekan had decided to sell their factory in Paris, Fidde said. They were working hard preparing it for a good sale. And he had also made a decision to sell his golf club in Fribourg, to his members, he said, when they were ready. And he would come to live here permanently. He laughed a deep, resounding laugh when I showed surprise. 'Perhaps I'm running out of dynamism to be leaving Fribourg at last, Patricia!'

If his house wasn't finished soon, he might even rent somewhere here for the winter, he said. He looked at me. He hated leaving, loved being here, he continued. It would be a short but significant step towards his goal. And he could be around to push the builders along, cajole the architect, move things forward. Pia laughed knowingly. 'Even if you're *in situ*,' she said, filling another pancake and speaking with authority, 'not a lot changes, Fidde!' He laughed. 'Patricia! These are fantastic!' boomed Ekan, taking another pancake from the basket and filling it. 'Delicious,' said Pia. Fidde held up his glass, his eyes dark and sparkling. 'Thank you, Patricia' he said. '*Skol.*'

Days later, Pia and Ekan's eldest son, Peder, and his fiancée married in the small country church opposite my house. Although Saussignac, where Pia and Ekan lived, had a church, it didn't have the simplicity and beauty of Gageac's and although Peder and Susanna lived in London, they wanted the wedding here.

The service was as simple and beautiful as the church, decked with white flowers and candles. It was the first time Fidde had been inside it and he loved it. Two life-size wooden angels knelt at either side of the altar, with a statue of Our Lady to the right and one of Joan of Arc to the left. Wicker chairs lined the interior. 'It's such a quiet church. So simple — so beautiful,' he whispered as we waited for Peder and his bride to walk back down the aisle together after the service.

He looked around at the walls and the candelabra hanging from the ceiling. 'Why haven't I been in it before now?' he asked me. 'Why haven't you shown it to me before?' I looked around too, pleased that he found its simplicity and peacefulness as striking as I did. For me it was familiar, an integral part of my life. I often sat in it on my own, or simply wandered in for a few minutes to experience its coolness and calm in summer, or its comfort and peace in winter.

We watched as Peder and his bride walked past us down the aisle, past the flowers and candles and the large, wooden cross on the wall, their forms framed in light as it flooded in through the open door and they stepped outside. We left our places and followed them.

The wedding banquet held in the tower at Saussignac was magnificent and Swedish. Dark and creamy black mushroom soup was served as the entrée, the main course fillet of venison. My sweet wine accompanied the wedding cake and we drank champagne as we stood outside in the courtyard with the bride and groom. A fireworks display over the towers of the château in honour of their wedding lit up the black sky with fountains of light, shimmering and cascading down towards us.

Within two months, Fidde found a house to rent nearby. He moved in swiftly. '*Hej*, Patricia, I'm back!' he said on the phone. 'Are you free? You don't have far to drive, as you know . . .' The house was here in

Gageac. Situated on the top of the ridge, it had a view over towards the château, the church and my house. He opened the door with a flourish, laughed uproarously as I arrived. 'Welcome!' he said, sweeping me in.

The hall was crowded with boxes of belongings, along with some stereo equipment and as much as he had been able to fit in his car, having driven down with them from Fribourg. He was elated, happy to be one step nearer to his goal. On top of one of the cartons was a box of his cigars, each one in their tin holder, along with bars of dark, Swiss chocolate and pumpernickel bread. They looked so personal, so Fidde, much more so than even his clothes, hung on coat hangers and draped over the chair beside them.

We sat in front of the fire after dinner. He had returned from business in Fribourg, but only for tonight and tomorrow, he said. He had been to Stockholm beforehand and seen his sister, Agneta, who had decided to move back from the States and live permanently in Stockholm, where she had kept a house. Fidde was delighted with the news. He was also delighted with events at his golf club. He was moving nearer to a sale. Progress was painfully slow on his house here, which was a disappointment to him, but things would improve from now on, he felt sure. He smiled. 'And now I'm here, Patricia . . .' he said and roared with laughter again.

The following evening Pia and Ekan came to dinner too. 'Where are you, Patricia?' asked Fidde into the phone. 'We're waiting for you up here!' He laughed as he spoke. 'I've been saving dinner for you. Come as quickly as you can.' I rushed to shower, having spent the day working outside, cursing that I was still always late for everything, even Fidde. I guessed we'd be eating spaghetti bolognaise, which was something Fidde knew how to make and did so often. We ate golden caviar from Russia with cream and chopped-up hard-boiled eggs and drank aquavit and beer. '*Skol*, Patricia!' laughed Fidde.

———

'*Coucou!*' shouts Juliana as she bursts into my kitchen. She has brought with her some early raspberries just picked from her garden. I tell her of my fishing trip and the catch of all nations of fish that I am going to eat tonight at Michel and Monique's. '*La bonne friture!*' she shouts, bursting my eardrums. I don't really know why she shouts when there is only me in the kitchen. '*Ah, là!* They're wonderful as an *apéritif* with a glass of rosé or a *petit jaune!*' she bellows. She often cooked them dipped in flour and served like Michel when she lived in the Midi, before moving here to Gageac.

'*Et quoi de neuf?*' she asks, what's new? La Petite Venus rules their lives completely now, she says, laughing. Yves won't go shopping any more. The car's air conditioning has broken down so it will be far too hot for La Petite Venus. And the other day she was sick as Yves had given her titbits from the table, expressly forbidden by Madame de la Planche and not at all good for her. But at least Yves is now taking exercise, even if La Petite Venus isn't. She is mostly carried on Yves's shoulder. And at least Yves has taken an interest in the garden again.

The season is rushing on and we haven't yet planted our new vines. The young plants are ready and waiting for delivery and the land is prepared but the planting contractors can't fit us into their schedule for the moment. I remember as if it were yesterday the last planting four years ago. Two hectares of plants, one *parcelle* of merlot behind La Tabardy and the other near Madame Cholet's were pushed carefully into the ground on the last official day for planting. Gilles had exploded. '*Milledieux*! Why have they waited this long! They're making more work for you! You'll see! The plants will be desperate! You'll have to water them!'

A bulldozer passed through the *parcelles* beforehand to break up the bedrock that lay just below the surface of the soil. We gathered up trailer load after trailer load of huge boulders after the bulldozer had finished and each time we did so yet more appeared; there were mountains of them.

When the contracters arrived to plant the vines, it was in impossibly hot weather. There was no shade, simply barren expanses of land, heat reflecting from the white stones still embedded in the soil. They worked for three days, advising us as they left that the plants would have to be irrigated again in only two days time, and under their leaves rather than on them. It took what seemed like forever to irrigate, working in searing temperatures. The thought of doing so again is sobering.

Leaving the cover off the light above the kitchen door at La Tabardy seems to have resolved the problem of the owl with bowel problems. The starling population, if still evident, is less noisy. I guess that some have fled the nest and the rest must be well enough fed. The rabbits lope around periodically.

The tenants are now arrived at La Tabardy. The pool is sparkling and clear. They love the house, they say, they love rabbits too and show me a hole near the newly planted catalpa trees and the terrace. I nod. Yes, I say, rabbit holes are a problem. I peer down into it. A toad stares back at me, blinking. A family of them live over at Clos d'Yvigne, some of which are pretty big, but this one is enormous. It croaks, swelling out its body to even greater proportions.

Chapter 11

TODAY WE ARE PLANTING THE VINES. VINES PREFER STONY GROUND as it drains and warms up easily. And chalk in the soil to give a good bouquet to the wine. Clay in the soil gives alcohol, good colour, full body and tannins and the *parcelle* of land next to La Tabardy is stony, with chalk and clay. The tractor has finished levelling out the ground, now finely tilled. All that remains is to plant them.

The young plants have been delivered. Small tender green leaves sprout from their heads. Already woody, the young stems have a knob at their base where they have been grafted on to American root stock, essential since the outbreak of phylloxera in the 1870s. Thousands of them stand to attention next to the tasting room, each one in its own plastic pocket, grouped together in packs of ten.

They are quite extraordinary plants. They will take five years creating a root system before giving a harvest, and then only if they are carefully nurtured in the interim. If the first two summers are hot they will need regular watering. They will also need spraying in the same way as my adult vines do, and pruning each year. If the climate is right, they will flourish and eventually produce mature fruit and if the soil I have chosen for them is right, they will produce grapes of high quality. Thereafter they will go on giving me quality harvests for as long as they are cared for.

Benjamin and Alain are standing next to the contractors who have arrived with a lorry load of small wooden markers and a large machine that will measure, mark and guide the installation of them before planting the vines. '*Bonjour, Madame.*' The contractor shakes my hand, as do his team of eight men. Their hands are coarse and they are deeply tanned from a hot and dry planting season. They will plant the vines after the machines have bored the holes. '*On y va?*' and they unload both machines and markers.

We are a veritable crowd witnessing the beginning of another cycle of life in the vines. The tenants who are installed at La Tabardy have come out to watch and, in addition to Alain and Benjamin, Gilles and Michel are here. The contractors mark out rows with string, a machine guiding and measuring, ensuring that lines are straight, that markers are positioned properly, that holes are in the right place.

Gilles has his arms folded over his chest, nodding now and again or gesticulating, pointing out to the tenants where the lines will finish and what the contractors will do after having measured up the rows. They look at him, understanding nothing. Unconcerned, he gesticulates more forcefully and shouts more loudly, the better to make himself understood. I laugh, suddenly overcome by the absurdity of the situation. Gilles and Michel laugh too. 'Eh?' splutters Gilles laughing, looking at me and shrugging his shoulders then turning back to the tenants. They look at him in admiration.

The contractors work efficiently; men stride up and down the *parcelle*, measuring out and planting markers. Occasionally they stop and turn to shout out instructions or check on the distances between each marker. Slightly bemused by the crowd of onlookers, they look over now and again and talk among themselves, laughing. Our small crowd has grown into a larger one with the arrival of Juliana and Yves who have seen the lorry in the distance and come to investigate. La Petite Venus, a permanent fixture on the arm of Yves, is here too and Madame Briand, who just happened to be passing.

Even the artisans at Madame Cholet's stroll over to see the work in progress. A bevy of vans are crowded round the mulberry tree this morning and a huge digger is installing the *fosse septique* and drainage behind the house with plumbers, tilers, painters and electricians on site.

The young vine plants are dropped into the holes provided for them as we chat to each other. Gilles has great experience of all this, he tells the uncomprehending tenants in his booming voice, having planted more often than he can remember. He waves in the direction of the planters. They're not doing a bad job, he says, but he would do it slightly differently. Michel lent a hand replanting at Francis Queyrou's last week, he says. What with that and his vegetables, his back doesn't stand much of a chance at the moment. He and Gilles discuss vegetables and *chasse* and fishing as the workmen from Madame Cholet's wander back to their tasks.

One of them stops at the iron cross near Madame Cholet's and leans against its plinth. In animated conversation with the digger driver who stands nearby, he looks up at it now and again. The cross used to lean at an angle, dilapidated and uncared for, before I had it straightened. It may be a Compostela cross, a friend told me. He pointed out the scallop shell emblem on it that distinguishes it from other mission crosses, suggesting it may have marked part of a tributary path linking it to one of the four major Compostela routes through France.

The mission crosses marked the way for pilgrims en route to the cathedral at Santiago de Compostela where a tomb holding the relics of St James the Great, 'Santiago', are housed. For more than eight hundred years Christians have made pilgrimages there, many of them crossing the deep valley of the Dordogne.

Slowly everyone moves off. The tenants haven't had breakfast yet and Michel is heading to the pond to recover one of the bream he fished out of the Dordogne river. He and Gilles discuss wood pigeons and frogs as they climb into Michel's van. Juliana wants to see Madame Cholet's, she says. Have I time to show her? '*Ça m'intéresse aussi*,' adds Madame Briand. Could she come along too?

'*Oh, là!* What would Madame Cholet think?' exclaims Madame Briand as we stand in the large *salon*. She turns to look at me, her hand on her cheek. A small, thin woman in her eighties, she has flaming red hair that has the same frizzled style as that of Pamela Cholet's sister. '*Oh, là là!*' she repeats slowly, looking around the room and wandering into the kitchen area. '*Quel changement!*' She walks back towards us, looking up at the beams in the *salon* and over to the chimney which in Madame Cholet's day had a woodburning stove positioned in front of it and was largely hidden from view.

Her house is greatly changed. The ceiling beams, now painted, are lighter and the stone walls are clean and restful to the eye. The floor tiles, although yet to be treated, are laid throughout the house. The last time Madame Briand was in the house was a long time ago, she said. She and Madame Cholet had not been on speaking terms for many years. '*Oh, la pauvre*,' she sighs, referring to Madame Cholet and crossing herself, raising her eyes to heaven. She looks at us again then laughs, a jovial, tinkling laugh. Yes, she says, Madame Cholet would be greatly surprised at the change. I guess she would be greatly surprised to see Madame Briand in her house at all. La Petite Venus looks up at her from the floor, listening. She leaves a puddle on the tiles.

We walk back through the vines. Yes, says Juliana, La Petite Venus is indeed *très joueuse*. If I could see how she rushes up and down the stairs, how she steals socks, how she jumps on the sofa, which Chloë was never allowed to do. Madame Briand nods her head, red hair bobbing. She looks at the vines to the right and left of us as we walk back. Did I know, she asks me, that she and her husband used to own these vines many years ago? I didn't. Yes, she continues, they sold them to Monsieur Bellegrue.

Madame Briand no longer owns *parcelles* of vines, but *parcelles* of land. She has already sold one to Roland and Beatrice, owners of the hardware shop in Gardonne. It is near Les Bûchères, my *parcelle* of vines, with woods nearby where wild boar and deer reside, if Gilles is to be believed, and where my truffle tree is. I have not forgotten my truffle tree. Each time I visit Les Bûchères to inspect the vines there, I also inspect the tree and clear any undergrowth from around its base.

She has recently sold another *parcelle* next to her own house on which three new houses are to be built. Opinion is divided in the village on whether this is a good or a bad thing. Madame Briand herself is outraged as she sold the *parcelle* to someone who told her he was planning to build a solitary house on the land then promptly resold it for more money.

Madame Briand lives almost opposite Josianne, mother of Manu and secretary of the Mairie. Opinion is divided on her too. Voluptuous with large, dark eyes and a wide smile, she is treated with caution by most of the women in the village who worry vaguely about the safety of their husbands in her presence, and with admiration by the husbands in question who greatly enjoy their visits to the Mairie.

She is very unhappy about the recently sold *parcelle* of land as the new houses will be in full view of her own. I am unhappy about it too as I don't want the village to change. Gageac consists of three hundred or so inhabitants spread out over the ridge where

Jean de la Verrie's *vignes* lie and onwards towards Saussignac and Cunèges. The centre of the village is the church, Eida's field and the château. It is beautiful in its simplicity; a perfect rural village.

The church once had a large and beautiful presbytery. Geoffroy, the eldest son at the château and my friend, since gone, showed me photographs of it. It was magnificent with a mansard roof, a seventeenth-century staircase and ancient floor tiles. His grandmother wanted to buy it at the end of the war, he told me, to save it from falling down. It was already in a bad state of repair and was fast becoming a ruin. The *maire* had not refused to sell it to her, but suggested a price so astronomical that Geoffroy's grandmother, outraged, said it could fall down of its own accord, which it did. The staircase, the beautiful corner stones, the chimney and floor tiles disappeared mysteriously. Most of the remaining stones and rubble, according to Gilles, are now under the road in front of my house.

When I first moved into my house opposite the church, the only resident in its centre was Eida. Juliana's house was uninhabited and a ruin, the two small houses at the bottom of my garden were deserted and Geoffroy had not yet moved to the small house opposite the château. Now Juliana and Yves are installed, the houses at the bottom of the garden are inhabited and a new house has been constructed between the church and the cemetery, with another just up the road between my house and the Mairie. The new *maire* and his municipal councillors have new ideas, both for construction in the village and for revitalising it generally.

They and Geoffroy's youngest brother have given permission for a country festival to take place in the grounds of the château. Le Festival des Plouques will be held one evening in summer; two thousand or so people are expected. Opinion is divided on this too. Madame Briand is uncertain about having so many strangers in the village. Where will they all stay and what damage might be done to the *environs*, she is saying. What with that and the new houses to be built behind hers, the old order is changing rapidly and she's not sure she likes it.

Juliana says it serves her right. She refused to sell her land to the foreigners, owners of a large house nearby who wanted to buy it, simply to ensure that no houses were built there. In fact, I was interested for the same reason, but the price was too high. In any event, Juliana said, what will be will be. We walk along in silence for a minute. 'It usually is,' she adds, laughing and scooping La Petite Venus up from the ground where she is wilting with the heat and the effort of keeping up with us. '*Au revoir, Madame!*' says Madame Briand to me, jerking her head over towards La Tabardy and the planting team. '*Vous avez le travail maintenant!*'

Le travail we have at the moment in the vines, even without the newly planted ones, is keeping us pretty occupied. The wires are lifted and the *épamprage* is done, but the grass is high again between the vines. The vines themselves have grown considerably and now need trimming so that their energy can be directed into the fruit and not into clambering leaf and branch growth and so that the tractor can pass through the rows and spray against mildew. Some of the rows have already been trimmed. They look symmetrical and beautiful. Others look wild and rampant, their branches toppling over the top and middle wires of the canopies.

In the *chai*, the 2001 sweet wine tastes delicious. In oak barrels since its fermentation, it now has harmony between fruit and oak. The same is true of the 2001 reds. Firm and fruity, they now need to come out of oak before the tannins become astringent. Last year's barrelled dry white, the Cuvée Nicholas, has roundness and fruit and harmony. All three are ready for bottling

Madame Cholet's is behind schedule. In theory, the handover date from the architect is next Monday, but in reality it seems unlikely that either the architect or the artisans will be able to meet that date. Already, the plumber is behind. The mirror man can't install the mirrored walls until the bathroom sinks have been plumbed in and the electrician can't put the lights up until the mirror man has done his job.

The swimming-pool man announces that if we want a pool installed and running by mid-July he will have to put in the liner before the tiler lays the surrounds. We have given up on the tiler altogether, as there is no word from him. His answerphone is now blocked, probably from our daily calls to him. Mark, who did the building work at La Tabardy, has agreed to install the surrounds of the swimming pool.

He's also agreed to build a wall behind the house in order to hide the parked cars from future tenants at La Tabardy. And he's reluctantly, but with good heart, agreed to install the Ikea kitchen which he knows could drive a sane man to the edge of madness and which is sitting in boxes in the kitchen awaiting the Ikea installation team, who now can't come until the end of July.

The swimming-pool man is big. With a stomach of impressive proportions, one glass eye and large hands that feel like those of Gilou, a fat half-cigar hangs from his mouth. He puffs on it except when he has something to say. When he does have something to say and addresses me, I'm not sure if he's looking at me.

He and two of his workers have worked all day in the searing heat. They have drawn out the water stagnating over the last few months in the base of the cement hole and carefully laid in the hole a type of felt underlay which they soaked beforehand. Over it is draped the liner, attached firmly to the edges of the pool. They have spent at least half the day in the empty pool walking over the liner. Spreadeagled, they lay on its slopes smoothing out the liner with their hands and feet to remove the creases in it. Now a large industrial hoover with a pipe has been affixed to one end and is drawing out air from under the liner, drying the underfelt as the water fills up the pool.

The swimming-pool man is looking both at me and behind me and explaining that the hoover will stay on until the water in the pool reaches the level of the first step. He takes his cigar out of his mouth. This will take a day or so, he says. They have dispersed most of the creases and those that are still there will disappear within the hour as the weight of water increases. The liner will eventually fit perfectly into the form of the cement hole. If we could turn off the hoover once the water level reaches the first step and then call him, it will save him coming all the way back from Marmande, some seventy kilometres away, before it is necessary.

Marie, the daughter of some friends, is staying. She and I nod as we listen and look down into the immense pool. The expanse of white liner with mosaic edges gleams in the sun, as does the small amount of fresh water already in its base. The swimming-pool man puffs on his cigar and looks down into the pool too. '*Bon. On y va!*' he shouts and he and his team depart, doing a nine-point turn around Madame Cholet's tree with clouds of dust rising from the wheels of their lorry. The terrain there has just been levelled out, top-soiled and strewn with grass seed. Marie gasps and stares at me in horror as we look at the devastation left behind; there are huge ruts in the soil and most of the grass seed is embedded in the tyres departing down the road.

Situated on the top of the ridge at Monbazillac, the terrace at Le Moulin de Malfourat gives a spectacular panoramic view over the valley of Bergerac. Marie Rougier is the chef there and her husband, Paul, front of house. It's a hot, balmy evening and Marie, Odile and I are dining there. A summer haze hangs over the valley, the sky suffused with pink from the setting sun as we chat to Paul who has brought us the menu. He and his wife have just returned from Paris, he tells us. They had a wonderful weekend there; a welcome break for them before moving into the full summer season at the restaurant.

He has been cleaning his mushroom wood, he tells us, in

preparation for next season. During the autumn, the menu at Le Moulin often includes mushrooms gathered from his wood with wild *gibiers* caught by local *chasseurs*. I still remember the wood pigeon I ate there last season, served with *cèpes* and *morilles*. It was memorable, I tell him. He laughs. Yes, he says, there's nothing like locally caught wild game and nothing like the *cèpes* gathered from his own wood.

In a strange way, although he is far from being a rural peasant, Paul is not dissimilar to Gilles and Michel. I watch him as he talks to us, dressed smartly in a jacket and trousers, order pad in hand with enthusiasm for his private mushroom wood and his vegetable garden and the *gibiers* and the seasons bubbling out of him. Gathering mushrooms can become an obsession, he warns us; you must beware of it happening to you. 'You don't sleep if there's a possibility of gathering some in!' For the moment, we tell him, there's not much chance of that happening. He laughs.

All the same, he says, he has had to enclose his private wood against '*les obsèdes*', who scour it for mushrooms, especially his *cèpes*. And if they see mushrooms around the edges of his wood, he continues, in spite of the risk of being caught, they simply can't help themselves. They lift the wires and crawl under his fencing to gather them in. 'And they get there before you!' he exclaims, irritation on his face. 'They sell them these days.' Yes, he says with regret, it's now become a commerce instead of a pleasure. Or an obsession, I say.

'You jest,' he continues, 'but blood has been shed over them, I can assure you.' He has our attention. 'I promise you. I nearly did so myself! People guard their mushroom gathering areas jealously.' He looks around, then adds conspiratorially, 'If a car from another area is seen there, the first thing they do is to slash their tyres!'

Paul didn't slash anyone's tyres or shed anyone's blood. Two men came up to the Moulin, he recounts, to sell him *cèpes*. 'Do you know how much they cost, *les cèpes?*' he asks us. He bought fourteen kilos of newly gathered *cèpes* from them at great cost only to discover from a friend later that the *cèpes* in question had been gathered from his own wood. He glares at us. 'You can only imagine . . . !' he splutters. As a result he has fenced in his wood. Odile draws deeply on her cigarette and sips her *blanc cassis* as she listens. Marie gazes at him, wide-eyed. I commiserate. '*Je vous jure* . . .' he splutters. More customers arrive and he rushes off to welcome them.

We look out over the valley as we choose our meal. The view is spectacular, a huge panorama of undulating countryside with gentle slopes of vines, fruit orchards and houses dotting the landscape. The vines of Monbazillac, St-Laurent-des-Vignes and all villages up to and past Gageac are spread out in front of us. Bergerac can be seen in its centre, the spire of its church rising up out of the low-lying haze of the summer evening. We sip cool, crisp white wine with the gentle hum of conversation from neighbouring tables and the clink of glasses a pleasing backdrop to the view.

Odile, too, has been occupied all day with builders who have just finished pointing the wall in her *salon*. She's delighted with it. 'I'm attacking the bathroom tomorrow,' she says. Marie relates to her the story of the swimming pool. The plumber is behind with the bathrooms at Madame Cholet's, I tell her. At least the electrician will be there tomorrow and the tilers, too, to put a seal on the floor. Hopefully we can catch up on the work. '*Oh là!*' laughs Odile. '*Tu parles!* You'll never catch up. It's just not possible!' Marie looks over at me with large eyes and sympathy as I feel a sense of doom pervading the evening, the tranquillity of a moment ago gone.

In fact, only the electrician turns up the following morning. He is already at work when Marie and I arrive to check the pool. He had a slight problem, he said, with one of the rooms which had a live electrical wire but the problem is now resolved. The tiler will come at the end of the day as the sealant to coat the tiles needs a twelve-hour period with no one walking on it.

Even before we reach it, we can see great creases hanging like huge curtain swathes in the liner of the pool. We stare at it in horror. 'Quick!' says Marie. 'Ring the swimming-pool man!' I look at her, the pool and the electrician, who is also staring at it. '*Quoi?*' shouts the wife of the swimming-pool man down the phone. '*Ce n'est pas possible*! When he left everything was fine! Is the hoover still working?' Yes, we say. 'He'll be over straight away!'

'*Ce n'est pas possible!*' he bellows, when he arrives. Clouds of dust and seed rise up from the braking tyres, his lorry having driven over yesterday's newly resewn grass seed in front of the house. He looks down into the pool and yells '*Meeerdee!*' His voice echoes across it and back to us. We stare at him. We must have done something to it! he shouts. No, we say. The liner is probably ruined! he is shouting. They cost a fortune! he bellows. He throws his cigar on the ground as his men stand around, shifting their feet. He looks around wildly, shouting '*Merde! Merde!*' then directly at me and behind me simultaneously, fury in his face. Something must have happened! he shouts. A silence as he stares at me. Did we switch off the electricity?

We look at each other and the electrician, who looks back at me with fear and alarm in his eyes. The electrician is young, has only just begun his own business and probably hasn't sufficient insurance for such things and definitely switched off the electricity to rectify the problem of the live wire. The swimming-pool man is big, has a large and successful business and will definitely have cover insurance. '*Non!*' I say. 'But it was very thundery last night.' Marie looks at me in incomprehension. 'We often have electricity cuts when the weather is uncertain,' I say, looking up at a clear blue sky with nothing in it but an intense, bright sun. I feel my face burning as Marie stares at me with a mixture of astonishment and admiration. The electrician looks at me with something akin to love.

'Get in!' bellows the swimming-pool man to us, pointing at the pool. His men are already in, balancing themselves on the shelf halfway up and spreading their arms over the liner, pushing it up and out, already ironing out creases. Without a moment's hesitation, both Marie and I jump into the pool in our clothes and stand on the shelf. 'Push it back in with your feet!' he bellows and we do as we are told, shuffling the liner back on to the shelf. With short, hopping steps and facing the walls, we slowly chug round the circumference of the pool, hanging on to the edges with our fingers, heads bobbing over the edge of the pool.

Chapter 12

JULY, AND THE YOUNG PLANTS NEWLY INSTALLED NEXT TO LA Tabardy look small and vulnerable, dwarfed by tall sémillon vines on one side and merlot on the other. Benjamin is worried about them because of the heat, but more especially by the dryness. It is very dry. Gilles was right about getting the vines in as quickly as possible. They are looking parched and in need of water.

An impossibly hot morning and I have a long day in front of me. Driving along the D936 towards the furniture shops of Bordeaux, I mentally run through the list of requirements for Madame Cholet's house. I have all bedding, cutlery, crockery and glasses. I have no cupboards, no beds, no sofas, no seats, no tables, no carpets and no peace of mind. Serge, the antique dealer, has promised to keep an eye out for a good quality *armoire* for the *salon* and a table for the kitchen.

'*Bonjour, Madame Atkinson! Bienvenue!*' smiles the lady at the furniture shop. She remembers me well, she says, from last year. I smile weakly. Yes, I say, and I'm here on the same mission for another house. '*Aaah, bon!*' she smiles. We wander through the store as I buy lamps here, carpets there. Do I have outside chairs, she asks.

What about lavatory brushes? Had I thought of place mats? We move from floor to floor while my mind turns from Madame Cholet's to the bottling on Monday. Have I ordered enough labels? Will the corks arrive in time? Are the cartons long enough to hold the newer, elongated bottles we'll be using? Will I ever get through this weekend?

The contrast between the baking heat of Bordeaux with the insides of furniture shops and Georges and Christine's garden at Arcachon couldn't be greater. I feel transported to another place in another country in another time. White star-shaped clusters of gardenias hang over glossy green leaves, blowsy cream-coloured roses cascade down the trellissed walls of the house and great clumps of huge blue and pink hydrangeas surround the small swimming pool constructed in its centre. Exotic thornless cacti create form around it and the dark purple flowers of clematis 'Jackmanii' ramble along the tops of plants and spill over the roof of Georges's study built in a corner of the garden.

'Of course you'll get it finished in time!' says Georges as I recount my worries about Madame Cholet's house to him and Christine, his wife. He pours out a glass of cold rosé and we sip it next to the pool. We are sitting in low, luxurious fabric chairs around their swimming pool. Georges has run off from his computer some photos he took on our trip to the oyster beds. I look at images of Gilou working the oyster rows, of his boat, beauty and simplicity in pale rose and blue wood, and of Zaza standing next to me in the water. Gilou is well, he says. He saw him only this afternoon when he went to buy oysters for this evening. He said to say hello. '*Aux huîtres!*' he laughs, raising his glass. '*A Gilou!*' I reply. 'To Madame Cholet's!' says Christine.

The impression of having been transported to another time and place is reinforced as I drive back up the hill to Gageac at midnight. Transformed from a sleepy village to a seething metropolis, cars are parked everywhere I look, on both sides of the road as far as the eye can see. They are outside the church and among my rows of vines that now look like huge assembly lines for car-manufacturing plants rather than a vineyard. They are in my drive, surrounding the swimming pool, behind the *chai* and in my garden. They stretch up the road that Gilles helped lay as far as and beyond the Mairie. The Festival des Plouques is being held in the grounds of the château of Gageac. People from Gageac and the surrounding villages as well as hippies, festival-goers and Parisians are here.

I leave the car and walk down the road from my house to the château surrounded by loping teenagers, some in groups outside the church, others wandering down past Juliana and Yves's house. Smoke from roasting meat and barbecues hangs in the air. Opposite Geoffroy's and my house at the bottom of the garden a traditional gypsy caravan is parked, its apricot silk curtains drawn, flickering candlelight from inside sending soft light on to the hedge opposite. It looks surreal, magical. I approach the low wall of the château and enter another world for the third time in one evening.

White lights draped along it lead down to the immense sloping lawns of the château. Before me, six narrow nine-metre-long tables are crowded with people who look as though they have been transported from a Breughel painting to the grounds of the château. Some are leaning back on their chairs, some have their arms spread out and others are eating: all are animated. White tablecloths draped to the ground and stretching along the tables' lengths decked with plates of food and glasses look extraordinary against the backdrop of the château walls, accompanied by noise, laughter, music and coloured lights.

To the far right, fire belches into the air from three huge barbecues; one, a spit with a roasting wild boar, looks medieval cast against the black night sky. Hot ashes, red and white, dance in the air above them, the crackle of wood and the spitting and hissing of hot meat a backdrop to the two thousand or so people milling about on the lawns of the château who are dancing, laughing, interacting, partaking in a celebration.

High above them, along the immense back wall of the château, a singer lit up by light bellows, '*Ça va toujours, Gageac?*' through the microphone. '*Ouiiiii!*' responds the crowd. Coloured light floods over the group and the pale stone walls of the château. I follow the low wall to the gate and enter the grounds.

Inside and between the avenue of beech trees along the side entrance of the château, a round iron tyre rim hangs from a chain for children to play in or simply to bang on as a gong. Laughter echoes from a wooden childrens' windmill constructed nearby. They rush in and out of it and the tepees standing behind it, tumbling on the ground, running after each other, shouting with joy.

People loom in and out of the darkness, some with painted faces, ethereal and glowing. The stars in the night sky, coloured lights hanging along the path and trees that send strange flickering shadows on to their faces, add to the dream-like sensation of once again passing in and out of time.

'Patricia!' shouts a winemaking friend. He is playing next, he says, part of a jazz group. A neighbour's son smiles next to me and greets me with a kiss. '*Ça va?*' he asks. I walk down the slope towards the tables and the crowd. Around the wine kiosk I see my friend and neighbour Francis Queyrou who sold me the house at the bottom of the garden. He waves me over. He is delighted to see me here, he says. Why didn't I come earlier?

'*Salut*, Patricia!' shouts Michel, waving. He is basting the roast boar, his face lit up by the golden flames of the fire. A huge Catherine wheel bursts into sparkling, swirling light as I greet him. '*Torre de Fuego!*' shouts a Basque Espagnol standing next to me. He is small and thin with burnt brown skin, an angular face and thick black, curly hair. He wears yellow suede boots, shorts and a red shirt. A blanket wrapped around his torso is tied at his waist by a leather belt.

His burnt legs are sinuous and he looks nomadic and medieval, like a shepherd from another time or a pilgrim en route to Compostela. He laughs raucously, his face illuminated by the glow from the fire and raised upwards to the sky, his mouth open, two huge gaps in his teeth. He and his companion, a thin, tall man with a long white beard and a large beret, break into an ancient Basque song. They sing in harmony, one arm on the shoulder of the other.

Manu waves, wandering over to us. He is smiling, bashful, with his girlfriend on his arm. The Basque Espagnol sways now to the music being played by the group ranged in front of the vast wall of the château. It is futuristic music accompanied by red and blue strobes that flicker over the wall. The outside of the château presents its inscrutable face, solid and beautiful and awesome, the past and its secrets hidden in its walls.

The Basque Espagnol sings again as a man with a bare torso dances round like a whirling dervish with long torches of fire in his hands. A small crowd watches him. He is heat and light and movement, the past and the present. High above him the singer from the group has taken off his top and is also bare-chested. He ranges round and round like the man with the fire torches, the château walls a backdrop to his slow dance and the dull thud of electronic music.

Michel hands me some wild boar wrapped in a toasted baguette, melting cheese falling out of its sides. Francis hands me a glass of wine as the Basque Espagnol bursts into another Basque song with his friend, probably one as old as the château, harmony in their voices and ancient heritage manifest in their forms.

I wander round the grounds, walk back up to the château I know so well. Slipping along its flank and past the beech trees I open the grey side gate into its courtyard and close it behind me.

Inside it is virtually silent, peaceful, as I had guessed it would be. A feeling of history, of permanence, hangs in the night air. The pale grey stone of the château is almost translucent. Its towers stretch up towards an ink-black sky, a panoply of sparkling stars and the moon.

Benjamin, Francis and I taste the wines about to be bottled. The barrelled dry white has everything in it we would wish. It is fresh and alive, with well-balanced fruit and wood. The reds have concentration and fruit and the sweet wine tastes of honey and apricots with a liquorice finish. Francis is pleased with his barrels and Benjamin delighted to have the bottling day here.

The familiar clink of bottles hits our ears as the machines start up. They dance round the conveyor belt, empty one moment, full the next. The corking machine hisses gently as it releases a cork into a wine-filled bottle and the capsule machine thuds dully as it compresses the capsule over the cork. Huge rolls of self-adhesive labels swirl round, expelling labels on to bottles as they pass by. The bottles swirl too, dancing in a row like so many chorus girls as they disappear through the brush curtain that seals the labels firmly to each side of them, where they are finally whisked off the line by workers who stack them into cartons.

'*Salut!*' says Gilles, smiling and giving me a kiss in greeting as I stand in front of the bottling lorry. He has been to the frog pond, he says, and taken a look at the new plantation of vines on his way back. He watches the bottles dancing round the conveyor belt and shouts hello to two of the men he knows who are working on the lorry. '*Salut!*' he bellows and my eardrums vibrate again. Returning to the subject of the young vines, he nods, arms folded. They are well planted, he says, but they need water. We know they do, I tell him. Alain is filling the spraying machines with water as we speak. 'Not before time!' he shouts.

Gilles still takes a proprietorial interest in the vines and the property generally. 'Which spraying machine is he filling?' he bellows. 'The big one!' I shout. I'm not sure why I find myself shouting whenever I'm talking to either Gilles or Juliana. Gilles and I are in the kitchen now and the only noise apart from our voices comes from the bottling plant: a dull clink of bottles and the gentle hiss of the compressor. 'And who's going to water them?' he asks.

The watering of young plants is back-breaking work. Their leaves are still only three inches or so above the ground; watering underneath their leaves is the only way to avoid burning them. We will be a team of three, I tell Gilles. One to drive the tractor slowly through the rows and two, one on each row, to water each vine. Rods attached to long rubber hoses leading from the spraying machine will be directed underneath each plant. He nods. '*Bon!*' he shouts. '*Alors, bon courage!*' and he and the wet bag of frogs are gone.

We finish spraying the young plants with stiff backs and three shades darker in colour than we were before we started. The sun beat down relentlessly. At close quarters, and after working two long rows, they no longer seemed like millions of identical plants as they had when we started. Some vines seemed to be planted higher, some lower, some seemed to be growing much more quickly and all looked very different from each other.

I willed each one of them to establish root systems immediately. I willed the soil to give nothing to the vine, to aid it on its way down to greater and longer root structures, to penetrate deeper and deeper into the earth. And I willed them all to thrive and grow and be healthy and vigorous.

Walking back through the vines, exhausted after a long day, I pass Madame Cholet's without a second glance. The vines I walk through look gigantic after the young plants we have just been watering. Huge and healthy, their deep green leaves are enormous. Their flowering is over and the berries have closed in loose clusters; they will now start to grow and ripen. I look at them and calculate that we will be out in the vines by next week thinning out bunches. The idea of cutting off a potential harvest is always painful to me and I peer at them closely as I pass through. They must be cut off, I tell myself. For quality.

The few remaining loose bottles of Saussignac are slotted into cartons by the bottlers and the cartons sealed up. The roads leading to Gageac that have been closed for over two days because of the bottling will soon be open again. Two workers wash down the lorry, others roll up pipes and return them to the *chai*, transporting the last of the pallets to their resting home and piling up discarded cardboard and clingfilm for burning. Even with water running off the lorry and through the pipes, diluting the last dregs of sweet wine from them, aromas of honey and apricot pervade the air.

The new plantation of vines looks beautiful and well-nurtured. We have watered them again and now the leaves stand pertly up and outwards towards the sun like a battalion of well-drilled soldiers, their stems bare and erect. I walk through the rows, verifying that none of them have buckled with the heat or perished. The sun beats down on my head and shoulders and pricks the backs of my legs, concentrated heat; burning and relentless.

It is almost mid-July. I wake up to the sound of a million birds arguing outside my window. Each morning as I open the shutters and the sun rushes in, birds fly out of the virginia creeper surrounding them in their scores chirping and fluttering in the air, disturbed by the newly opened shutters. Eida's field is flooded with golden sunlight. She looks up at me expectantly from her habitual spot in the corner of her field. Juliana's voice echoes down the road; her shutters are opening too. *'Patriciiaaaa! Bonjour!'* I hear the insistent bark of La Petite Venus. *'Venus! Tais-toi!'*

This morning I am a driven woman, a woman on a mission. It's not good enough. Not good enough that there are no cupboards at Madame Cholet's. Not good enough that the furniture remains undelivered. Not good enough that I no longer sleep due to worry and stress about it. Two days of telephone calls, pleas and threats and Madame Cholet's house is suddenly bursting with objects. They are everywhere.

Beds sit in cartons on the floor. Huge component parts of sofas and chairs wrapped in cardboard and plastic film are stacked against walls. Bedside lamps and paintings join the sheets, towels and duvets on the bedroom floors and we are suddenly in a whirl of activity. Mark and his worker unwrap cartons of bed sections, bedside tables, chests of drawers and cupboards. Mark's wife and my secretary, Karen, and I cut away swathes of thick protective polystyrene and polythene from sofas and chairs. Benjamin and Alain tear off coverings of table lamps, carpets, teak tables and mirrors. We construct beds. We fill drawers. We unroll mattresses. We create a house.

Serge, the antique dealer, arrives with cupboards, tables and chairs. He looks around at the transformation. In spite of the mound of discarded cardboard and plastic film piled high in the centre of the *salon*, it is undoubtedly and indisputably a furnished house. Light floods in from the French doors and windows. The terracotta floor gleams. The kitchen shines. The mirrored bathrooms shimmer. Outside Benjamin and Alain unwrap sun beds and parasols, Mark and his worker fill pots with flowers, Karen and I plant beds with lavender and Michel plants six olive trees in the garden.

'*C'est quand même incroyable!*' says Odile, taking a nicotine fix as she stands in the *salon* at Madame Cholet's. She looks around at the pale walls, the gleaming terracotta floor, the large sofas and chairs, the glass table and the paintings. She walks through to the kitchen flooded with evening sunlight where the French windows are open on to the terrace and the swimming pool sparkles, prisms of light from it dazzling our eyes. She stands in the upstairs master bedroom and looks out at the spectacular view. She walks through the downstairs bedrooms and into the bathrooms with walk-in showers and mirrored walls. '*C'est quand même incroyable!*' she repeats. '*Bravo!*'

When Fidde eventually moved into his own house, it was only after high stress levels and endless missed deadlines by electricians, plumbers and deliverymen. Renting a house here hadn't been particularly useful as far as being on site for builders and architects was concerned, as most of his time was still spent away on business, either in Paris, Fribourg or further afield. Furniture arrived from Sweden and Fribourg as well as America some time in advance of the house being finished.

Agneta had decided to use the small *pigeonnier* in the courtyard as a retreat for her trips to France. Her furniture joined the growing pile of possessions stored in the large barn attached to the house. It was rapidly filling up as deadlines passed and time moved on. Cartons of valuable wines sent from Fidde's cellar in Fribourg were stored in my *dépôt de stockage* rather than in the barn.

During the summer his sister, Regina, and her husband, Christian, along with two friends; called by to see the house. I took them over and we walked around it, wandering through room after room, each one in a partly finished stage. Large cartons holding sinks and bidets for bathrooms sat awaiting plumbers and cumbersome reels of electric wire were piled up forlornly in corners while yet more deadlines passed.

Fidde's happiness when he did move in was palpable. It leapt out of him, spread over all of us. 'Patricia! *Hej!*' he shouted as he arrived at my house with Ekan to take some of his wine over to the newly finished cellar. He was bursting with energy, exhilarated, elated. He would only take some of the wine for the moment and leave the rest until later, he said. He kissed me, holding my hands in his. 'Can you come to dinner tonight?' he asked. 'I'll be cooking for you myself so you may want to refuse!'

'Come in, Patricia!' he shouted as I arrived at the door, taking my hand dramatically as I stepped over the kitchen doorstep and sweeping me inside with a swirl. 'My house,' he said, laughing. Delighted to see me, to show me the finished project, he watched my reaction as we moved from room to room.

It was exquisite; simple and elegant. The *salon* was large and inviting. A sofa and chairs surrounded a glass table in front of the large chimney, a fire burning in its grate. Behind the sofa was an old oak chest from Sweden. The dining table in the far right-hand corner was already laid for two with pewter plates and large white napkins. The cutlery shone and the glasses sparkled against the polished mahogany wood.

On the wall near the table were paintings of his ancestors, one of the oldest families in Sweden. At the other end a large, modern painting, striking and strangely in keeping with the ancient walls of the house, contrasted with a rich, deeply coloured carpet spread out on the terracotta tiles beneath it. A door next to the painting led to the hall and the wood-burning stove set into the wall and to his office, painted dark green and already equipped with his computer.

He smiled at me, pleased with my reaction. 'I've been working hard here!' he said with a self-deprecating laugh.

The kitchen was plain and functional. He would change it soon, he said. A large oven and hob was already on order and he had plans for the rest of the room. The hallway, equipped with cupboards already neatly filled with towels, sheets and blankets, led to a huge bathroom, then on to Fidde's bedroom at the far end of the house, large and spacious. A sideboard there was already dressed with silver-framed photos of Ebba, her small son, Fredric, Gustaf and the rest of his family. Upstairs was a drawing room with bathroom and bedrooms earmarked for future visits from his children and his first grandchild.

'It's wonderful,' I said, astonished at the speed with which he had transformed the house after the builders had moved out. 'I'm so glad you like it,' he laughed, putting his arm around my shoulder as we walked back towards the *salon*. I felt his contentment, his happiness. 'Come, let's have a drink.'

We drank an *apéritif*, looking out on to the sloping lawn that led down to the poplars and the river that sparkled through the trees, light dancing along its surface.

Chapter 13

'*QUAND MÊME! BRAVO!*' SAYS JEAN FROM l'IMPARFAIT. HE IS HERE
with Philippe, his chef. The tenants at La Tabardy want to give
a dinner for sixteen on the large terrace there and l'Imparfait will
be providing the meal. They look around the house, inspect the
kitchen and terrace. 'You know, you'd think the English had
never lost France!' Jean shouts to Philippe, laughing and looking
around.

He turns to me. 'We'll provide the tablecloths, the candelabra,
the crockery, the cutlery, the food and the ambiance.' He chuckles.
'*Et voilà, notre patrimoine!*' he pronounces loudly, nodding his head
and gesturing dramatically at the house and its surrounds with
his arms open. 'No, seriously,' he adds. 'You've restored part of
France's heritage that would otherwise be lost.' We stand in the
salon. 'This will be here long after you and I are gone – and it's
magnificent. *Bravo.*'

The grapes are growing. Their small green nodules are
swelling out to grape size. They look healthy and clean. We have
sprayed infrequently this year thanks to the good weather and
so far we are free of any diseases on them. The same is true of

Michel's vegetables. A basket of new potatoes, spring onions, cucumbers and tomatoes has been left outside my door. They look as healthy as my grapes. I bite into one of the tomatoes. It is sweet and rich. I cut a slice of cucumber. It is crunchy, fresh and juicy.

Sales from the *chai* door take a leap forward with the arrival of holidaymakers. They park their cars around the church and up the side road of Clos d'Yvigne. Some are return visitors, others new. Many of them have tasted the wine already at either the Moulin de Malfourat or l'Imparfait and been sent on direct to the source by Paul and Jean.

Sometimes they come with children, sometimes with other groups. They taste the wines with me. I put my nose into the glass as they do and describe what I find in each wine. Citrus fruits and flowers in the whites, raspberries and strawberries in the rosé, cherry and rich, ripe fruits in the reds and honey, apricot and liquorice in the sweet.

Occasionally I take them into the vines to show them the grapes. I explain how the vine wakes up from its winter dormancy. How the buds begin to swell. How I worry about frost burning their clusters of delicate leaves when the bud breaks. How we spray the vines against mildew, oidium and other maladies.

How the vine flowers. How the fruit sets. How the shoots are trained on to the wires. How we cut off the shoots growing at ground level to ensure all the goodness goes into the vine. How the vegetation is trimmed back so that all the goodness goes into the grape and not in leaf growth. How we cut off and thin out bunches in order to limit the final crop and concentrate what's left. How the colour change takes place. How we need an abundance of sun to ripen the fruit. How we love and care for and protect them.

As I explain, they peer at the grapes. They touch the leaves. They marvel at the cycle of growth. They commiserate at the hard work. They are engrossed and it's a delight to me that they find wines and vines as fascinating as I do.

'*Coucou! Patriiciiaaaaa!*' yells Juliana as she opens the kitchen door and bursts in, a large dish of *pistou* in her hand. She hands it over with a kiss. It looks dark and rich, the tantalising smell of basil, garlic and olive oil reaching my nostrils as she takes its clingfilm cover off. '*Quoi de neuf?*' she booms. Madame Cholet's house looks wonderful, she says. She was over there this morning. '*Chapeau!*' she congratulates me.

The first tenants are installed, the finishing touches completed only twenty minutes before their arrival. I took them over. They walked in and murmured in appreciation. I watched their reaction with delight and relief. It looked very beautiful. Flooded with light, the *salon* was cool and elegant with its graceful limed beams. The children with them rushed in and out of bedrooms and into bathrooms, then through the kitchen and out towards the swimming pool, squealing with delight.

Juliana's *pistou* tastes as delicious as it smells. Bruno and Claudie are here for dinner. They have bottled their first Pomerol vintage and brought a sample along to drink with our meal. They bought their half-hectare of vines in Pomerol nearly two years ago now. Their *vendange* was a small one with the picking over in less than two hours and no one other than themselves needed to pick it.

Bruno and Claudie, Benjamin and I heaved and pushed the small *pressoir* that I use for my sweet wine into a hired van a few weeks after their harvest. We wedged it between a radiator, some plastic sheeting, a small stainless steel vat and four barrels, prerequisites for their vinification. They pressed the grapes, housing the juice in the stainless steel vat for the first fermentation, in barrels for the second. To keep the temperature warm and constant, they stood a radiator next to them and encircled plastic sheeting around both. It aged '*en toute tranquillité*', as Claudie put it, until it was bottled.

We sit in the garden catching up with our lives since we last saw each other as the sun sets. The sky, streaked with gold and saffron, turns magenta as a magnificent red orb slips down behind the château and the trees. It is hot and sultry. They are just returned from their vineyard in Pomerol where they have been working in the vines.

They know the road to and from there like the backs of their hands now, they say, trips back and forth time-consuming but obligatory. We open the bottle of Pomerol with our meal. Two years ago, when the second fermentation of it was over, we went to pick up the press and taste the wine together. Then it already had aromas of violets and ripe fruit. It has developed since and is now suave, wooded, with round and velvet tannins and the voluptuous taste of ripe cherries and fruit.

———

Fidde had no sense of smell at all, he once told me. I was astonished. He loved Pomerols, Médocs and Bordeaux wines in general. How could he tell the difference, I asked him, between the rich plumminess of Pomerol, the fullness and denseness of Pauillac and the softness, delicacy and elegance of Margaux? We were sitting in front of the fire at his house, drinking a bottle of Vieux Château Certan from Pomerol, rich and velvety with a concentration of fruit. 'In my teeth!' he laughed.

He was back for a few days from Paris. It had been cold in the city, he said, and the factory was depressing. We moved into the kitchen with our glasses of wine. Fidde was cooking spaghetti bolognaise for supper. Lifting up strands of spaghetti from the pan with a fork and with steam rising from the boiling water, he turned his head towards me. 'I'm testing it,' he said. 'There's a right and a wrong way to do this, you know ...' It was just about the only dish he could cook, I told him, and he ought to be good at it, the number of times he had made it for us. He laughed softly. 'Well, I'm also good at Swedish meatballs,' he said, 'and frozen Swedish potatoes from Ikea ... as you know.'

He smiled, chuckling, peering into the simmering pan of bolognaise. He leant over it, feet together and standing slightly too far away from the hob; more a golf stance than a comfortable cooking position. Wearing a striped apron over his corduroy trousers and jumper, he looked the part. He was happy to be back. As he cooked, we ate small rounds of dark pumpernickel bread and Gruyère that he brought back with him periodically from Switzerland.

He was still having some difficulties with the architect here, he said. Although the house was finished, there were small faults that needed rectifying. The wood-burning stove in the entrance hall wasn't functioning properly. It was a nuisance. He was hardly here at the moment and hadn't the time to chase the plumber himself. In fact, he hadn't a moment to himself, he said, what with the business in Paris and his golf course in Switzerland.

'You know, Patricia' he said suddenly, turning to me. 'It's only by not stopping, never looking back, being determined, that you've achieved what you have in your vineyard.' His eyes were serious, questioning. 'It's a great achievement.' I looked back at him. 'Do you ever stop and consider where you are now? Where you are going?' he asked.

I could feel again the still atmosphere of his car that summer evening on the way back from Bergerac. Weightless, motionless, a silence enveloped us. The fleeting shadow of a cat passed by the door outside. Fidde looked vulnerable standing there, this time his dark eyes finding in me a mirror image of himself.

Frozen in time, there was no sound. Unnerved, he turned towards the bubbling pan and our dinner. 'I feel it's time for us now,' he said, breaking the silence. Life crowded back into the kitchen; the hiss of the gas hob, the ticking of the clock above it. 'Let's eat,' he said, laughing gently.

<hr>

Hot days follow sultry evenings and we are almost at the end of July. Eida looks up at me each morning as I open the shutters, her field aglow with morning sun. Juliana bellows her greeting down the road and La Petite Venus barks. This morning as I gaze from my bedroom window past Juliana's house, one of the tower rooftops of the château has sunlight glinting on its tiles, splashes of rich brown and terracotta reflecting back at me. The cypress trees in the cemetery look peaceful, dark and brooding, already with a summer haze hanging over them.

The grapes are plumping out and changing colour. It is fascinating to see. The white grapes are no longer sharp bright green, but a delicate and honeyed green, slightly translucent. On the outer edges of the red bunches, one or two of the grapes have changed colour to mauve or pale rose red. Occasionally the middle of the bunch changes colour with the outer grapes still green. Within a few weeks, they will all be a uniformly dark, rich purple, then black.

'Milledieux! C'est la canicule!' bellows Gilles as he pulls from his head the old cloth cap that inevitably accompanies him in summer. It is too small for his head. He has worn it ever since I have known him. Frayed and faded now, it protects his crown from the sun. He closes the kitchen door against the hot rays of the sun that send a path of light and heat across the floor. Yes, he'll have a cup of coffee.

'*Milledieux!*' he repeats as he sits down. He is wearing his faded black espadrilles, shorts and a T-shirt. '*Quand est-ce que les filles arrivent?*' he asks, referring to Amy and Beth, who are always here in summer, usually on days such as this. They adore Gilles as he does them. One of my overriding memories of spraying the vines in the early days of my life here is of Gilles and the girls. Gilles had come to help attach the spraying machine on to the back of the tractor and stayed to check that the nodules on it were operating as they should. Turning at the top of a row and working down the next, I saw Gilles's form in the distance, watching from the bottom of the row with Amy and Beth beside him. They were looking up towards the tractor and me, one on each side of Gilles, each with a small hand enveloped in his large working hands.

He's finished his wall at last, he tells me. He's hoping it will deaden some of the noise from the tractors that beat their way to the Cave Co-operative next to his house during the *vendange*. They roll up day and night, he complains. It was something he hadn't considered when he bought the house. Does he regret buying it now, I ask him. Does he regret leaving La Tabardy? '*Milledieux, non!*' he laughs. Noise of the tractors apart, he likes living there. And it's right next to the main post office where Pamela works. He has a life there now, he says. He's often in the Cave Co-operative during the *vendange* to see what they're doing.

The *vendange* will soon be upon us, he says. The grapes are plumping out. The colours are changing on the reds, he noticed the other day when he was walking through my vines. Does he miss the vines, I ask him. He often turns up during my *vendange* when we're tipping grapes from the trailer into the de-stalker. Or

241

when we're picking noble rot. A bit, he says, but not the hard work involved. And certainly not the *fonctionnaires*. With all the new forms to fill in and the complications the *fonctionnaires* put in the way of a man who's simply trying to make a living, it's no longer worth it.

I understand Gilles's frustration with 'les *fonctionnaires*'. They require precise details of each winemaker's area of production, grape varieties and quantity of yield for each harvest. As well as declarations of stocks and yields in the *chai* or in the *dépôt de stockage* at any one time. And before the wine can reach a bottle at all, it must pass its '*labelle*', a quality control which gives it the right to be listed under an *appellation*.

Things started going wrong only when we let the *fonctionnaires* rule our lives, he is saying. They've taken our lives away. Not all that long ago, as late as 1976, his father didn't even have to have a *labelle* for his wine, he tells me. I'm surprised to hear this. I had assumed it was obligatory since the *appellation contrôlée* institute came into being in the mid-1930s.

'*Non*,' he insists. In 1976 you didn't need one. Life was different then. 'In those days,' he says, 'we didn't even know what the *malo* was!' The *malo* is the second fermentation of the red grapes, essential to the stability of the wine. *Malos* take precedence in my mind as a major stress factor. During the vinification of the harvest, everyone who makes wine worries about every vat until each has finished its *malo-lactic* fermentation. Even after fourteen years, the worry is as fresh as ever. 'We picked it all!' he is saying. 'Sweet, dry, red; we threw it in vats, made it and sold it!' He looks at me. 'The *malo* did itself! *Je te jure!*'

The sound of Alain on the tractor spraying the vines and turning at the end of a row can be heard on the air. He gesticulates with his thumb in the direction of the noise. 'And we didn't put anything on the vines either, apart from copper and lime — and that we did by hand. Treatments didn't exist!'

He is warming to the subject. The grapes were clean. They didn't rot when it rained. There were no maladies on them. They only had natural products. No fertiliser; only cow dung. It was clean and healthy . . . 'and the wine was good!' he shouts. 'There was no *labelle*. The wine was bought by quality then, by a *négociant*. If the wine was good he bought it and if it wasn't, he didn't.' How different it is now, I say. '*Milledieux!*' he shouts. 'Once they introduced the *labelle*, *c'était la bordelle!*'

For his marriage in 1966, he says, his parents opened an old barrel of sweet wine from 1929. It wasn't filtered. Wasn't clarified. It was black in colour, like oil, he said. During the feast they drank only that and it was delicious.

After his marriage, he moved into La Tabardy and his parents moved into Madame Cholet's. They had chickens, geese and two pigs for the year, one for his parents and one for him. The pigs were fattened on chestnuts, cabbage leaves, beetroot and potatoes; they were stuffed, like his geese. He worked eighteen hours a day in those days, he said.

'You worked ten times harder then – that's why our generation is half-dead.' I look at him. He lights a cigarette and looks back at me. 'At fourteen I had a *hotte* on my back,' he says. A *hotte* is a large, elongated bucket strapped on the back of one of the *vendangeurs* at harvest time. Pickers empty their grape baskets into it. With every basket of grapes and resultant weight increase, the straps cut into your shoulders and back. When full, the contents of the *hotte*, still on the carrier's back, are tipped into a trailer, stretching his back muscles and twisting his arms. The process is repeated until the end of the working day. In Gilles's childhood it wasn't a trailer but a handcart they were emptied into, pulled by his parents' cows.

'With bare feet,' he continued. 'We pressed all night, got to bed at 2 am and had to be up again at 5 am to milk the cows . . . only three or four hours' sleep during the *vendange* . . . you had to be there. It had to be done and you had to do it.' A pause. 'But you ate well,' he said. '*Milledieux!*' He smiled. 'It was in your interest to eat because you worked!' He looks at me earnestly. 'Today's kids couldn't do it. If they worked like we did for only two weeks, they'd all be dead!'

We laugh. 'It's true!' he bellows. As soon as they could, all the young people left for town, so hard was life in the country. 'Who's left here from my epoch?' he asks, then answers for me. 'Only Jean-Lis and me.' He is no longer smiling. '*Non*, I didn't have a *vie en rose* as a child. I had to work. I wasn't paid by my parents and I had no money.' He looks at me. 'One day a week I could work for someone else for a bit of pocket money, but only once the *vendange* was over because during the *vendange* they needed me day and night . . .' He pauses, looking down at his feet, remembering his childhood. 'I used to work at my aunt's who lived nearby in Lamonzie St Martin . . .' He fiddles with the rim of his hat on the table. '. . . she paid me four francs.'

'In summer there used to be summer balls here on the village green with an *orchestre*.' He laughs. 'An accordion and a trumpet . . . on the grass around the church.' He gesticulates with his thumb towards the church. 'Saussignac one Sunday, Gageac or Monestier the next . . . My pocket money paid for the *fête* but I had no money for a drink. The La Grange kids went to the dance and could buy a drink as well. Their parents gave them some *sous* . . . same with everyone else.' He smiles. 'I would go along after I'd milked the cows and just dance.' A silence. 'Yes, I had a strange youth . . . I've always worked. My mother worked and she expected me to work.'

'When I was sixteen I got a *permis de chasse*. I worked to buy my own gun – one season of harvesting to buy it.' A silence. 'My pleasure was to *chasse* on my own every Sunday.' He looks down at the floor. 'Yes, it was a real pleasure for me to *chasse*.' He looks at me. 'I was free – I was on my own, no one to shout at me, no work, silence.' I feel inadequate and humbled. I look back at him, words insufficient. 'I had silence there,' he said. 'I could relax and roam the countryside.'

I don't know what to say. It often happens when Gilles recounts stories of his childhood. He was the oldest of two boys. It was decided that he would stay and work the land while his brother went to school, trained to be a tiler and, unlike Gilles, earned money. Gilles started his vines with two cows and a plough. He looks at me. 'Honestly, I wouldn't do it again . . . I was the oldest and it was just decided that I would work the land. My brother did other things; he escaped.'

'When I was called up for the army, my friends came round to take me to the *fête* the night before; it was a Sunday. I couldn't go — wasn't allowed to.' He laughs dismissively. 'My mother told them so, then sent me to bed so that I would be *en forme* for the army.' He looks at me and laughs again. '*En forme* for the army!' he repeats, rubbing his hand over his hair. 'Yes, for other people the army was hard. For me it was a real holiday, a piece of cake.' He stands to leave. 'My youth was hard,' he says, shrugging his shoulders and smiling weakly. 'But that's what it was like in those days.' And with a kiss he's gone.

Fidde elected for national service in Sweden as a young man. He spent two and a half years in the cavalry regiment stationed in Umea, ten hours' drive from Stockholm in the far north of the country, he told me. He had inherited his father's love of horses, rode whenever he could and chose the cavalry for that reason. And he chose Umea because he loved cross-country riding. His regiment spent weeks up in the mountains in mid-winter with their horses on training manoeuvres.

I was surprised there was still a cavalry regiment, I

said. 'Yes, it was a bit outdated even then,' he said. 'Horses rather than tanks. But I enjoyed it. And as well as having the freedom of the land you got to wear nice old-fashioned uniforms that you looked good in!' He laughed, mocking himself.

We were sitting in his *salon* in front of the fire that sent out gentle heat, flames licking the logs that Fidde had just added. On the chair opposite us was a small white kitten sitting on a yellow blanket. She looked at us calmly, her front paws crossed. A feral cat, thin and long with a tabby tail, she had arrived at Fidde's door a few months before. 'She won't go away, Patricia!' he had said on the phone. 'Each time I open the door she comes in . . . and I don't even like cats!' She didn't go away and when Fidde did, he rang me daily to find out how she was, whether she was still there, whether she was taking the food he had left for her in the barn next to the house. He christened her Missy and he loved her. 'Of course, I don't let her in the bedroom,' he said. 'She's not allowed anywhere near the bed.' She looked at us as we discussed her.

He had returned from a trip to Paris, Fribourg and his golf club, but only for two days. Various hitches in both businesses were causing him stress. 'I'm waiting,' he said with a sigh. 'Waiting to sell the businesses and live here. Waiting to live a proper life.' He looked at me sideways, humour in his eyes. 'As you know,' he said, smiling, 'I'm a patient man.'

We looked at the flaming logs, basking in the gentle heat given out by them. 'Your friends Gilles and Michel, Patricia . . .' he said. 'They don't know it, but they're rich – Juliana too. They have real values.' I agreed with him. 'They have the freedom of the land,' he said. 'But they don't ride around in the mountains on beautiful horses wearing old-fashioned uniforms,' I said. We laughed uncontrollably.

Fidde left the following day for more meetings in Switzerland and Paris as I headed into another *vendange*. On each of his subsequent visits there was both a pick and pressing of grapes and the vinification of them in the *chai* that took me well into the night, with people installed in the house for the duration of the *vendange*. His visits were brief. Occasionally he came to eat with us.

'Patricia!' he said on one of his phone calls from Switzerland. 'I never get to see you on your own now. It's not good enough!' It was true, but the sale of his golf course was proceeding, along with the sale of his and Ekan's business in Paris, both of which were taking up almost every second of his time. As was my *vendange* for me. Neither of us had time for anything. He hardly knew himself when he might be back and when he was it was only for a day and a night, or sometimes not even that.

'You know, Patricia,' he said on another of his calls, 'it's not good enough. You're surrounding yourself with those *vendangeurs*.' He laughed gently into the phone. 'And they're the wrong men, Patricia. Why doesn't someone make a smart decision round here? You need me!' I threw back my head and laughed. He made me laugh with his mock arrogance, with his sense of humour. He understood things at a primal level, which made his honesty refreshing and direct. He made me respect him with his sincerity, made me look into myself and understand myself with his own honesty. 'I'll be back soon,' he laughed. 'I'll call you.'

He did. He called me one evening as Odile and

Christianne were celebrating my birthday with me. Odile had brought a home-made birthday cake with her and Christianne their joint present. 'But I've got your birthday present here,' he said on the phone. 'I'm just arrived.'

'No, I don't want to see you with other people,' he replied when I suggested he join us for dinner. We hadn't seen each other on our own for some time and this seemed like yet another opportunity lost. Even more frustrating, I had committed myself weeks ago to a dinner the following evening that I simply couldn't cancel.

'No, I don't want to sit with people I don't know tomorrow. I want to see you,' he said, disappointment in his voice. 'And I'm leaving early the following morning.' I felt sad and frustrated. Sad not to see him and stung by his unspoken resentment. And frustrated not to have known until that moment that he was back. I had almost to pass by his house on my way back from dinner the following evening, I told him. 'If it's not too late, I'll call by on my way home,' I said.

'*Coucou!*' bellows Juliana as she bursts through the kitchen door. '*Alors*, what a beautiful day!' she shouts. '*Mais, ah là là, les tomates cette année*,' the tomatoes this year! 'I've stuffed them, I've cooked them, I've made purées with them and they keep on coming. Do you want some sun-dried tomatoes, Patricia?' She deposits La Petite Venus on the floor. She turns towards Gilles who has called for some wine and is rising to leave. '*Non!*' she bellows. '*Assieds-toi!*' and he sits back down again.

'Have you picked any mushrooms yet?' There is an interrogatory tone in her voice. She fixes Gilles with an intense look then turns to me. 'He knows where to find *cèpes* and *chanterelles* here, don't you, Gilles?' and she winks, laughing raucously. Most of the locals and all the *chasseurs* are mushroom pickers. Competition is keen, with no one keener than Juliana. In fact, no one knows better where mushrooms are to be found than her.

'Over in the woods at Les Bûchères or Les Ruisseaux, *peut-être?*' she asks him. 'He wouldn't tell me anyway!' she pronounces, her eyes narrowing. A silence, then Gilles laughs. 'Well, if I told you, it wouldn't be a secret!' he booms, lighting a cigarette and rising to leave again. '*Attends*,' she shouts as he reaches the door. She rummages among the sorrel leaves in her basket and extracts a large, plastic bag. Picking it out with a flourish she walks back to the table and empties the contents of the bag on to it. '*Eh voilà!*' she says as a cascade of coral-coloured mushrooms tumble on to the table.

'*Mon Dieu! Les chanterelles!* That's early!' exclaims Gilles. '*Mais non!*' she replies nonchalantly. '*Les chanterelles* are often around in summer. You just have to look harder for them.' She looks at me and winks, turning back to him. 'Don't tell me you don't know that?' She scoops some of them up from the table and into the bag, handing it to Gilles. '*Avec mes compliments*,' she says, laughing as he kisses us goodbye. With a '*Salut*' he is gone. 'He knows perfectly well where to find them!' she laughs. 'Just like Michel!'

Michel and Juliana have a mutual respect for each other. He will almost certainly have gathered in some *chanterelles* and probably a few *cèpes* too. His secret places remain so, providing him and a small coterie of his lucky friends with annual feasts of fresh, firm mushrooms of all descriptions. *Chanterelles, cèpes, trompettes de la mort* and *pleurottes* are only some of the varieties I have sampled from his mushroom forages. They are usually deposited outside my door in a plastic bag hung on the door handle, awaiting my return from the vines or the *chai*.

Juliana has been mushroom hunting since dawn, she says. The

forest was singing again. '*C'est beau, la fôret!*' she says. 'Often I think there's someone behind me. But no, it's the sound of *la nature*. The sound of the forest awakening.' She looks at me with excitement, a smile on her lips, her eyebrows raised.

Les champignons emerge with the first light and the morning mist, she tells me. Leaves on the ground appear to swell before her eyes, then fall away revealing mushroom heads that gleam, almost translucent in the first rays of the day. This morning, she says, the first mushrooms she found were just outside the wood. They had come out of the woods in search of light. '*Il faut l'ombre et le soleil dans la forêt*', you need shade and light too. 'If it's too dark, you find nothing!'

She found kilos of them today, she said. 'Of course, you don't leave them if you haven't any more *sacs!*' she retorts in answer to my question. She had found a path of mushrooms in the wood. The more she gathered, the more she spotted – a treasure trove. She quickly ran out of *sacs*. 'You use your cardigan or your coat!' she shouts. Mushrooms had been crammed everywhere, even into the cardigan she normally wore on her shoulders.

This morning she saw a *sanglier*, a wild boar. '*Mais non!*' she laughs when I ask her whether she wasn't frightened. '*Ils s'échappent*', they run away. 'It's only if they're wounded that they attack.' In any event, she said, this *sanglier* wasn't interested in her or the mushrooms. It was heading towards the vines in search of grapes. I wonder with alarm if the mushroom hunting was in the woods next to Les Ruisseaux or Les Bûchères and whether it was my grapes the *sanglier* was heading for.

It wasn't only *chanterelles* she found this morning. '*Regarde!*' she whispers once Gilles's van has disappeared down the road. Her whispers are loud. With a conspiratorial glance towards the door, she gathers up her shopping bag and tips mushrooms from the cavernous depths of it on to the table. '*Cèpes!*' she declares.

I recognise them although, unlike the *cèpes* Michel leaves me, with their velvety brown caps and pale-coloured, spongy pores, these mushrooms have caps that are almost black. '*Têtes de Nègres!*' she pronounces with pride. 'They're very rare,' and with a broad smile she proclaims, '*oui, ça commence, la belle saison!*'

Chapter 14

TOBY HAS LARGE EYES, A LONG BLOND COAT AND A WAGGING TAIL. He lives at the Moulin de Malfourat restaurant and is Paul Rouget's Labrador. He is wagging his tail now as we don our wellingtons and head down towards the locked gate of the mushroom wood. There is a possibility, says Paul, that *cèpes* are abroad.

Cèpes are *boletus edulis*, mushrooms. They grow exclusively in the forests and their flavour and texture are greatly prized in the south-west. Their large, bulbous stems are as good to eat as their caps. They are filling, they are rich, they are meaty, they are sought-after. *Cèpes* cost a lot of money. *Cèpes* are the mushrooms everyone covets. *Cèpes*, Paul reminds me, bring about madness in the local population.

According to Paul, you need at least ten millimetres of rain followed by eleven days of fair weather before the first crop appears, fair enough for the sun to pierce the leaf cover on the floor of the wood and heat the earth. If it rains in between, the water washes away the mushroom spores. 'But,' he warns, 'even with ideal conditions and even if they are there and right in front of you, you won't necessarily find them and there won't necessarily be any.'

He has a basket over his arm and a long stick in his hand as we approach the gates.

It's just over eleven days since the last rain, when we had not just rain but violent hail. Luckily my vines escaped any damage from it, although vineyards in Sigoulès near Gilles were badly affected. He came to see me the morning after to check that I had no damage. Bruno rang up too, as did Francis. Since then the weather has been fair.

Paul's wood is of oak and chestnuts. A bird sings as we enter. We must be careful where we step, Paul warns, as we tread softly along the forest path. 'I really don't know whether we'll find any,' he mumbles as he looks from right to left. We must keep our eyes wide open. We must step carefully over brambles and dead branches.

'You can be ten centimetres away and not see them,' he continues, searching, surveying the ground and using his stick to delicately turn over leaves. 'They're the same colour as the ground . . . they hide themselves.' He peers closely at the ground as he speaks and we tread softly along the path. I peer closely at the ground too. I'm not sure what I'm looking for, but I'm looking intently, nevertheless. Paul stops suddenly, his face lighting up. '*Alors!*' He turns to me with a look of triumph. '*Voilà!* Try and find them!' he says. 'They're around you!' I stand stock still. I see nothing. 'Look carefully,' he insists with a large grin on his face, trying not to give any clues, obviously delighted. 'You're only a metre away.'

I scrutinise the ground and see only leaves, ivy, dead branches. Suddenly, amidst the foliage I see not one but two *cèpes*, appearing as if by magic. I thought I had already scoured the area they now sit in. Round and bulbous with a smooth, velvet cap of chestnut-brown, they are young and perfect, absorbing nourishment from the earth, from the oak leaves, from nature. Paul kneels down to cut them at their bulbous feet and hands one to me. I hold it. It is firm to touch and beautiful to look at. Its cap feels luxurious, like velvet, and its spores are a creamy white. He places them carefully in his basket.

We walk on, the only sound the crack of dry branches underfoot and the solitary song of the bird. A dense but delicate wood, low branches and dappled light highlight tall, thin trunks of oak trees. A shaft of sunlight filters through the wood as I catch sight of a mushroom in its path. I call to Paul, uncertain. It's probably not a *cèpe*, I say. Paul rushes back towards me. '*Mais oui!*' he shouts in delight. '*Bravo!*' He bends down to cut it and whistles slowly. '*Grande qualité*,' he says with reverence.

He points out to me mushrooms with dark orange caps and peachy undersides as we range round, carefully searching for *cèpes*. These resemble *cèpes*, he says, indicating with his stick, but are not the right type. He points out *pleurottes*, a very fine variety of *cèpes* with long, delicate stems, and *champignons de châtaigne*. He discovers a *blancharde*. '*Oh là!*' he says with excitement, stepping back in surprise. '*Quel plaisir!*' He bends down and picks it out from the ground delicately, with care. '*Comme une belle fille*', like a beautiful young girl! he exclaims with appreciation, turning it over in his hand. 'It has finesse, cleanliness, beauty! *Extraordinaire*. A perfect specimen.' What type is it, I want to know. '*Excessivement fin. Très, très fin*,' says Paul, gazing at it and ignoring my question.

I am hooked. I am driven. I search around the bases of oak and chestnut trunks. I walk delicately. I scrutinise leaves. I turn back after having left a tree trunk in case the *cèpes*, like Gilles's hare, are waiting for me to pass by without noticing them. It is humid but warm, a summer wood; a still wood harbouring carefully, naturally camouflaged young and beautiful *cèpes*.

Toby rushes towards me through the undergrowth, on the scent of something, tail up, nose down. He reaches me, then turns tail back towards Paul, ears flapping, tongue hanging out, revelling in the sheer pleasure of running. I see Paul in the distance checking the borders of his wood, bent over, scrutinising the ground.

I turn back to my plot and see in front of me not *une belle fille*, but one, two, three ceps in a row. Their round caps are a pale, velvety brown colour, their creamy white spores raised up from the forest floor. As I bend down I see more, one, two more. I call Paul. He is ecstatic. They are perfect specimens, he says. '*Oh là. C'est trop beau!*' he exclaims with laughter and excitement in his voice. 'And if we had a good bottle of Burgundy, some pâté and some bread now, we could celebrate!' We laugh as he cuts them out of the ground. I am just as ecstatic as he is.

His large basket is filling up. We find another, dark brown and enormous. It grew quickly and burst, Paul tells me; you can see that its cap is split yet dried. On it are what look like large cream spots where slugs have taken chunks out of it. This is not a bad sign, says Paul, far from it as it guarantees its edibility. He cuts it from the ground and shows me its underside, pale green and yellow. '*Non!*' he says, looking at my face. '*C'est bon!* The old ones are full of flavour. That one's for sauce.' He smells its underside. I do too. It smells of fruits of the forest, pepper, faintly truffle-like. 'But of course' says Paul. 'A young *cèpe*, cut finely and eaten raw, tastes like a summer truffle. *C'est un délice!*'

We walk on, ranging round the wood. I spy another. Paul turns back, annoyed that he missed it. 'You see how you can pass by and not notice?' he remarks, stooping down to cut its base and scoop it into his basket with the others. 'There!' he shouts as he spies another two, illuminated by a beam of gentle light from the sun. They are nut-brown and pale cream. Their undersides, like all the others, don't have gills like other mushrooms, just smooth, spongy spores.

We are a team now. I am a *cèpes* hunter. I have passed the test and it's fair to say I am obsessed by them. Paul is leaving me to scour a section of the wood on my own while he checks the outer perimeters of his wood. I slip under twisted, low-hanging branches as I range round. The wood is still. Pale green shoots of new oak contrast with the dark ivy spread out over mossy ground. Dappled sunlight falls on light grey trunks. High up through the canopy of leaves at the top of the trees the sky can be seen. One tall oak, older than the rest, sits on its own. It has a thick, straight trunk, solid, magnificent and proud.

And it gives me two more *cèpes*. Next to them is a red *cèpe* with pure white spots, slugs having eaten into it. Toby is streaking through the wood towards me again, panting, racing with the joy of life. Paul is bent and walking slowly around a tree trunk. His spectacles are on the end of his nose and his hair flops in his eyes, making him look younger. Suddenly, he falls down on bended knee; I guess he has found his reward.

We walk back through the wood together. '*Regarde-moi ça!*' says Paul, stopping and pointing out an *au range* mushroom. I recognise it as Juliana gave me one last year. Oval, its cap is flame-orange like the yolk of Madame Briand's eggs; indeed, it looks like a boiled egg and it feels like the fresh, rubbery skin of one, firm to the touch, its stem white and creamy. It is delicious either raw in a salad or grilled with a little oil, says Paul. It has a fine and extremely delicate taste. He scoops it up and adds it to his basket.

Paul's basket looks like an oil painting. He holds it on his left arm. Bursting with perfect specimens of freshly picked mushrooms, small clusters of young *cèpes* and large caps of older ones are piled high, shades of brown, pure white and cream. They emit a delicate scent as we walk back towards the car and home, our harvest gathered in for the day.

Driving back from dinner with friends and knowing
I had vats of wine to rack early next morning I debated
only for a second whether or not I would call in on

Fidde. I turned into his drive, parked and switched off the engine. Walking up the drive to the kitchen door, I could see golden light from the windows spilling out into the darkness and on to the gravel of the courtyard.

I could see Fidde sitting on the sofa watching television, a bottle of red wine half-drunk and some chocolates on the table in front of him. He leapt up and smiled his wide smile as I opened the door, striding towards me with an arm outstretched to take my hand. 'Patricia!' he said, laughter in his voice, kissing me. 'I'm so glad you've come!' He was glad; his face and his manner showed it in every gesture. He hugged me. 'I wasn't sure you would.'

He was exhilarated to see me. 'Come!' he said, drawing me into the *salon*. 'Have a drink', and he poured out some wine from the bottle. 'I've missed you!' he smiled, looking over at me with dark, glistening eyes as I walked towards the hall near his office to hang up my jacket. As I did so, I heard him call me back, his voice insistent and urgent. 'Patricia!'

'Patricia,' he said, looking up at me from the sofa, sprawled over it. 'My arm . . .' Raised above him, he gazed at his right arm in incomprehension, touching it lightly with his left hand as if he had never seen it before. 'Like pins and needles . . .' he said faintly. He was white, his face bathed in a cold sweat. 'My feet are cold . . .' he said, turning his head slowly to look at me. His chest was tight. He didn't understand, couldn't comprehend. 'Am I having a heart attack?' he said softly, more to himself than me.

Suddenly galvanised into action, I grabbed Missy's blanket. 'No,' he cried, his face convulsed in pain as I placed it over his feet, the weight and harshness of the wool hurting him. I rushed to the cupboards in the hall for softer cotton towels, wrapping one round his feet and wiping his face with the other. Even the displacement of air as I moved caused him pain, I could see it on his face.

His eyes were closed. I knelt next to him as I spoke to the emergency services on the telephone. The white mask on his face receded, his body relaxed and he sank back into the sofa in relief, opening his eyes and looking at me weakly as I gave them the address. 'It's easy to miss,' I said. 'You could pass by the house and not know it was there.' Fidde's secret place, hidden away from the world.

The flashing light from the ambulance waiting in the courtyard flickered over us as the ambulancemen knelt on the floor next to Fidde. They took his pulse, felt his heart. 'What are they doing to me?' he said quietly as they lifted him off the sofa and on to a stretcher.

His body tensed suddenly in a second spasm of pain. His eyes closed in concentration against it, in a desire to live. 'I'm here, Fidde . . . I won't leave you,' I said as they picked the stretcher up and we rushed him through the kitchen towards the door and the waiting ambulance. Fidde's eyes opened and glazed over before they reached the door. He left his house. Left the world. Left me. 'No! Stop!' I screamed at the ambulancemen. 'Give him oxygen! Make him live!'

'What's his name?' asked one of the ambulancemen as he pumped his heart in the ambulance. 'Call him!' 'Fidde,' I said quietly. 'Fidde!' shouted the ambulance-man. 'Fidde! Fidde!' I shouted desperately as I stood next to him. 'Fidde! Come back!' One of the ambulancemen moved me to one side. 'You must leave now, Madame' he said. 'We need the space.'

The ambulance swayed as they fought to give him life. I stood outside in the black night. Time froze. The sky was black. Stars hung in it, distant and timeless. 'Madame,' the doctor said as he walked slowly from the ambulance and stood in front of me. 'I'm sorry . . .' I looked into his face, watched his lips move, understood nothing. He gestured towards the ambulance. I walked towards it and stepped inside.

I spoke the words into the telephone; flat, wrong. I heard Ekan's insistent voice on the other end of the line. I heard my words yet it wasn't me talking. I stood in the courtyard yet I wasn't there. It didn't happen. 'Fidde's dead,' I said.

Pia put Missy's yellow blanket over my shoulders as forms were signed. The undertakers took away Fidde's body. We were left behind, immobilised and empty. Pia and Ekan sat on the sofa where Fidde had lain. We stared at the dead embers of the fire. 'You must come home with us, Patricia — you can't go home on your own,' said Ekan quietly.

I had to. I drove home through the black night, a silence in my head. As I climbed into bed I lay on my stomach, cold and in shock, my hands and arms underneath my body. I closed my eyes and felt suddenly the warmth of Fidde wash over me. I felt it fleetingly but surely as sleep overtook me and I knew it was him.

A violent wind that has come from nowhere carries away garden chairs. They scoot across the courtyard like feathers. The kitchen window bursts open as I stand in front of it, sending glasses sitting on a kitchen surface hurtling across the room, scattering into a million pieces. Doors that were open slam shut through the house and shutters bang on and off the wall. A deep purple sky, menacing and violent, has suddenly replaced the hot summer one of a moment ago. From the trees and the ground leaves dance in the air, swirling in circles like marionettes in front of me.

The tall acacia tree in the garden bends like a blade of grass, its branches swaying as a crack of thunder bursts directly over the house. A searing, white, jagged light soars across the sky at the same instant as torrents of hailstones fall with incredible force. They are the size of marbles, falling diagonally as the wind tears through the sky. I watch as the acacia stoops for a second time, its top branches almost touching the ground. It bounces back up again in a second, then jerks backwards and forwards like a swirling feather. The curtain of hailstones hammers into the shutters and on to the doors. A crack and one of the windows is broken, the sound of hailstones like a thousand kettledrums echoing around the house.

It stops as abruptly as it started. As if it were a figment of my imagination, the sky is blue again. The tree is standing upright. Leaves scattered over the kitchen floor stir at my feet. The silence after the bombarding hailstones is deafening. A screech inside my head temporarily roots me to the spot in front of the kitchen window. I gaze at the tree for a moment, then rush out to my vines.

They are devastated. The broad green leaves that were full of health and sun and goodness less than four minutes earlier are now ripped through, gouged with huge holes. They hang in tatters. I stare at them in horror. I touch them, put my fingers through the holes, hold one in my hand. The grapes are bleeding. They have great gashes in them. I can see the pips in their centres. What were ripening bunches of grapes hanging like jewels from the vine are now limp and damaged, pitted with holes and already dying. They have been raped, torn open by the force of the hail-stones. Those that aren't pierced are bruised and will open with the first rain. I touch one. It falls off the vine and on to the ground.

The damage is replicated on each of the vines I look at as I wander up the row. Hot tears prick my eyes and sting my face as they dry on my cheek. I wipe them away in anger and frustration as Benjamin rushes up. He looks at the vines in horror. '*Ce n'est pas vrai*,' he says quietly.

All the work of the season, from pruning to budding, from flowering to fruit set, from thinning to spraying, from trimming to ripening, all the care and attention they were given was for nothing.

'Maybe not all the *parcelles* are affected,' says Benjamin. As I look up the row I see only tattered leaves on the ground, witness to the devastation.

A night's sleep does nothing to alleviate the numbness and shock. The *parcelles* of merlot near the house and the sauvignon at Les Bûchères are obliterated. Some of the vines at Les Ruisseaux are badly affected, others not at all. Today they look worse than they did yesterday. Their ripped leaves are dessicating, their grapes are more shrunken and some have the beginnings of rot on them.

I walk up and down the rows, calculating what percentage of my harvest is lost to the hailstones, what percentage can be salvaged. Morning sun, already hot and relentless, beats down between the rows and on to the vines, a white, burning orb against the cloudless blue sky, highlighting the devastation.

Benjamin and Alain, each with a tractor, course up and down the rows spraying bruised, battered vines with insecticide. The rhythmic drone of their tractors sounds like a lament. The searing heat beats down on them and the vines. I watch, the sun stinging the backs of my legs, then walk through the vines and over to Les Ruisseaux.

I stand on the ridge and look out into the valley, deep below. It is peaceful, timeless. The vines in the foreground sweep out towards fruit trees, leafy woods, the meandering river and fields of ripe corn. It shimmers, quiet and untroubled. Tears prick my eyes, spilling out over my cheeks. The thunderstorm has already passed into its history. The valley is dazzling, a summer haze hanging over its lush contours. The sound of droning tractors drifts towards me as Alain and Benjamin head slowly towards La Tabardy and the vines of Les Ruisseaux.

The children are here. 'Grandma!' shouts Amy, rushing into my arms. I am at the airport waiting impatiently for them, longing to grab them and cover them in kisses. 'Hi, Grandma!' and Beth is beside me. Now twelve and ten, they are tall and beautiful with peachy complexions and long limbs.

The customs men at Bergerac airport have let them through the barrier, even though Chantal and John are still on the other side waiting for luggage. The children jump up and down, happy to be here, eager to be off. 'What's La Petite Venus like?' 'Can we have a swim when we get back?' 'Are you getting a puppy?' 'Can we have a go on the tractor?' 'Hi, Mum!' and John and Chantal are through customs with bags and baggage. I've been longing to cover them in kisses too. 'God! The whole world was on the plane!' complains Chantal with a laugh.

Amy and Beth know Gageac well as every summer of their lives so far has been spent here. They are loved by the village, which rings with the sound of their voices each August. Squeals from the pool, the sound of their bicycles racing up and down the road, their visits down to Juliana's and back for sweets and their calls to Eida to give her titbits fill Gageac with life — and noise.

'*Quoquillooooo, mes enfants!*' bellows Juliana to them each morning. '*Bonjour*, Juliana!' they yell back. '*Bonjour, La Petite Venus! Comment, ça va!*' they shout. Their voices echo up and down the road, bouncing off the walls and flooding Eida's field. She rushes over when she hears their voices, having changed camps from me to them with the sudden increase in quotas of carrots, bread and sugar.

La Petite Venus has long since been inspected, cooed over, had her hair combed, had different coloured ribbons placed in her topknot and generally been manhandled with love. She is visited daily and benefits greatly from the doling out of sweets by Juliana to the children.

Amy and Beth love the vines too. They run through them, or take coloured pencils and drawing pads into the vines to draw pictures of them. Or help pull off leaves from around the grapes. Amy has cut off shoots at the base of the vines more than once. And they love tutored tastings with customers in the tasting room. They put their noses into the glass to try and find aromas of raspberries, lemons, cherries and oranges; they chatter to the customers.

I still feel bruised from the horrors of the hailstones. It hit the land and the vines in a thin corridor of devastation, missing most of the other vineyards in and around Gageac. We have calculated that around twenty-five per cent of the harvest is affected, not nearly is bad as our original estimation. Apart from one night of rain, the weather has remained hot and dry. 'The poor grapes,' says Amy. She and Beth inspect them closely. Those that had been gouged open by the hail are now dried and shrunken, but still raw and damaged. 'I can see their pips,' says Beth.

Francis Miquel, his wife, Sandrine, and their two children, Sylvio and Romano, live near Marmande, a three-quarter-of-an-hour drive from me. Their house is bathed in evening sun as we drive through the open gates and into the meadow in front of it where

Sylvio is rolling on the grass with one of the puppies, his younger brother, Romano, laughing next to him. They are in pyjamas and look like puppies themselves. Francis greets me with a kiss. '*Salut*,' he smiles, happy to see me. We are invited '*en famille*' to eat *lièvre à la royale*. 'I'm so sorry about the hail – and your vines,' he says.

Amy and Beth stand shyly beside me, looking over at the children who sit up on the lawn and look back at them. '*Bonjours mes filles*,' Francis says with a smile, kissing them. 'Let's go and say hello to the boys', and he leads them over to the grass, the puppy and his children. They look back at Chantal, John and me uncertainly for a moment, then stroke the puppy self-consciously. Sylvio chatters to them in French, the ice is broken and within seconds they too are rolling around, all four chattering in English and French.

Francis's house is an old barn that has been modernised. Full of light, rather like Jacques and Marie-Christelle's, the sun streams in through its windows and glass doors. Aromas of cooking pervade the house as Sandrine greets me with a kiss. She looks Spanish and exotic this evening with long, black hair tied back tightly and kept in place by a black hairpin. She has large, dark eyes and is dressed in black. '*Salut*, Patricia!' and she kisses me. '*Les enfants!*' she shouts as she doles out supper for all four children in the kitchen. Francis's young assistant, Pascal, is here too, also an ex-sommelier.

Francis has found a good foie gras for his *lièvre à la royale* and has been cooking both all day. The hare has been de-boned, seasoned and wrapped round the foie gras, then enveloped in layers of aluminium foil and a tea towel, where it has been simmering gently in *vin rouge* and a *bouquet garni* for more than seven hours. The bones, too, are simmering in red wine and onions and herbs, cooking slowly to make the sauce that will accompany the hare.

He inspects them from time to time as we chatter together,

lifting out a thermometer that sits in a huge casserole beside the hare and its liquid from time to time to check the heat. I look into the saucepan next to it; the sauce is simmering and glistens, the bones having given not just taste, but sheen. Next to the hob is an open tart, Francis's favourite accompaniment to game. Its base of shortcrust pastry is spread thinly with *échalottes*, mushrooms, maize, *crème fraîche* and paprika. You need nothing else with the *lièvre*, he says.

Marc arrives. An *oenologue* friend of Francis's, he is large and in his fifties with a gentle, round and pink face, a white, close-cropped beard – hardly even a beard, more an unshaven look – sandy hair and small, round spectacles. His eyes shine out from behind them, intelligent and sparkling. '*Aaah! Bonjours mes filles!*' he says gently to the girls who are now well-versed in French habits and rise to give him kisses. '*Bonjour tout le monde!*' and he shakes hands, gives kisses.

It is Sandrine and Francis's wedding anniversary and he has brought with him a huge bouquet of flowers. Sandrine loves the display. 'Happy anniversary,' he says, throwing his hands in the air and laughing. His laugh is infectious. He looks round at all of us, inviting us to share in his enthusiasm for life.

We drink a glass of champagne together in celebration as we amble out to the terrace where we will eat. The children rush back to the lawn and the dogs. The terrace is long and wide. Oak posts run along its length, deep red roses and honeysuckle clambering up them, round them and onwards over the roof. 'It's lovely here, Mum,' says Chantal, looking out from the terrace at the children and on to the large expanse of open lawn and further on towards golden fields of corn. In the distance, the evening sun strikes gold into the gentle yellow and pale brown shades.

'You can't find better!' Marc is saying, looking at the young, new potatoes from Michel's garden that I have brought with me for Francis and Sandrine. He's heard, he says, that home-grown vegetables in gardens today are more polluted than shop-bought ones because of the overenthusiastic use of chemicals. He looks again at Michel's potatoes. 'These have had no *traitements*,' he says. 'You can tell.'

He loves home-grown vegetables. His grandfather had a wonderful kitchen garden, he says, and although his parents weren't interested at all he loved nothing better than to spend hours there, helping to plant or dig up vegetables or making conserves of them. He recounts anecdotes of his grandfather amid bursts of laughter. The children appear to listen and laugh with him.

He has been making conserve of lamprey this week, he says, with '*les poireaux monstrueux de quarante ans*'. What are they, John asks. 'Monstrous leeks, of course!' He looks at him and laughs. His laugh spreads over us, making us laugh too, the children joining in from the lawn. They are a particular variety of huge leeks with a strong taste which you need, he explains, to marry with the *lamproie* and *vin rouge*. Not only must you have *le vin rouge*, he continues with enthusiasm, but also the leas of *vin rouge*, to give body and structure as well as taste. 'Of course, the older the pâté, the better,' he concludes. I tell him about Gilles's pâtés and how he prefers to eat them older. 'Wonderful!' he bubbles, hands in the air and laughter in his voice.

The aromas of hare and onions hang in the air as Francis recounts in his deep, slow voice the dinner he made last year for sixty people. After the hours of work preparing, de-boning, wrapping and cooking seven hares, it took all of ten minutes to be devoured. He did manage to save a *morceau*, however. It was delicious the next day, cold, '*avec un grand blanc*'. Marc nods enthusiastically. Strong, dark meat eaten cold with a good white Burgundy is a sublime combination. '*Oh, que c'est délicieux!*' he reiterates, laughing and raising his hands in the air, then placing them between his knees.

Sandrine and Chantal disappear to the kitchen and reappear with the starter of carpaccio of monkfish. *Baies rose* peppercorns and *fleur de sel* are scattered over the white, opaque flesh, finely sliced and surrounded by lemon quarters. The dish is sprinkled with green fronds of *aneth* and delicate trails of golden olive oil. '*Oh, que c'est joli!*' exclaims Marc. The children arrive to inspect. '*Oui, c'est joli,*' says Amy, laughing.

Francis opens a bottle of Sancerre, a Cuvée Edmond. We all savour the taste of richness, minerality and flint, providing vivacity with the carpaccio of monkfish that is fresh and delicate. It melts in our mouths. 'God, it's delicious,' says John. '*Oooh, que c'est bon, le carpaccio!*' says Marc. How did he make it, he asks Francis. The olive oil on it is delicious too. He has recently been to Italy, he tells us, for a professional tasting of olive oils. They were excellent, mineral, with good texture and aromas. 'Often if black olives are picked too ripe, the oil is heavy and it loses its perfume,' he says. 'The stage of maturity is very important.' Yes, says Pascal, supermarket oils are sometimes bitter and *brûlant* whereas if you search out the *grand crus* you get something '*haut de gamme*'.

Francis pours some of the olive oil used in the carpaccio on to a spoon for me to sample. It has fruit and length and minerality. Pascal tastes it too and is ecstatic. '*Que c'est bon!* Didn't I give you this bottle, Francis?' He turns to us. 'Often I make fish *en papillote* for myself. All you need to do after you've taken it out of the oven is to open the packet and dribble some olive oil over it! Nothing more!' He takes another helping of carpaccio and dribbles more olive oil over it. 'Did you know,' he says, savouring the fish and relishing its taste, 'that in Tuscany you often take a bottle of olive oil to dinner for the host rather than a bottle of wine?'

We change wines to a Meursault Genevrière from Burgundy. 'God, Mum. Have you tasted it?' says John in admiration. His French is improving as the evening moves on and he launches into conversations with Francis, Mark and Pascal. Marc's enthusiasm for wine and life positively bursts from him. He talks of great vintages, the importance of wood in wines. 'Richness comes from the difference, the sucrosity,' he says. 'The difference is in the nuance.' His hands are in the air again, his red face with small, round spectacles and sparkling, intelligent eyes gripping us all.

Francis brings out the *lièvre à la royale*. Dark and rich, as Francis cuts into it the rich aroma of truffles fills our nostrils and hangs over the table. As I taste it, my mouth is filled with the mellow richness of game, the dissolving luxury of smooth foie gras and the forest fruits, velvet and cream of truffles. The sauce, dark and rich and tasteful, marries perfectly with it. And Francis was right when he said that the open maize tart was all we needed with it. We savour the taste in silence for a moment. *'Que c'est bon!'* says Marc.

Francis has opened two bottles of red wine. The first is deep rose-coloured, fresh and acid and obviously a Burgundy. 'Is it Gevrey?' asks Pascal. 'It's more like . . . Geantet? It's not Gevrey.' 'Is it Geantet?' Vincent Geantet's wines remain fresh in my mind, along with his Harley man sartorial style. It is absolutely one of his with the unmistakable flavour of pinot noir married with his style. With finesse and delicacy, it is subtle and deep and delicious.

Night has fallen as we sit around the table. Sylvio and Romano have long since fallen asleep and been deposited in their beds. Beth is asleep on the sofa in the *salon* and Amy is on my knee. The stars are out in force, glittering and sparkling in the night sky. Cicadas are singing and an owl swoops and flies off near the terrace. 'It's la Dame Blanche,' says Sandrine; she loves owls. They swoop in and out of their terrace at the moment, like the *hirondelles* and *martinets* which are feeding their young.

She and Francis looked after a baby *martinet* that had fallen from its nest last year, she tells us. They fed him with a matchstick and he stayed for over a month. Eventually, he stopped eating. It was time for him to fly away and she cried when he left. Today two *hirondelles* rest and sleep in the honeysuckle on the terrace. They're lovers, she says laughing. Amy half-listens, sleep about to overtake her.

The roses and honeysuckle along the terrace emit perfumes that merge with the aromas of hare *à la royale* as we taste the second wine that has been carafed. It is expressive, fresh and generous. 'It has *terroir*,' says Marc as we all smell, taste and savour. 'It's *grande*,' says Francis. They talk of winemakers I don't know and how they make their wines, where they are situated in relation to each other. 'His father was dreadful,' Marc is saying. 'And now his father is no longer here, is it a surprise that it's so much better?'

We try and guess the second wine. Darker and denser in colour than the Burgundy we have just tasted, it smells of ripe, spicy fruit, leathery and rich with a distinguished finish. Pascal is beside himself with curiosity and leaves the table to go in search of the bottle. 'Ha!' he exclaims from inside the house. 'Guess what it is?' as he returns to the table with the bottle. It's an '89 Château Montrose from Ste Estèphe. 'I would never have believed it!' he exclaims. Marc is laughing again with his hands in the air.

Sandrine disappears to Francis's wine cellar with a Pomerol carafe in her hand. She will choose the wine for the pudding, she says. I didn't know that different shaped carafes denoted different types of wines. 'It doesn't actually make much difference,' says Francis, laughing as Sandrine returns with a golden-coloured wine to be drunk with the *nougatine* and ice cream that is now on the table. From its aromas of apricot and honey I recognise my own wine.

'*Regarde les petits amours*,' says Sandrine as she looks into the honeysuckle at the birds. Francis laughs and gets up from the table, returning with his guitar. He sings in his deep voice traditional songs of Georges Brassens, Jacques Brel and Henri Salvador. '*Les gens qui se bécotent . . .*' He sings gently and we all sing along.

The starry night, the cicadas, his deep voice and the wine are intoxicating. '*C'est une plage . . .*' he sings, smiling occasionally and looking at Sandrine or me or Marc as encouragement to sing along. '*Le pastis d'abord . . .*'

The phone rang only hours after I fell into sleep following Fidde's death. Agneta cried into it. 'Thank you for being with him,' she sobbed. Ebba rang, Regina and Ika, disbelieving and as shocked as us. I dressed in a daze, a dull buzzing in my ears, a light trembling in my body. 'Patricia,' said Ekan on the phone. 'You must come over now and be with us. We must be together. I'll come and get you.' We sat in the kitchen at Saussignac where we had so often sat with Fidde, empty and uncomprehending.

Ekan had rung Fidde's family after I left and they were on their way; Paul, his brother from America, his youngest brother, his sisters, his children, his wife Carola, Tom and Megan, Bobby. The phone rang constantly. Ekan handed it to me. I heard Arvid's voice on the phone, cracked with emotion. 'Patricia,' he said. I listened to his words, wished that the pain would go away, not just for me, but for him, for all of us. I looked at Pia's face looking at mine as I held the telephone to my ear. In it I saw our anguish.

Three days later Fidde's family and friends gathered at my house. The sky was black and clear with bright stars, as it had been on the night of Fidde's death. A pale, translucent moon hung over the church. Inside it, I placed a large white sheet over the altar. We put two framed pictures of Fidde on it and lit up the church with candles. And we said goodbye to him together. I read a poem. 'Death is nothing at all ... I have only slipped away into the next room ...' I began.

As I read on falteringly, thoughts of Fidde flooded my mind. His laughing face, his love of friendship.

Little could he have known when he met me that I would be present at his death. Little could he have known that the simple church in Gageac would welcome him in this way, that those he held most dearly would be sitting here, gathered together in grief to remember him.

I told them that the Fidde we knew and loved was the one we should remember. And we did. We remembered his vitality, his joy of life, his generosity, his sincerity, his love. He loved this church, loved the simplicity of it. Loved Gageac. We loved him.

Chapter 15

ALMOST THE END OF AUGUST AND THE CHILDREN ARE LEAVING. Sun-drenched days around the swimming pool and sultry evenings with suppers in the garden, coupled with dinners with Odile, Bruno and Claudie, Michel and Francis, along with sweets and presents from Juliana, have come and gone. Their stay has passed quickly and I'm sad to see them go, as I am each year. They always leave with the last of the summer, with the still summer haze, with the heat waves, with the end of the growing cycle in the vines.

They are sad to be leaving too. 'Bye, Grandma,' say Amy and Beth, hugging me for the last time before being whisked away by Ryanair. 'Bye, Mum,' say John and Chantal, doing the same. 'We've had a lovely time.' And with a kiss they're gone. Rain spots the dusty windscreen of the car as I drive back along the valley road to my vines and home.

It rains for the rest of the day and some of the night and when it stops the atmosphere is humid and hot. I look at the merlot grapes. For the moment they don't appear to be suffering. Those that aren't damaged by the hail have plumped out and look like jewels hanging from the vines, black and lustrous.

Two days later and I see the unmistakable signs of rot on the grapes. They glisten with minute grey and white specks, mostly at the point where one grape touches another. The weather forecast is not good. Jean-Marc, my *oenologue*, inspects them. Yes, he says. You must keep an eye on them in case you get galloping rot in the vines. The spots on my scalp are back in abundance.

I inspect the white grapes. Without a doubt, there is more rot on them than on the reds. Not helped by the sudden change in atmosphere, warm, misty mornings add to the humidity already present in the vines and aggravate the situation. We gather a team and start to work through the white grape *parcelles*, manually cutting off rot as we find it.

The week that follows sees us permanently in the vines. 'We can't keep up with it,' says Benjamin. Some of the *parcelles* are ripe enough to pick, others still have some greenness. The shame is that the rot we are cutting off is good, noble rot. We can't pick it for the sweet wine as it's not yet at the right stage of ripeness, and if we leave it until it reaches that stage we won't have any dry white grapes and will undoubtedly have ignoble as well as noble rot on them.

The *vendange* arrives swiftly as a result of the devastation. We pick the first *parcelle* of undamaged sauvignon grapes in the cool of the morning, followed by two *parcelles* that have had their rot removed. The others follow in quick succession, as quickly as we can knock the rot off. The sémillon and muscadelle *parcelles* follow the same path, rot removed and gathered in immediately. Tractor loads rumble in from the vines bringing with them the culmination of our year's work outside, radically reduced in quantity.

In the vines, the half-nobly rotted bunches of grapes that have been cut off lie on the ground in abundance. I look down the rows and see them scattered along the paths. They are everywhere, immediately beneath the vines, in the middle of the rows.

I look at the waste: the waste of potentially delicious dry white wine, the waste of potentially wonderful noble rot, the waste of all the care given them since they burgeoned forth as delicate embryo grapes. It saddens me. In the *chai*, we macerate the juice we have gathered for eight hours, then taste it. With relief, it is clean, fresh and untainted; rich, too, and concentrated. But there is hardly any of it.

'*Milledieux!*' exclaims Gilles. He has come to suggest next Sunday for the *chasse au sanglier* with Manu. 'Hailstones, *c'est le pire*,' he commiserates. His neighbour in Sigoulès doesn't have any harvest at all as a result of it. He thought he'd lost fifty per cent at the time, but rot has taken everything. No, I can't go on the *chasse* on Sunday, I tell him. The reds are starting the same thing.

We look at the *parcelle* of merlot nearest the house. '*Milledieux*,' says Gilles quietly. 'You can't wait any longer. Get them in as quickly as possible.' They look sad. They look shrunken. They hang limply from the vines. I can't pick them yet as they are not ripe enough, I tell him. Benjamin joins us. The weather forecast is good for the next two days, he says. He is tempted to wait. '*Milledieux!*' bellows Gilles. 'You won't have anything left!'

<hr>

We kept Fidde alive in our hearts in those first days after his death. Inextricably bound to him and to each other, we didn't want to let go, couldn't somehow. Carola recounted stories of the early days of their marriage. She laughed and cried. Ekan told us stories of their student days together. Agneta told us childhood family stories, remembrances of him as a small boy, as a young man, and his older brother, Paul, recounted stories of the *hôtel* they once owned together in the Alps. Ebba and Gustaf were quiet and contemplative, Tom too. Fidde would have been happy to have

275

everyone together there, glad to have known how much he was loved. When everybody had gone, I took Missy, his cat, home with me.

The emptiness I felt after his death would hit me when I least expected it. At the lab for no reason memories of him would engulf me. At a tasting or driving along the road in bright sunlight or driving back from Bergerac at night his absence would take my breath away. A starry night would bring a flood of memories and accompanying tears. I let go slowly, with pain.

Pia, Ekan and I had supper frequently together then, as we do now. Inevitably, Fidde would dominate our conversation, wash over our lives again. It wasn't fair that he should be gone, wasn't just that he wasn't here with us. We relived moments with him, repeated memories we had of him and remembered him with love.

The following summer I went to Sweden. Agneta picked me up from the airport at Stockholm and we drove to Rottneros where much of Fidde's childhood was spent, four hours' drive from Stockholm in the north-west of Sweden. The Bishop of Stockholm planted a tree in the park there in memory of him.

Agneta took me to Sunne, where his ashes were buried next to his parents in front of the simple country church overlooking the beautiful lake of Fryken. Seeing it, I understood why he loved the church at Gageac. We visited his school in Lundsberg where I saw photos of him everywhere on the walls, an ice hockey and ski champion year after year. We drove back via Arvid's summer home and stayed overnight with him and Shirstin. We returned to Stockholm and Ebba's house, bought for her by Fidde, for the name day of her second child, born just after Fidde's death. All the family were there, Ekan too.

We returned to Agneta's house where she gave a small, touching wedding dinner for Arvid and Shirstin. They were married only months before in a quiet ceremony after living together for years. On the sloping lawn and beside the archipelago in front of Agneta's house, they danced a wedding dance in the evening sun. Golden light from the sun silhouetted their forms and sent sparkling light over the sea behind them. Two small children seated in a wooden wheelbarrow nearby clapped in delight, part of the wedding group.

I felt humbled to be included and honoured to be part of their celebration, part of Fidde's commemoration, part of Ebba's daughter's name day. Fidde would have been happy, I think. Happy that I had gone to Sweden, to Rottneros and especially to Sunne. Glad that Ebba had brought another grandchild into the world. Glad that Gustaf was surging forward in his life, running his business successfully. Glad, too, that Arvid and Shirstin were married. Happy that he was remembered with love by so many. He loved real friendship.

We wait longer than two days to pick the red grapes. We look at them daily. We peer into the hearts of bunches. We touch the outsides, we tempt fate. We knock off rot. We *vendange*. The first trailer load of ripe merlot, gathered in at night and tipped into the de-stalker, soars through the pipe and into the vat, filling it up as more trailer loads arrive from the vines, the tractors beaming flickering light into the night sky.

Three days later and the *chai* is filled with fruit aromas. All the vats are fermenting. Juice run off from the merlot to make rosé emits raspberry and strawberry perfumes with citrus fruits and melon from the whites. The merlot vats exude red berry fragrances and the amalgam of all of them pervades not just the *chai* but the house. As I climb the stairs at night for much-needed sleep, so do the aromas, heady and pleasing. As I close my eyes, their scent carries me swiftly to another place.

'*Patricciaa! Coucou!*' shouts Juliana from her window. '*Eh la pourriture noble?* When are we picking?' It's October and we have finished picking the cabernet sauvignon and cabernet franc grapes. Long pendulous jewels of ripe, black fruit hung from the vines with not a hint of rot and were picked swiftly and cleanly. They sit safely in the *chai* along with the rest of the harvest, gently macerating before starting their fermentation.

At Monestier as I open the door of the car, parked at the top of the noble rot *parcelle*, a faint smell of vinegar hangs in the air. I know before I get to the first vine that there will be nothing left to pick. In place of noble rot grapes are orange, empty skins and the overriding smell of vinegar. They have been decimated by vinegar fly. Clouds of them rise into my face as I peer at the grapes. The hail that had opened some of their skins let the flies in. I walk down one of the rows, desolate at the sight of vine after vine of vinegar. At the bottom of the row, two or three chickens from a nearby house systematically peck off the few grapes still left with the vestiges of noble rot.

I charge through the noble rot *parcelles* at Gageac cutting off any bunches with vinegar fly, inspecting, smelling, cutting. Juliana follows on an adjacent row, with Benjamin and Alain doing likewise, up and down the rows. 'Cut it off!' I shout when Juliana protests that there is some doubt as to whether or not it smells of vinegar. 'Don't hesitate!' I yell when Alain says the grapes are faintly orange but taste sweet. 'Cut them all off!' I bellow when Benjamin says that some bunches on a vine have them, the others he's not sure about. Bunches fall to the ground accompanied by clouds of vinegar flies, some with noble rot and the beginnings of vinegar, some pure vinegar, some, by mistake, pure botrytis. It doesn't matter. Anger has replaced depression, tears and impotence. We will cut out the vinegar now before it runs rampant. All of it.

A week later and we pick noble rot. We pick basket after basket of it, pure and luscious. The vines look magnificent. Autumn sun strikes gold into the canopy of leaves above the grapes, pale yellow and red, highlighting the black vines with their small jewel-like bunches of noble rot in all stages of evolution. Violet, purple and pink grapes, shrivelled and ripe for the picking are gathered in with not a hint of vinegar.

We have come full circle. The *chasse* is open again and we hear the shots of the *chasseurs* as we *vendange*. '*Oh là!* Another pheasant gone!' shouts Juliana, laughing, and '*Bonjour, Monsieur!*' she bellows as another picker arrives to join the team. As we pick at Les Bûchères, I glance over at my truffle tree. It is still without weeds at its base, still stunted and gnarled.

The weather is wonderful with day after day of morning mists and hot afternoon sun, essential for the development of noble rot. Three picks later there is a temporary halt to wait for the last of the grapes to develop. The birds wait with us. They sit on the telegraph wires, they line up on rooftops, they hang around the trees.

'*Regarde! Patricia!*' shouts Juliana. We are in the beech wood near Cunèges where tall trees lean towards each other, criss-crossing at their summit. Leaves fall periodically like large golden snowflakes. They pirouette slowly downwards through the still air and land gently, silently, on the ground as we walk through. Pearly leaves from the few oak trees and small patches of dark green ivy contrast with the thick carpet of amber beech leaves on the forest floor.

Juliana is dressed in a yellow jacket, a small figure in wellingtons marching purposefully towards where she thinks there may be easy pickings. She holds an empty plastic bag in one hand and a walking stick in the other. Occasionally, she displaces leaves on the forest floor with her stick, as Paul did in his wood, delicately inspecting the ground underneath and around them. Yves, like her, scours the *environs*.

'*Viens! Viens voir!*' she shouts, waving her stick as I walk towards her. '*Cherche!* Find them!' she shouts excitedly as I peer at the ground in front of her. We are looking for *trompettes de la mort*, horn of plenty mushrooms in English and trumpets of death in French. 'They're in front of you!' she yells.

I look. I search. I see nothing. The forest floor is scattered with ochre and amber-coloured leaves interspersed with soil, ivy, moss and small branches. '*Ce n'est pas très évident,*' mutters Yves, bent over and scrutinising the ground like me. 'I'm not gifted at this,' he continues. '*Oh là là!*' Juliana bellows, impatient, incredulous that we can't see them. She has one hand on her hip, the other waving her stick. '*Ce n'est pas vrai! Là! Là!*' she insists, pointing with her stick at the ground. I bend over to inspect more closely. I see only leaves and soil and crisp sprigs of moss. '*Oh là – ce n'est pas vrai, mes enfants!*' she repeats, laughing now.

Our search is temporarily halted by the unmistakable and wonderful sound of cranes overhead. Through the tops of the trees we catch sight of a huge flock migrating southwards in convoy. Hundreds of them fly in formation high in the sky, their outstretched wings flapping slowly. '*Oh, que c'est joli,*' says Yves, relieved to be looking upwards, thankful to be released from the task of hunting mushrooms. We watch them in admiration for a while. Yves rubs his back. I gaze up at them. They are extraordinary, beautiful. '*Viens!*' says Juliana. '*Maintenant, les champignons!*'

I kneel on the floor to look more closely for the mushrooms and suddenly see them, scattered among the leaves. What I thought were sprigs of moss are transformed into rich, curly-headed *trompettes de la mort*. With long black and dark grey stems they rise from the forest floor, delicate and extraordinary. Some have ochre-coloured, frilled tops, camouflaged among the leaves; others are small, dark and trumpet-shaped, perfect black tubular forest flowers.

Others have rich brown or black, or pale grey velvet heads. Some are larger than others, shaped like miniature black irises. Some are simplicity itself, delicately shaped forms everywhere, black, beige, one like a sponge, dark brown and black inside, others grey and beige. A faint aroma of truffles pervades the air.

Juliana laughs uproariously as I exclaim in amazement at her find. I gather one up from the forest floor. It is dry to the touch, delicate and fine. A mushroom next to it is exactly the same colour as the leaves, and yet another darker still, with curling frills at its top. The leaves on the floor are wet, the mushrooms utterly dry. They look like velvet. They even feel like velvet; curling clumps of rich velvet. I look into one of them. It is perfect: a tubular velvet flower with a deep, black interior reaching down to its very base.

I am hooked. I can't leave my spot. Just when I think I have gathered everything, I see another path of them. Juliana has moved off to another spot, Yves is somewhere else in the wood. He is not gifted in mushroom hunting, says Juliana, not at all or in any way. She has to force him to come in search of them. They can be right in front of him and still he sees nothing. I hear Yves muttering, '*Non, il n'y en a pas,*' when Juliana asks him whether he has found any. 'I don't believe you!' she shouts. 'I know there must be some there!' Her voice echoes around the wood.

I move off through the woods, scouring, searching for more. They appear suddenly, as if by magic, on the forest floor in front of me. '*Oh là là!*' I shout out and my voice echoes around the wood too. 'Juliana! Come and see!' I yell as I scrabble on hands and knees gathering in huge bell-shaped *trompettes de la mort* with pale grey and black stems. I scoop up amber sprays with grey stems like charcoal and delicate black forms like spring crocuses in clumps of four or eight or even more, great clusters of bell-shaped, curly-leafed mushrooms.

The truffle-like smell is intoxicating. Each time I rise, thinking I have them all, I see yet more. One has a white base, its pale grey stem turning gradually to a darker grey, then to charcoal black at its head. On my hands and knees again I realise that these are moments of pure and utter pleasure. As I pick another I see next to it a delicate, gossamer-like spider's web spun between two leaves, glistening drops of water held in it. They sparkle like diamonds next to yet another clump of *trompettes*.

'*Tu n'a pas le vertige?*' asks Michel as we climb the ladder of the sixteen-metre-high *palombière*, an edifice of corrugated sheeting, landings and ladders attached to a tree. 'Best not to look down,' he advises. Already halfway up, it shakes and sways dangerously as we continue our ascent. There is no going back. There is no looking down. I look at my hands and nothing else as I clamp each of them firmly to the rung above me, positioning my feet on those below by touch.

I tell myself it's no different from the ladders in my *chai*. Except that this is eight times their height and swaying dangerously the higher I get. As I clutch at each rung with my hands, I stoically look ahead and reach with relief the relative safety of the trap door and open cabin at the top. I clamber in and stand up. A slight feeling of what I imagine must be *vertige* is actually the swaying of the *palombière* in the wind.

Michel, who climbed ahead of me in order to open the trap door, is already hauling up his gun, attached, before our terrifying ascent, to a hanging rope coiled on the ground. His van has been parked nearby under a makeshift overhead covering of wire with dark green plastic leaves woven into and over it. Looking down on to it now from the *palombière*, the van is completely hidden from view. 'So the birds don't see it,' says Michel, chuckling.

We are a long way up, at the very top of the highest oaks in the *forêt*. The view is extraordinary. A panoramic vista of St Philippe, Gardonne, Le Fleix, Gageac and Pomport lies before us. The colours of autumn are vivid; the vines are changing colour with giant brush strokes of red, yellow and green sweeping across the landscape. Trees and woods add rust and golden hues to them and in the distance a blue haze blurs the horizon where land meets sky.

The open cabin of the *palombière* is two metres long by a metre wide and is itself camouflaged around its parapets by lalindi branches, woven in and around it. A *bidon* of wine with a tap attached to it is perched on a small shelf in one corner. A table in another has a frying pan, casseroles, plastic cups and knives arrayed on it. Underneath is a stock of food: *bocaux* of pâtés, jams, cheese, bread and chocolate *noisettes*, plus a small gas burner. Michel empties the bag he has brought with him of his favourite *gâteaux*, chocolate biscuits filled with orange, along with fresh bread and a *saucisson*.

Positioned at the top of our tree, two long wooden poles leading from the *cabane* into the branches have plastic pigeons attached to them. They look absurd. 'It attracts *les palombes*,' says Michel unconvincingly, turning the handles and causing the birds to swivel slightly. He chuckles. 'Yes, they're not very good . . . but we're not allowed to use our own birds as decoys any more.' The birds he refers to are tame pigeons trained to attract flights of *palombes*, wild pigeon. 'If they're not trained they just put their heads down and flap their wings in fright each time we tug . . .'

Michel shows me one of the small leather thongs and laces used to attach the tame pigeons' legs to a string. 'It doesn't hurt them at all,' says Michel calmly. 'Look! They're coming!' he whispers and he drops the leather thong and cocks his gun suddenly, aiming it into the sky towards a flight of wild pigeons. 'Too high,' he says with disappointment as they fly higher and he lowers his gun. *'Mais c'est joli à voir, n'est-ce pas?'* He hands me a pair of binoculars. They are very beautiful, flying in formation across the grey sky with purpose.

'La casse-croûte,' Michel laughs, opening the packet of *chocolat* and orange biscuits. He cuts up some bread and spreads melon jam over it, watching the sky as he does so. *'Sers-toi,'* he says, picking up his gun again. 'Look, there's the *saloperie* that eat your grapes and my cherries before they're ripe,' he says, nodding in the direction of a flock of starlings and eyeing them with resentment. 'Too hard to eat,' he says with regret, then qualifies this, adding, 'Well, you can, but it's hard work.' I look towards them and feel resentful too; they're probably on their way to my vines now.

I'm getting used to both the height and the swaying of the *palombière* and no longer feel unsafe. Michel has cocked his gun a number of times at high-flying *palombes*, with no reward. We gaze into the sky, always facing the vista of villages on the horizon. Sometimes crows fly by, often flocks of grape-eating starlings and occasionally a seagull. None of them appear to notice the plastic pigeons. We eat chocolate orange biscuits and bread with Michel's home-made melon jam.

The north wind brings with it the sounds of birds, distant tractors, a train passing through Gardonne on its way to Bordeaux. We see its winding path, a silver snake moving slowly along the landscape in the distance. We need a southerly wind, says Michel, as the *palombes* will fly lower with it. They are en route to Spain and Morocco, he tells me, rolling a cigarette and lighting it. He stands in front of the sky looking southwards through the trees, gun in front of him, his *casquette* with embroidered wild boar on his head.

The *palombe* lasts is only a month, he continues, occasionally peering through the branches of lalindi, looking up at the sky. *'Il faut de la patience,*' he says calmly, '. . . like fishing.' We wait, patiently. 'I used to speak to my pigeons . . . but they didn't speak back.' He turns to me, chuckling, then cocks his gun skywards again. '*Bouge pas!*' he says. '*Zut!*' as another flight of *palombes* flying high turn off to the right as they approach our *palombière*. We hear the sounds of *chiens de chasse* echoing up to us on the wind. '*Chevreuils,*' says Michel, looking over towards a dense wood on the other side of our *palombiere.*

In the distance a lone figure strides through the vines, his two dogs white streaks along the horizon. 'It's Lionel,' says Michel. A young friend of Michel's who moved here from Agen where he was a butcher, he used to come and work in my vines now and again. Tall, well-built and large like Manu, he is fresh-faced with short, black hair. The same age as Manu and, to some extent the same type, he too loves the *chasse*. Now married with a child, he lives in Razac de Saussignac and does odd jobs for a living.

The sound of a horn calling dogs to heel echoes across the countryside. Lionel's head turns towards the sound as the wind rises. It will be colder now, says Michel, looking up, but will bring the birds. I look up at the sky empty of birds, at the vista of land meeting sky and sky which has become land. Another flock of *palombes* passes by, too high to shoot at. They come from England, from Norway even, Michel tells me, on their long journey to the sun.

Lionel is striding in our direction in his large hat, gun on his arm, white streaks transformed into two English setters which gallop towards the foot of the oak tree and the *palombière*. Now below us, I look down. We are a long way from the forest floor. I see the crown of Lionel's broad hat and his boots. '*Salut!*' shouts Michel. '*Tu montes boire un coup?*' Lionel smiles, holding on to his hat and straining his head and neck to look up at us. '*Ah, on peut! On peut!*' he shouts. He climbs up the ladders, the *palombière* shaking with every step he takes.

'Patricia!' he says with surprise as he reaches the cabin. '*Ça fait un moment!*' He kisses me. It is some time since I last saw Lionel, at least six years. '*Ça va*, Michel?' he says, breathless from the ascent. 'What's new, Patricia?' and he rubs his hands together. It is much colder since the wind rose. '*Tiens*, Michel, I hunted woodcock and hare yesterday ... *Mon Dieu*, the *bécasse* took one look at me and left! I was only thirty metres from it!' Michel laughs.

'*Regarde ce vol!*' he exclaims suddenly, pointing upwards and we watch with regret and admiration as a flight of *palombes* high in the sky turns and heads southwards. 'They were probably at Orly this morning,' says Lionel, looking at me. '*Ah oui*,' he continues, sighing and looking up to the sky. 'You can't know when they'll come. You can spend all day here and see nothing, then stay at home and see flocks of them!' He looks from me to Michel earnestly. '*N'est-ce pas*, Michel?' he adds. 'You have to be here on the right day,' he says, turning back to me.

'You know only one per cent of *palombes* are killed in France,' he continues. 'It's not *énorme!*' he says, with feeling. His voice is slow and articulate, lowering slightly with the last syllable of the last word of his sentences except when he is speaking with passion, when it goes up. Which it is doing on this subject. 'In Espagne, they kill them by the thousands!' He takes a glass from the table and fills it with red wine from the *bidon* in the corner. '*N'est-ce pas*, Michel?' Michel nods, looking out towards the sky. 'Gayard!' Lionel shouts suddenly, looking down over the parapet at his dogs. He whistles loudly. Gayard has run off in search of something. She hears him and returns, the sound of crackling leaves and bracken as she races through the wood echoing up to us.

He turns back to us. '*Tiens*, Michel. I caught a *lièvre* yesterday,' he says. 'Five kilos three!' He rubs his hands together. He wears pale khaki trousers tucked into boots with buckles on their sides, a large loose jacket and his broad hat. He rolls up a cigarette. '*Un coup de rouge?*' he says to Michel as he pours himself another. '*Viens ici!*' he shouts down to his dogs as they run off again. *Chasse* dogs howl in the distant woods.

'Yes, he was sitting right in front of me!' he recounts, returning to the subject of the hare he caught yesterday. 'Gayard passed right by him!' He and Michel talk excitedly of hares, *bécasses*, *palombes*. 'I saw Manu yesterday,' Lionel remarks, draining his *coup de rouge*. 'He was ploughing one of the fields with his tractor. *Mon Dieu*, he worked like a maniac . . . didn't stop 'til he'd finished . . .' then, changing the subject, '*Tiens*, there are *sangliers* at the moment,' he says, turning to me. 'Did you know? They're everywhere. You can smell them!'

It is noisy suddenly with dogs barking in the woods, the sound of horns, birds, gunshots, a train passing. Michel and Lionel look up into the sky. 'Did you see the cranes the other day, Patricia?' Lionel asks me. '*Magnifique, n'est-ce pas?*' he says. 'What a noise! They were chattering! What a flock! Half an hour of them! I never saw so many . . . could hardly hear myself speak for them!' A silence as we look up into the sky. 'You hear their voices first,' he continues, slowly, 'then the sound of their wings . . . *Oui, magnifique*,' he repeats looking at his empty glass. The sound of gunshot cracks through the sky from a distant *chasseur*.

'*Tiens*, have I finished my *coup* already?' says Lionel. '*Un coup de plus?*' and he pours himself another. The sun shines weakly through grey clouds, dappled light falling on Michel's face as he gazes skywards, hands in pockets, cigarette in his mouth. Occasionally he taps the tip of it to remove dead ash and relights it. The *palombière* shakes with the rising wind. 'Yes,' says Lionel, looking up into the sky with him. 'The cold sends the birds southwards . . . I wonder if it's snowing in the Pyrénées?'

Leaves rustle in the tops of the now familiar trees, their golden, green and pearly tan colours creating a backdrop to flocks of skylarks, *alouettes* and starlings. '*Alouette, gentille alouette*,' sings Lionel softly. 'Yes, you must be philosophic for the *palombes*,' he sighs, laughing. '*Mais on est bien à campagne, n'est-ce pas?*' he laughs, looking at us. 'I much prefer *la campagne*. Even Bergerac is too much for me,' he says. A ray of sun pierces the grey sky and shines down on a pale yellow patch of vines, lighting it up and changing its colour to a deep ochre.

'*Eh bien*,' says Lionel, looking around the *cabane* and rubbing his hands together. 'I think I'll *chasse* for woodcock in the *forêt*.' He looks at me. 'If you catch one of those, you merit it, believe me! They're crafty.' He pauses. '*N'est-ce pas*, Michel?' Michel laughs. '*Oh oui!*' he agrees. '*Tiens*, you should have seen the *joli bécasse* that escaped yesterday . . .' rejoins Lionel. '*Bon . . . Un dernier coup et je descends!*' Lionel pronounces with decision. It's not yet 9 am. '*Ne bouge pas!*' says Michel as two *palombes* fly low. They rise higher in the sky and turn as we watch. 'Come on, *les filles!*' shouts Lionel looking up at them. 'We're waiting for you!' He raises his fist, laughing. 'Some of them come from as far as Russia,' he says, peering into the grey sky then looking at me earnestly.

'*Mon Dieu!*' he laughs. '*C'est le* Titanic *ici!*' as the wind rises and the *palombière* shakes violently. The tree tops sway. '*C'est bon ce petit vin*,' says Lionel looking into his empty glass and eyeing the *bidon* of wine in the corner. '*Allez, un dernier!*' and he pours another. '*Eh voilà*,' he says, emptying it in one and placing his glass back on the table.

'*Bien*,' he says, rubbing his hands together again and glancing fleetingly at the *bidon* of wine. '*Bon*,' he adds. Then '*Allez!*' he says with finality, giving me a kiss. '*Je descends!*' Michel warns him to be careful descending. 'There's still some of the day left,' he says, more to himself than to us. He looks down at the dogs seated on the ground beneath our tree house. 'Maybe I'll catch a *bécasse* for dinner,' he muses, sitting on the floor of the *palombière* next to the open trap door, legs dangling through it, his feet searching for the first rungs of the ladders. '*J'arrive!*' he shouts to his dogs as his head and hat disappear through the aperture. '*J'arrive!*' he shouts again and descends, the *palombière* shaking as he does so. He reaches the ground, lurches slightly and is gone. We see him swaying in the distance, broad hat, gun on his arm, flashes of white.

Our patience is not rewarded as the northerly wind rises and the sky is emptied even of starlings and *alouettes*. The occasional crow flies overhead. With one last look at the sky, Michel empties his gun of cartridges, puts the cover on it, attaches it to the rope and lowers it gently to the ground. 'We'll come back,' he says, disappointed that he was unable to catch any *palombes* today, but philosophic. '*On a des jours comme ça,*' he says with a smile.

As we drive back along the valley road to Gageac we see a flock of them fly over. They look beautiful, a pale grey mass sweeping low over the dark red leaves of the merlot vines. '*Zut!*' says Michel with regret. '*Tant pis pour nous.*'

The last noble rot pick is a pleasure. We still haven't found a solution to the waiting birds on the telegraph wires. They succeed in stealing some but we gather them in now in clusters rather than individual grapes. I hear Juliana's shouts of '*Oh, que c'est bon!*' from a distant row. '*Des vrais bonbons!*' she shouts. 'Come and have a look at this! A whole vine full of it!' she bellows. We pick it greedily, gathering it in quickly now as though the starlings might steal it from our hands as we pick. '*Hah! C'est nous qui gagnons!*' laughs Juliana raucously, shaking her fist at them as they sit on the wires watching us. 'We need Gilles and his gun next year,' remarks Benjamin, laughing.

Walking back from the vines, sticky with sugar from the last pick, Juliana and I linger at the walnut trees. 'Stop!' bellows Juliana, pulling me back. 'Don't tread on them!' We laugh, pick some up and crack them, sitting underneath the tree to eat them. We are exhausted, happy and relieved to have the *vendange* over. Leaves from the tree send dappled sunlight flickering on to

Juliana's face. She looks part of the landscape, at one with nature, part of its cycle. '*Oh, que c'est bon!*' she says, chewing a walnut and throwing the shell to the ground. '*Je te les laisse devant . . .?*' '*Non!*' I shout. 'Not in front of the door!'

Chapter 16

THE *CHASSE AU SANGLIER* RENDEZVOUS IS AT THE *CHASSEURS'* *cabane*, a long plastic polytunnel with a table running its length and benches positioned alongside it. Situated at the end of a road and down a long lane bordered by oak and hazelnut, it lies at the very edge of Gageac. A mist hangs over the woods on the ridge opposite the *cabane* and surrounded by box and oak hedging, the sloping meadow in front of it is white with frost and dew. Two cars are already parked there, three men chattering quietly together next to them.

One is unusually tall, wearing a multicoloured knitted jumper with a vivid hunting scene on it. Across his chest are black boars running across a bright green valley with a blood-red sky. He wears a hat like Michel's but with two embroidered pheasants on it rather than a wild boar. An older man dressed in khaki stands next to him with another, a large man in his forties, standing nearby. '*Salut!*' says Michel.

We walk towards them as an enormous flock of *palombes* flies across the sky. '*Regarde! Regarde!*' they shout excitedly, pointing up at the sky. A second, then a third *vol* circles and swirls around, searching for a resting place in the trees of the nearby woods. They look beautiful, their bodies highlighted against the cold sun piercing through the mist. 'Listen!' says the man in the multi-coloured jumper, gazing up then looking at us. 'Listen to the song of the *palombes!*'

A man walks slowly towards us with his dog, cigarette in his mouth. '*Regarde!*' they shout to him, pointing up to the sky. '*Et voilà le tueur!*' says Michel. He also wears a jumper with a hunting scene emblazoned across it and a hat with an embroidered pheasant. He smiles, patting his dog and shaking hands with us. '*Le tueur*' is the hero of the moment, having shot a wild boar just last Monday, the first of the season.

A small van hurtles along the track, sweeps round the sloping meadow in an arc and with a screech of brakes comes to a halt next to us. A younger man jumps out excitedly, his dogs tumbling out behind him. '*Félicitations!*' he says to the *tueur*, striding over to him and shaking his hand warmly. '*Quelle bête c'était!*' he exclaims, looking round at us. 'It was a pure breed! It's a long time since we saw one like that!' Another car arrives. 'Venus!' shouts the young man, Pierre. His puppy Venus, a Griffon Bleu de Gascogne, not in any way resembling La Petite Venus of Gageac, leaps up at a white van and barks at the three dogs inside. The driver gets out, shakes our hands, almost crushes mine with the force of his handshake, and congratulates the *tueur*.

Hands in pockets, cigarettes in mouths they talk together. Everyone smokes. We are now eight. '*Oui, c'était un joli mâle,*' says the *tueur*. '*Il était beau!*' shouts Pierre in appreciation. 'It was a two-year-old, a pure breed! Seventy-seven kilos! Short but stocky. *Très carré!*' he continues, gesticulating. 'He was running wild, alone,' says another. '*C'est normale!*' exclaims Pierre. 'His rump was gored. He'd been fighting! *C'est tout a fait normale qu'il était seul!*' He looks around at the group for agreement on the normality of a wild boar, gored and running alone. They talk excitedly together. 'His primolars weren't out,' says one of them, 'so he couldn't have been more than two years old.' 'He ran alone by the light of the moon the night before,' says another. 'We could see by his tracks!'

The *tueur* speaks, smiling, proud. 'He fell into a hole in front of me,' he says laughing. 'I could see his rump. Of course, I didn't shoot when he got caught up. I waited . . .' They listen. '. . . I waited until he dug himself out . . .' Two more *chasseurs* arrive. '*Salut! Félicitations!*' they shout to the *tueur* who begins his story again. 'Two bullets it took,' he concludes, smiling. Edward Aublanc, president of the *chasse*, arrives. Everyone shakes hands and discusses again the *jolie bête* that was killed heroically by the *tueur*.

Edward has three teams looking for traces of wild boar this morning. They have with them their *chiens de pied*. Manu saw fresh footprints last night, he says. Everyone murmurs. The boars aren't running yet as the maize hasn't been cut. Everyone is smoking and we are now fifteen. The majority of the *chasseurs* have emblazoned caps with hunting scenes on their jumpers. Only a shy, thin man wears a plain green sweatshirt, sleeves rolled up with a large knife in a leather holder attached to his belt. He looks cold and incongruous without his jumper. I am very cold with three jumpers and a coat. I stamp my feet from time to time.

It's the same boar that has been in the area for the last three weeks, Edward continues. Three weeks in the territory and they still can't find him! The *chasseurs* discuss. He's intelligent. He's crafty. One of them saw footprints just the other day. The boar was out looking for chestnuts. It had rolled in the water there, he continues, so he knew it had passed by. Once the maize is cut they will have fewer places to hide, says Edward; the maize is keeping them safe. 'Why should they run if they have enough to eat where they are?' says another in agreement.

Edward, too, has an embroidered wild boar swathed across his chest and bullets slotted into special bullet holders on his coat. Fresh-faced and slim, he has a gentle countenance. Another *chasseur* arrives and walks towards us, a belt of bullets encircling his waist. '*Salut le tueur!*' he cries and shakes hands with *le tueur* and everyone else. It runs at night, the *sanglier*, Edward is saying. I listen, shrinking visibly with the cold. Michel hands me his khaki waistcoat.

Two more *chasseurs* arrive with dogs, two of the team of men looking for the traces of *sangliers*. Their van screeches to a halt beside us with the sound of six barking dogs in the back. Manu and his dogs appear and everyone falls silent. '*Voilà l'artiste!*' shouts one of the *chasseurs* as Manu gets out of his van with Benoît, Edward's son. He strides towards us. With his arrival, the atmosphere moves into a different dimension.

Manu is a presence, a force. The bulk of his large, muscular frame, the assurance of his gait and the unspoken respect he commands charges the atmosphere as everyone waits, looks at him. Has he come with news of new traces? Is the maize cut over at Cunèges? Are the boars running? Are the traces he found last night of a solitary boar or a *troupeau*? Manu is silent, his face gives nothing other than a slight frown. He shakes hands with everyone, kisses me in greeting then walks up the slope of the meadow taking his mobile telephone out of a pocket.

His huge Griffons Bleus de Gascogne fall out of the back of the van. Next to them Venus looks very much a puppy in comparison. They sniff, bark, range; dogs are everywhere. The *chasseurs* look up to the sky as another flock of *palombes* heads towards the woods. They regret they can't aim at them. They're not allowed to if they're hunting wild boar. It's against the rules. They can't even have shot cartridges for them in their cars, they complain. But the rules must be respected. Michel talks of mushrooms. He gathered *trompettes de la mort* the other day, he says. He found paths of them on the forest floor.

Manu ranges around at the top of the meadow talking on his mobile telephone, shoulders hunched. 'The dollar's dropped, the yen's rising!' shouts one of the *chasseurs*, to laughter from the rest. 'Not a grain in their necks,' I hear one of the *chasseurs* saying of the *palombes* he caught the other day.

With large, wide strides and his hands deep in his pockets, Manu descends the slope and gets back into his van without a word. The dogs leap into the back, Benoît closes the door behind them, jumps smartly into the seat next to him and they tear off down the lane, mud flying. We regroup in a large circle. '*Milledieux!*' says a *chasseur*, watching the van as it disappears behind trees. A silence, then another remarks, 'If anyone can find *les traces* it's Manu.'

It's already one o'clock and we haven't moved from our meeting point. '*Ah, c'est le plus dur,*' says one of the *chasseurs*. 'It's the hardest of the hunts. You can wait all day and not have a sniff of a wild boar. You must wait for the teams and the dogs to find *les traces*. You need patience.' Three vans arrive, a fourth, and then Manu, returned from a fruitless search for fresh traces. They screech to a halt and the full contingent of *chasseurs* is here. Dogs fall out of cars; large *Griffons Bleu de Gascogne*, spaniels, labradors, pointers, dogs of all colours and sizes.

Edward takes from his car a large box containing pâtés and *apéritifs*, the *tueur* carries a cold box into the *cabane* and the prelude to lunch is here. Two huge breads and a plastic *bidon* of wine are already on the table, along with bottles of whisky, martini and sweet wine. Michel has brought some *saucisson*, cut up into slices and already on the table beside the bottles. Everyone takes an *apéritif*. They stand around, dogs weaving in and out at their feet. Michel lights a large bundle of *sarments* that he has brought with him and adds vine stumps to them. The fire bursts into life, bringing with it the comfort of real flame and some heat. The *chasseurs* take off their coats. Everyone apart from the man in the green sweatshirt has an animal on either their jumpers, gilets or hats.

Large *bocaux* of pâté appear on the table, along with paper plates, and we sit down to eat. A gas burner is lit in the far corner and the smell of cooking meat pervades the *cabane* as we eat wild boar and venison pâté. I am starving. I have hardly moved since we arrived at 8 am but the cold and damp have given me an appetite. The pâtés taste delicious and the bread we eat with it is fresh and crusty.

Everyone has their own knives, hunters' knives, apart from me. Michel hands me one. The pâtés come round again, along with a *bocal* filled with a lighter coloured mixture of tubes and unidentifiable brawn and gristle. It is made from head and brains of boar, which I decline – it's just too much for me and for Michel too, who passes it on without plunging his knife into it as the others do.

The ambiance is warm as bottles of wine are opened in addition to the *bidons* already on the table. The sun shines weakly through the plastic roof of the *cabane*. A sudden smell of vinegar and the large pan sizzling on the gas burner is passed around. It contains the liver and heart of last Monday's *sanglier*, cooked in fat with vinegar added to the pan at the last minute.

'*C'est la bonne franquette!*' Edward shouts over to me as I reluctantly take a thin but large slice of liver of *sanglier*. There are no small slices. The man with the crushing handshake hands me a wooden fork made from a branch of wood from the tree nearby and everyone watches as I bite into a mouthful of liver. It tastes of liver, but stronger than any I've tasted. A pregnant silence then the *tueur*, smiling at me, asks, '*Ça va?*' They laugh uproarously as I swallow it. '*C'est bon, très bon! N'est-ce pas?*'

Michel takes a *morceau* of heart and Manu, sitting on my left, a slice of both. He had a feast of *grives*, thrush, the other day, he says as we eat the heart and liver of wild boar. He cooked them in a kebab over the embers of the fire. Everyone listens. When Manu talks there is silence. How many do you need, I ask him. 'Normally three or four per person,' he says. A silence, then he adds, 'I find I need seven or so.' He eats everything, he tells us, bones included.

A murmur of approval. This is obviously the right way to eat them.

Manu has his own *bidon* of wine on the floor beside him. He takes my glass and discreetly empties it of the undrinkable wine that was poured into it earlier, replacing it with some of his own. 'I only kill what I want to eat,' continues Manu, returning to the subject of thrushes. 'Fifteen for two days,' he continues. 'Three days in the fridge is the maximum you can keep *gibier*.' '*On peut les garder dans le congélateur!*' shouts someone at the far end of the table. Manu looks over at him, unblinking, and shakes his head. '*Non,*' he says. 'The freezer reduces meat to dust and paper.'

A heated discussion on the merits of freezers follows. *Gibier* is better eaten fresh, insists Manu. What is the point of killing an animal in the wild when it's fresh, then storing it away to become stale? It shows a lack of respect for the animal. A *civet* of *sanglier* or venison, he concedes, can be stored in the freezer for a time, but even then, longer than a few months there and it's virtually inedible. 'Freezers are fine for pizzas, but nothing else,' he pronounces. 'They're not worth the space they take up in the kitchen.' You may have waste without one, but so what? 'You should see what my dogs eat,' he says. '*Ça fait pitié les gens qui mangent moins bien.*' The table erupts with laughter.

I watch Manu as he eats and talks. Still only twenty-five, he is a throwback to another age, his life dominated by hunting *sangliers* or *chevreuils* or '*les gibiers nobles*', his opinions formed by a series of rituals and by the rhythms of the seasons. From the age of four he followed Gilles and his *chasse* party on their hunts. As a child, Michel took him fishing, or on *palombes* shoots, or *bécasse* hunting and hare coursing. Gilles did the same. At the age of seventeen he went on his first *sanglier* hunt. Pierrot, Michel's great friend, father of the local stonemason and then president of the *chasse*, told Manu then that if he wanted to hunt wild boar, first and foremost he must be valiant. He never forgot what Pierrot said.

Manu took me with him to look for *les traces des sangliers* a week ago today. His huge dogs ranged around in cages in the back of his van as we drove to where he had seen traces the night before. He showed me a large puddle made from the passage of tractor tyres in which a *sanglier* had rolled, indentations of its knees and thighs clearly visible where it had climbed out. It probably passed by at dusk, said Manu, in any event it must have been some time ago as the water was no longer muddy. He pointed with his foot to more recent hoof prints, gazed at them for a second then walked calmly towards his and the dogs. As he opened their cages, they leapt out, circling in front of us. Manu lit a cigarette, touched the huge belt of bullets round his waist and turned to his dogs. '*Cherche le cochon,*' he said under his breath. They circled around his feet then rushed off down a row of vines, already on the scent of wild boar.

The trail was warm. We watched as they coursed down rows of vines, over the road and up a hillside, swift and fleet like two arrows. Turning right in perfect unison with noses to the ground, they raced onwards through bracken on the edge of a wood, over a ditch, past a row of poplars then left towards a wood of burnished gold. Their speed was extraordinary. Manu inspected a bank on the edge of the road, glancing up now and again at the dogs coursing on towards the wood, in unspoken assurance of their prowess. The *sanglier* that passed here was a *gros mâle*, said Manu, pointing nonchalantly to the bank. He could tell by its imprints. It was probably the one they had been tracking on and off for the last three weeks.

Long, deep howls emanated from the wood. Manu set off suddenly up the hillside, racing, me behind him. Davy, another *chasseur*, joined us with his dogs who rushed onwards, overtaking us as birds flew up over the woods. We reached the edge of it, dense thickets of brambles barring our way. Everyone stopped, Manu only momentarily. He stepped in through a tunnel of brambles and trees, their leaves and branches cascading downwards like yellow fountains to the empty lair, the *bauge* of a *troupeau* of wild boar.

Surrounded by dense and tall thickets of brambles, the interior of the *bauge* had overhanging branches and a ceiling of leaves. Within its refuge an expanse on the forest floor, devoid of brambles and leaves, had a series of large and small indentations where wild boar had lain, the outlines of their bristles evident in the dark soil. The smell was sour and strong. 'They left only hours ago,' said Manu quietly, looking down at the furrows then up and through the branches towards a ridge outside the wood on the other hillside. The dogs ranged and sniffed.

We left the wood and descended the hillside, picking off and eating some *chasselas* grapes still left on the vines on our way down. Five or six bunches of them hung in solitary splendour among the *parcelles*: cold, transparent pearls, delicious and thirst-quenching. The boars had passed to the other slope, said Manu as we ate the grapes, and we walked in great strides down the hillside.

Last week, he said, they were tracking *sangliers* and surprised a whole *troupeau*, twenty-three of them running together. They separated in two, there were boar everywhere, he said. Everyone left the wood, he continued, the *palombes*, the *merles*, anything that moved; they flew up in the air in fright, flocks of birds hovering above the wood.

The dogs surrounded the dense thicket where one of the *troupeau* was hiding. They were courageous, knowing they were in danger, he said. They could easily be cut in two by the powerful jaws and teeth of a wild boar, or gored by them, or trampled. They stop howling when they surround the boar, when they sense danger, Manu said. A combination of fear, courage and bravery drives them on.

'Like Davy,' he continued. 'When Davy is about to shoot a boar, when he's waiting for it to leave its lair, the hairs on his forearms stand on end in fear and his face goes pale.' Manu looked at me with a level gaze, smoking his cigarette. 'For him,' he said, 'the thrill is in the chase, in that moment before he shoots – in fear.' He and Davy had killed three of them that day and wounded one, which escaped.

We didn't find any *sangliers* after our discovery of their *bauge*. They had run to the other hillside and even further afield, past Monbazillac, in the time it took us to descend our slope. The dogs searched in vain for a warm trail. Manu put them back into his van. '*Il faut de la patience*,' he said, looking at me again. '*Le gros mâle* is here somewhere. We'll find him sooner or later.' His level gaze was calm, unblinking; a hunter, a predator in search of his prey.

At the *chasse* lunch, a huge cheese is being passed round the table, followed by two willow baskets filled with apples, shining and delicious. Down at the bottom end of the table raucous laughter erupts.

The man with the multicoloured jumper has a black cigarette in his mouth, only an inch of it left. '*Nom de Dieu!*' I hear someone shout amidst laughter. Coffee, *eau-de-vie* and *alcool de prune* are passed round. 'Take this sugar lump,' says the *tueur*, placing one carefully in my hand, 'and hold it over your coffee cup.' He pours *alcool de prune* over it. 'Now eat it,' he says. 'It's good for you. Alcohol preserves!' he says, and the *cabane* is ringing with laughter.

Chasseurs stand up and don their coats, paper plates are gathered up and deposited into huge plastic bags, bottles disappear and the baskets of apples return to where they came from. Speedily the table is emptied of its contents. We regroup outside. Manu and Benoît are gone, Pierre and his dogs too. '*Il est plus fort que nous*,' says Edward of the *sanglier* as the wind rises. 'Only good for the *palombes*,' says Michel when I ask him if the wind will be helpful to the teams looking for *traces* and the dogs searching for smells of the *sanglier*. '*Eh encore!*'

The hedging to our left flashes with red and gold as the sun pierces through the sky momentarily and sends golden light flooding on to it. I look up towards the ridge as we stand next to the embers of Michel's fire and see the *tueur*, a lone figure, hands behind his back, his dog running beside him. He takes long strides. A flight of *palombes* passes overhead, the sun catching the under-sides of their delicate bodies in its light.

The man with the crushing handshake recounts past glories of *sangliers* caught, seen, left. 'I don't know what else to do,' says Edward. 'This one is more intelligent than us . . . three months he's been in the territory.' He looks around at the group then up at the sky where three *palombes* fly overhead. 'The problem is that there are too many people around,' he complains. 'It's the season for *les gibiers* – pheasants, *palombes*, *lièvres*, *bécasses* – *ils n'arrêtent pas.*'

The unmistakable sound of Manu's dogs howling halts all con-versation. We look towards the wooded ridge as the distant howling continues. The dogs at our feet bark, tails up, noses quivering in the air. The crackle of the fire seems very loud as our ears strain to identify the area from which the sound comes. The sound carried on the wind is of Manu's horn bringing his dogs to heel and Edward turns to us excitedly. 'He's found it!' he exclaims.

A van careers along the lane. Pierre jumps out, rushes towards us. '*Ça y est!*' he shouts. 'Manu has found it.' He explains where Manu is, in which woods, what *traces* he has found. The *chasseurs* head to their cars as Edward gives them their positions. He talks to Manu on his mobile telephone. Michel and I are directed towards Pomport next to the water tower and opposite the dense wood where the wild boar, Manu and his dogs are. Within seconds *chasseurs* are in their cars, racing off down the track and heading to their posts.

As Michel and I drive to Pomport we pass *chasseurs'* vans and cars parked at strategic positions. Occasionally we see a *chasseur* standing on the edges of the wood, gun already in hand, orange *casquette* and *blouson* now donned over their coats and hats to make them more visible, a requirement of the Fédération de Chasseurs au Sanglier.

We arrive at our position next to the water tower, vines to our right and a dense wood on the other side of the road. I, too, have an orange *casquette* on my head. We get out of the van and inspect the soil around the vines and near the tower. '*Ça y est*,' says Michel, pointing to the soil at the end of a row of vines.

I peer down and see two thick and oblong indentations side by side, then another only a short step away, then more, the fresh imprints of wild boar. '*Regarde*,' says Michel, pointing at the bank opposite. The unmistakable signs of an animal's exit and entrance into the wood are evident in a path up the bank of dried mud. We walk up and down the road scouring the bank for further signs.

Michel points out great gouges in the grassed path between two rows of vines, as if someone had kicked over large tufts of soil and grass. The *sanglier* passed by here, he says, tossing up soil with his snout to root out worms and roots, or just for the sheer pleasure of doing it. I look at them in astonishment. I often find the same marks over at Les Ruisseaux between my rows of vines.

We wait. I look out over hectares of golden-leaved *parcelles* of vines interspersed with green and rust woods as Michel wanders up the road. Some of the *parcelles* of vines have changed colour, this morning's frost shrivelling the leaves. I look back towards Michel who is waving, walking back up the road. Behind him, the wood is momentarily highlighted by the sun, rose and golden hues on its copper leaves. I hear the howling of dogs, shots that crack out violently, Manu's horn drifting on the air.

The *sanglier* has been killed, on the other side of the wood not far from the Moulin de Malfourat near Monbazillac. It is being transported to Bernard's garden, one of the *chasseurs* informs us as he passes by in his van, slowing down to give us the news. He lights a cigarette, his engine still running. He was not far from the kill, he tells us. '*C'était un jolie chasse,*' he says. '*Très jolie. C'était le gros mâle.*' Manu was the *tueur*, already gone to hunt *bécasses* now that the *sanglier* is caught. We climb into the car and drive to Bernard's garden.

The wild boar lying on the ground in Bernard's garden is huge. Magnificent, prehistoric, its chest, front legs and neck are muscled and powerful. A solid mass of force, it is almost two metres in length and a metre to the shoulder. Jet-black bristles with white flecks cover its body and violent yellowing tusks protrude from under its mouth. Its head is colossal, with large ears and an elongated, bulky snout, almost as huge as its body. Its eyes are closed, its mouth slightly open as it lies motionless on the ground. It was powerful, intelligent, matchless in the forest, with no other predator than man.

It weighs ninety-eight kilos, Pierre is saying. Another pure breed, it was already wounded when Manu found it. The dogs were head to nose with it in the brambles then backed off, sensing it was dangerous. They encircled it, rooting it out, showing courage and bravery. It charged at them once, mad with rage, then dug itself in. I only half-listen as I stare at the dead animal on the ground in horror and fascination. Its teeth and jaws can cut a dog in two, they are saying. It can gore and kill them on the spot. This one was particularly dangerous, mad with rage, they conclude.

A cold, winter sun shines weakly as four men heave up the wild boar with difficulty, tying its back legs to a large, thick branch of a tree. They groan with the effort. The boar hangs down, its head almost touching the ground, congealed blood dripping periodically from its snout. There is hardly any blood, in fact; most of it is in the back of the van in which it was transported. Dogs run around the garden, their breath sending clouds of steam up into the cold air; they circle the boar, sniffing it occasionally. A *chasseur* is hosing the blood from the floor of his van. Two men lean against a tree, their desultory conversation drifting over to me. A flock of guinea fowl in a pen nearby screeches loudly, rattling and alarming.

Two *chasseurs* with knives approach the tree and the dead animal. With one swift and continuous cut, they slit open the boar, from its hind legs down to its neck. They cut and peel back skin from its chest, its hind legs and down to its ears then over its face and snout, pulling it off with brute force, occasionally slicing carefully through white fat to do so. They remove it in one piece. The skin lies on the ground beside them, a shadow of its former, running, wild self.

Its two front hooves are chopped off and its breastbone sawed through. They remove lungs, kidneys, intestines, liver and heart. They saw off its head, pull out its stomach, then cut through its backbone. It's so tender, they say, they hardly need a saw. '*Voilà. C'est fini*,' says one of them, standing back. 'You can wash it now.' The two men wash their bloody hands down with the hose in the cold air, steam rising from them, then turn the hose on the carcass.

What was a wild boar less than twenty minutes ago is now two sides of fresh pork hanging from a tree. Edward washes them down with a hose. One of the *chasseurs* picks up the skin and runs round the garden with it, dogs pursuing him. The sides swing gently on the tree in the wind.

At the Moulin de Malfourat my *vendangeurs* and friends arrive in groups and gather in front of the counter. '*Que c'est bon un petit blanc cassis!*' laughs Odile, lighting a cigarette and sipping her wine. 'Gilles!' bellows Juliana as she bursts in through the entrance. She looks extraordinarily chic. Wearing a leather suit with a pale, silk blouse and decked with jewels, she is transformed. She steps back, looks at us all then shouts, '*Oh là, qu'il fait chaaauud!*' running her hand slowly over her forehead, diamond rings sparkling, her gold watch flashing. Yves arrives behind her, La Petite Venus on his arm, replete with red ribbons in her hair. 'I couldn't leave her behind,' he says quietly. 'She doesn't like it.' Juliana wants Gilles to know, she shouts, that she found some *cèpes* the other day! Has he found any yet? She looks over to Michel. 'I know you have!' she yells.

Michel and Monique are talking to Manu who has brought his girlfriend with him. Gilles walks over to them. 'Manu!' he bellows. 'Gilles! *Ta voix!*' whispers Pamela, smiling and following him to the bar. Georges has arrived with Christine from Arcachon, but without Gilou, who is busy with his oysters. Jacques and Marie-Christelle are here too, as are Jean and Annie, Benjamin, Alain, Bruno, Claudie, Francis and Sandrine.

We have moved full circle. A golden, autumn evening and the tables are laid with its rich fruits. Michel's burnt-orange and ochre-coloured gourds decorate the centres, along with walnuts. A large plate of ripe figs, each one slit delicately with a peeled walnut in its centre, has been placed on a side table next to a bowl of shining, lustrous chestnuts.

'*Asseyez-vous!*' Juliana's voice booms out over the hubbub of noise. Paul has given up on the hopeless task of ushering people over to the tables. Everyone has much to say to each other as they drink their *apéritifs* and the level of noise is high. Juliana's voice, however, rises about the babble with ease. '*Milledieux!*' I hear Gilles bellow at the same level, followed by raucous laughter.

We sit down to dinner. A *velouté* of pumpkin soup, buttery, rich and creamy, is followed by slices of foie gras, one cold tasting luxurious and fresh, the other sauteed and served with hot apple puree. The noise is deafening as people laugh, shout, eat and drink. Gilles approves of the foie gras, he says. It is pure, he confirms, looking at Michel who is chuckling, wiping his knife on his bread and taking another mouthful of my sweet wine.

The *magret de canard* served for the main course is voluptuous. Rose-coloured, tender and full-flavoured, the duck breast, cut into slices and fanned out on the plate, is served with a sauce made from sweet wine. Thinly sliced potatoes, crisp and deeply flavoured with juicy *cèpes*, complement it. Gilles approves of that too. He has already bought his *canard* for next year, he tells us. And this year they are the right size. '*Dieu merci!*' he yells.

The cheese plate comes courtesy of Monsieur Blanchard. A slice of Sans Nom cheese, one of rich and creamy Roquefort *fermier* and a chunk of Tomme de Chèvre are presented to each of us on separate plates. '*Quel bonheur!*' I can hear him say. A rich, crunchy walnut tart finishes our meal as Paul and Marie join us, the restaurant resounding with the sound of noise and people.

'A piece of cloth hanging from the mantelpiece to help draw the smoke up . . . all the older generation had them – thick, lacy things they were,' Monique is saying. 'Lift the base,' says Jean. 'There should be less distance between the fire and the chimney.' 'Demolish it and start again properly!' yells Gilles as we discuss the continuing problem of the chimney at La Tabardy.

'We used to have drunken thrushes in the vines during the *vendange* when I was young,' Gilles is telling us in response to my diatribe against the starlings that have a penchant for my noble rot grapes. 'Shame we couldn't stop *vendanging* and shoot them. There were hundreds of them!' We laugh. '*Je te jure! Milledieux!* Thousands of them!' he shouts. 'They were drunk from the grapes!' He takes a gulp of wine and laughs loudly too.

Francis has his guitar in front of him. He strums the strains of a song everyone knows. Juliana claps her hands then puts her arms up in the air. '*Oh là! Les chansons! La dance!*' she shouts, laughing. '*On va chanter!*' says Monique with a smile.

I look out of the window at the view. It is black night, the horizon lit up by the sparkling distant lights of Bergerac, Gardonne, Lamonzie-St-Martin and Gageac. The fertile valley there has come full circle again, one cycle ended and another beginning. The gentle slopes of vines that run up to the ridge have already given up their fruits.

I think of the château at Gageac, imposing, restful, beautiful. The stillness of its courtyard, the sun glinting on its rooftop in summer, the pale grey stone of its walls, its towers and its beech trees, the overriding feeling of history and permanence that resides in its walls.

I think fleetingly of Geoffroy, of Madame Cholet, *Comte* de la Verrie and lovely Edge. I look over at Michel with his patience and love of the land, his independent spirit. I glance at Gilles, proud, fierce, generous-spirited, whose life is so different from mine and yet so similar. And Juliana, laughing loudly. With her love of life and the seasons she is vibrant and alive.

And Fidde. I still catch my breath each time I think of him. A kernel of him is embedded in me. He was looking for real freedom, had almost found it. He's given it to me as his gift. An appreciation of what I have, an understanding of what I am. Fulfilment comes in many forms: my friendships here in France, my inter-action with the land, with nature.

The vines and the land of the valley in front of me are hidden by the darkness of the night. I can't see their forms, can't see the velvet contours of vines with their golden and flame-coloured leaves or the undulating countryside with its autumn display of colours or the beautiful woods with its wild boar and *bécasses*. I can't see the harvested fields, or the quiet villages steeped in history and tradition. I feel bound to them, inextri-cably linked to them. A feeling of timelessness washes over me as I dip back into its history. I am part of it, part of the passing of time.

Francis strums the opening strains of 'Domino' and everyone joins in with laughter. I, too, know the song from the Repas de Chasse when Odile's next-door neighbour reached the top note, the congregation singing along. '*J'ai besoin de toi! J'ai envie d'être aiméeeee . . . Domino! . . . Dominooooooo . . .*' we sing, followed by peals of laughter.

'*Il pleut sur le laque Majeur*,' sings Francis, changing again. '*Le plus beau voyage*', and Sandrine sings alone in her lovely voice. '*L'amour de droit*,' she sings, her arms folded on the table, wide black eyes fixed on Francis. I look at the empty glasses on the table, the babble of voices, the sound of people enjoying the ambiance of wine, food and friendship and understand how lucky I am.